CliffsTestPrep®

CSET®: English

by

Emily Hutchinson

Wiley Publishing, Inc.

About the Author

Emily Hutchinson holds a California lifetime standard teaching credential. She has been writing educational materials for students and teachers for about 30 years.

Author's Acknowledgments

Special thanks go to Sara and Erin Ahlich, my delightful granddaughters, who inspire me to keep a youthful outlook.

Publisher's Acknowledgments

Editorial

Project Editor: Kelly D. Henthorne

Acquisitions Editor: Greg Tubach

Production

Proofreader: Broccoli Information Management

Wiley Bicentennial Logo: Richard J. Pacifico

Wiley Publishing, Inc. Composition Services

CliffsTestPrep® CSET®: English

Published by:
Wiley Publishing, Inc.
111 River Street
Hoboken, NJ 07030-5774
www.wiley.com

Copyright © 2007 Wiley, Hoboken, NJ

Published by Wiley, Hoboken, NJ
Published simultaneously in Canada

Library of Congress Cataloging-in-Publication Data:

Hutchinson, Emily M., 1944–
  CliffsTestPrep CSET: English / by Emily M. Huchinson.
    p. cm.
  ISBN-13: 978-0-470-13969-1
  ISBN-10: 0-470-13969-2
  1. Teachers—California—Examinations. 2. English teachers—Certification—California. 3. Middle school teachers—Certification—California. 4. High school teachers—Certification—California. 5. English language—Examinations—Study guides. 6. CSET: Multiple Subjects. I. Title.
  LB1772.C2H87 2007
  371.12—dc22
                    2007028133

WILEY

Table of Contents

PART IV: CLOSING THOUGHTS

Introduction

So you have your baccalaureate (or higher) degree, and you've passed the California Basic Educational Skills Test (CBEST). Your goal of teaching English in a California middle school or high school is so much closer than it was a year ago. You just have two more things to check off your list: verify competence in English and complete a teacher preparation program, including student teaching. You know that you can verify subject matter competence in any one of three ways, and you've chosen what you think might be the easiest way: passing the California Subject Examinations for Teachers (CSET). Naturally, you want to pass the CSET the first time you take it, and that's where this book comes in.

The CSET is designed to demonstrate that a candidate has the basic knowledge needed to be a successful English teacher. The test is lengthy, comprehensive, and challenging, and it might cover material that you have not reviewed for many years. But don't let this scare you! If you use this book as a study guide, reviewing basic material and taking the practice tests, you can take the CSET: English with confidence.

What makes this book so valuable? It reviews the subject matter covered in the four subtests that make up the CSET: English. It also covers every type of question used in the subtests, suggesting strategies you can use to approach the questions.

Format and Content of the Test

The CSET: English test is made up of four separate subtests. Two of these tests have only multiple-choice questions, and two of them have only constructed-response questions.

Specific formats are shown in the following table.

Subtest	Domains	Number of Multiple-Choice Questions	Number of Constructed-Response Questions
I*	Literature and Textual Analysis	40	0
	Composition and Rhetoric	10	0
	Subtest Total	**50**	
II	Language, Linguistics, and Literacy	50	0
	Subtest Total	**50**	
III*	Composition and Rhetoric and Literature and Textual Analysis	0	2 constructed-response questions— 1 based on literary text, 1 on nonliterary text (extended responses)
IV	Communications: Speech, Media, and Creative Performance	0	4 (short responses)

*Subtest I is a multiple-choice test that covers the two domains of Literature and Textual Analysis and Composition and Rhetoric.
*Subtest III is a constructed-response test that covers the same domains.

Multiple-choice questions make up two of the four subtests. The typical multiple-choice questions present a question or an incomplete statement followed by four choices, labeled A, B, C, and D, only one of which is the correct answer or sentence completion. Multiple-choice questions may be based on additional material to which they pertain, such as an excerpt from a literary or nonliterary text.

Constructed-response questions make up two of the four subtests. One of these tests has two questions that require extended responses, and the other has four questions that require short responses. Most of these questions begin with an introductory paragraph, situation, quotation, excerpt, or other material, followed by a specific assignment related to it. For example, you might be asked to evaluate, analyze, discuss, interpret, or describe the introductory material or to compare it with other material presented at the same time.

How the Test Is Scored

The multiple-choice questions are scored electronically. Scores are based on the total number of correct answers, with no penalty for guessing.

Two sets of performance characteristics and two scoring scales are used to score the constructed-response questions. The reason for this is that there are two types of constructed-response questions on the CSET: English. The extended-response questions (Subtest III) are designed to be answered in approximately 45–60 minutes, and the short-response questions (Subtest IV) are designed to be answered in approximately 10–15 minutes. Here are the scoring scales for both types of questions:

Performance Characteristics for CSET: English Subtest III

The following performance characteristics guide the scoring of responses to the constructed-response questions on CSET: English Subtest III.

Purpose	The extent to which the response addresses the constructed-response assignment's charge in relation to relevant CSET subject matter requirements.
Subject Matter Knowledge	The application of accurate subject matter knowledge as described in the relevant CSET subject matter requirements.
Support	The appropriateness and quality of the supporting evidence in relation to relevant CSET subject matter requirements.
Depth and Breadth of Understanding	The degree to which the response demonstrates understanding of the relevant CSET subject matter requirements.

Scoring Scale for CSET: English Subtest III

Scores are assigned to each response to the constructed-response questions on CSET: English Subtest III according to the following scoring scale.

Score Point	Score Point Description
4	The "4" response reflects a thorough command of the relevant knowledge and skills as defined in the subject matter requirements for CSET: English. • The purpose of the assignment is fully achieved. • There is a substantial and accurate application of relevant subject matter knowledge. • The supporting evidence is sound; there are high-quality, relevant examples. • The response reflects a comprehensive understanding of the assignment.

Score Point	Score Point Description
3	The "3" response reflects a general command of the relevant knowledge and skills as defined in the subject matter requirements for CSET: English. • The purpose of the assignment is largely achieved. • There is a largely accurate application of relevant subject matter knowledge. • The supporting evidence is adequate; there are some acceptable, relevant examples. • The response reflects an adequate understanding of the assignment.
2	The "2" response reflects a limited command of the relevant knowledge and skills as defined in the subject matter requirements for CSET: English. • The purpose of the assignment is partially achieved. • There is limited accurate application of relevant subject matter knowledge. • The supporting evidence is limited; there are few relevant examples. • The response reflects a limited understanding of the assignment.
1	The "1" response reflects little or no command of the relevant knowledge and skills as defined in the subject matter requirements for CSET: English. • The purpose of the assignment is not achieved. • There is little or no accurate application of relevant subject matter knowledge. • The supporting evidence is weak; there are no or few relevant examples. • The response reflects little or no understanding of the assignment.
U	The "U" (Unscorable) is assigned to a response that is unrelated to the assignment, illegible, primarily in a language other than English, or does not contain a sufficient amount of original work to score.
B	The "B" (Blank) is assigned to a response that is blank.

Performance Characteristics for CSET: English Subtest IV

The following performance characteristics guide the scoring of responses to the constructed-response questions on CSET: English Subtest IV.

Purpose	The extent to which the response addresses the constructed-response assignment's charge in relation to relevant CSET subject matter requirements.
Subject Matter Knowledge	The application of accurate subject matter knowledge as described in the relevant CSET subject matter requirements.
Support	The appropriateness and quality of the supporting evidence in relation to relevant CSET subject matter requirements.

Scoring Scale for CSET: English Subtest IV

Scores are assigned to each response to the constructed-response questions on CSET: English Subtest III according to the following scoring scale.

Score Point	Score Point Description
3	The "3" response reflects a command of the relevant knowledge and skills as defined in the subject matter requirements for CSET: English. • The purpose of the assignment is fully achieved. • There is an accurate application of relevant subject matter knowledge. • There is appropriate and specific relevant supporting evidence.
2	The "2" response reflects a general command of the relevant knowledge and skills as defined in the subject matter requirements for CSET: English. • The purpose of the assignment is largely achieved. • There is a largely accurate application of relevant subject matter knowledge. • There is acceptable relevant supporting evidence.
1	The "1" response reflects a limited command of the relevant knowledge and skills as defined in the subject matter requirements for CSET: English. • The purpose of the assignment is only partially or not achieved. • There is limited or no application of relevant subject matter knowledge. • There is little or no relevant supporting evidence.
U	The "U" (Unscorable) is assigned to a response that is unrelated to the assignment, illegible, primarily in a language other than English, or does not contain a sufficient amount of original work to score.
B	The "B" (Blank) is assigned to a response that is blank.

Each subtest gets a separate raw score (points earned). The raw score is then converted to a scale of 100 to 300. You need a scaled score of 220 to pass, which means you need to get about 73 percent of the possible points in order to pass. You must pass all four subtests to pass the examination.

Time Management

The allotted time for the CSET: English is 5 hours (300 minutes). You may take any number of the subtests on the same testing day. Remember that Subtest III has two questions that are designed to be answered in 45–60 minutes each, and Subtest IV has four questions that are designed to be answered in 10–15 minutes each. So, you can guess that you will spend between 130 and 180 minutes on these two tests. Subtract that from the total time allowed, and it leaves between 120 and 170 minutes for Subtests I and II, each of which has 50 multiple-choice questions. Can you answer 100 multiple-choice questions in 120 to 170 minutes? If you think you can, then sign up for all four tests in one day. If not, spread the testing out. If you sign up for all four and complete only two or three of the tests, you will have to pay again the next time you register. So think carefully about how many tests to sign up for at one time.

Frequently Asked Questions

You've already learned a great deal about the CSET: English by familiarizing yourself with the format of the questions, planning how to manage your time on test day, and becoming familiar with the content covered on the subtests. But you probably have some questions about the test. Here are some frequently asked questions.

Q. How do I register for a CSET: English test?

A. Go online to the CSET Website at http://www.cset.nesinc.com and register. This option is available 24 hours a day, 7 days a week. Another option is registering through the U.S. mail or by telephone. Go online for details about these options.

Q. How do I know which CSET: English subtests to take?

A. You have to pass all four tests to demonstrate competence in English. The order in which you take them is up to you.

Q. How much does it cost to take the CSET: English subtests?

A. The cost is a total of $222. English Subtests I and II cost $55 each; English Subtests III and IV cost $56 each. (These figures were in effect at the time of publication of this book. Check at the CSET Website to see whether they have changed.)

Q. Can accommodations be made for certain test-takers?

A. Yes. Accommodations can be made for test-takers who have physical disabilities (for example, visual, hearing, or motor impairments; illness; injury), other-than-physical disabilities (for example, learning disability), or whose religious beliefs prevent them from taking tests on Saturdays. Go to the CSET Website for further information and for instructions on how to request special accommodations.

Q. What should I bring with me on the day of the test?

A. You need your admission ticket (which you received after paying the fees), several sharpened No. 2 pencils with erasers (no pens; pencils are not supplied at the test site), and proper identification (a current, government-issued identification, in the name in which you registered, bearing your photograph and signature). Acceptable forms of government-issued identification include photo-bearing drivers' licenses and passports. If you do not have a driver's license, you can get an acceptable photo-bearing identification card from the Department of Motor Vehicles. The following forms of identification are not acceptable: student and employee identification cards, social security cards, draft classification cards, and credit cards.

Q. What if I fail one of the subtests? Can I take it again?

A. Yes. You have to re-register and pay the fee again. After you pass a subtest, you do not have to take that subtest again as long as you use the score toward certification within five years of the test date. So, suppose that you pass three of the subtests and fail one. In order to use the passing scores toward certification, you have to pass the fourth subtest within five years.

Q. What's the best way to prepare for the CSET: English tests?

A. You've already started out well. Become familiar with the format, types of questions, and content of the test. After you're familiar with what to expect on the test, complete several practice tests (two complete practice tests are included in this book), correct them yourself (answer keys are provided), and study the content related to the questions you answered incorrectly. You can also find sample practice questions at the CSET Website.

Suggestions for Using This Study Guide

This book provides the following levels of support to help you prepare for the CSET: English.

Part I: Preparing for the Format of the CSET: English

This section offers step-by-step instruction and specific strategies for each of the three question types—multiple choice, constructed response (extended), and constructed response (short)—you encounter on the CSET: English.

Part II: Preparing for the Content of the CSET: English

As you know, the CSET: English tests have four broad categories of content: Literature and Textual Analysis; Composition and Rhetoric; Language, Linguistics, and Literacy; and Communications: Speech, Media, and Creative Performance. In this part of the book, detailed outlines have been prepared to save you time, offering a concise overview of the key areas covered in English instruction today.

Part III: Full-Length Practice Tests

This part of the book provides practice tests that match in length the CSET: English subtests. Complete each practice test, check your answers, and then study the detailed explanations. This is a good opportunity to practice your pacing for the subtests, thus giving you some idea about how many subtests you might want to sign up for during one testing session.

Part IV: Closing Thoughts

The last part of the book offers a few study-planning options to help in your preparations for the test. In addition, a list of resources and literary works gives you an idea of the content covered on the test and where to get more information if you need it.

PART I

PREPARING FOR THE FORMAT OF THE CSET: ENGLISH

This part of the book is divided into two sections that are aligned with the two question formats found on the CSET: English. As you know, those two formats are multiple choice and constructed response (extended and short). If you are preparing for only Subtests I and II at this time, you might want to focus on the multiple-choice section. If you are preparing for only Subtests III and IV at this time, you might want to focus on the constructed-response section. Of course, if you are planning to take all four subtests at one time, study both sections.

This section offers you specific examples and helpful strategies to approach the multiple-choice questions included on the CSET: English. Multiple-choice questions make up the following tests:

- Subtest I: Literature and Textual Analysis; Composition and Rhetoric has 50 multiple-choice questions.
- Subtest II: Language, Linguistics, and Literacy has 50 multiple-choice questions.

In this section, you learn about the formats and types of multiple-choice questions on the CSET: English tests. Multiple-choice questions require you to analyze passages, synthesize information, and apply knowledge, which can be time-consuming. Being familiar with the format of these questions prepares you to recognize the patterns quickly and answer each question with the most efficiency. This section also includes helpful tips to help you achieve your goal—a passing score on the CSET: English!

How to Approach the Multiple-Choice Questions

Be aware that five types of multiple-choice questions appear on the CSET: English:

- Complete the Statement
- Which of the Following
- Roman Numeral
- LEAST/NOT/EXCEPT
- Reading Passage

Often two types of questions are combined, as in a question that involves reading a passage and then answering a question about it.

Complete the Statement

In a Complete the Statement question, you are given an incomplete statement. You must choose one of the answer choices to make the completed statement correct.

Example: *Leaves of Grass* by Walt Whitman is written almost entirely in:

A. blank verse.
B. rhyming couplets.
C. free verse.
D. quatrains.

Answer: **C**

Which of the Following

In this question type, you read a short question that includes the phrase "Which of the following?" This is the most frequently used type of question on the CSET: English.

Example: Which of the following best describes the fiction of Virginia Woolf?

A. realistic
B. stream of consciousness
C. historical
D. imagistic

Answer: **B**

Roman Numeral

This format is used when there might be more than one correct answer in the list. You must use your critical reasoning ability to determine which of the answer choices contains all of the correct options. These questions take more time than most multiple-choice questions and appear infrequently on the CSET: English.

Example: Of the sentences below, which contain a subordinate clause?

I. T. S. Eliot, who was born in the United States, spent most of his life in England.

II. Eliot's poem "The Love Song of J. Alfred Prufrock" is written in the first person.

III. Eliot summarized his attitudes as "classicist in literature, royalist in politics, and anglo-catholic in religion."

IV. Although his literary output is relatively small, T. S. Eliot is considered a major poet.

A. III, IV
B. II, III
C. I, III, IV
D. I, IV

Answer: **D**

LEAST/NOT/EXCEPT

A LEAST/NOT/EXCEPT question contains a short passage and one of the three terms—*least, not,* or *except* (negative choices). This type of question is used in situations that have several good solutions or ways of approaching, but there is also a clearly wrong way to do it. You must select the choice that does not work. Be very careful with this type of question; don't forget that you are selecting a negative.

LEAST Example: Which of the following works is LEAST likely to be understandable to a tenth-grader?

A. James Joyce's *Ulysses*
B. J. D. Salinger's *The Catcher in the Rye*
C. Lois Lowry's *The Giver*
D. Pearl S. Buck's *The Good Earth*

Answer: **A**

> **NOT Example:** Which of the following literary works was NOT written by John Steinbeck?
>
> A. *East of Eden*
> B. *The Grapes of Wrath*
> C. *The Red and the Black*
> D. *In Dubious Battle*

Answer: **C**

> **EXCEPT Example:** Each of the following works of literature is a frame story EXCEPT
>
> A. *The Turn of the Screw*
> B. "The Minister's Black Veil"
> C. *The Canterbury Tales*
> D. *Heart of Darkness*

Answer: **B**

Reading Passage

Reading Passage questions are common on the CSET: English. For this type of question, you read a passage and then answer one or more questions based on it.

> **Example:** This sample question is based on the following excerpt from "The Cask of Amontillado" by Edgar Allan Poe:
>
> The thousand injuries of Fortunato I had borne as I best could, but when he ventured upon insult I vowed revenge. You, who so well know the nature of my soul, will not suppose, however, that I gave utterance to a threat. *At length* I would be avenged; this was a point definitely settled—but the very definitiveness with which it was resolved precluded the idea of risk. I must not only punish but punish with impunity. A wrong is unredressed when retribution overtakes its redresser. It is equally unredressed when the avenger fails to make himself felt as such to him who has done the wrong.
>
> It must be understood that neither by word nor deed had I given Fortunato cause to doubt my good will. I continued, as was my wont, to smile in his face, and he did not perceive that my smile *now* was at the thought of his immolation.
>
> Which of the following clichéd expressions is suggested by this passage?
>
> A. Slow and steady wins the race.
> B. Keep your friends close, but keep your enemies closer.
> C. Revenge is a dish best served cold.
> D. People who live in glass houses shouldn't throw stones.

Answer: **C**

Other Formats

From time to time, new formats are developed for multiple-choice questions. If you come across a format that you are not familiar with, don't panic! Read the directions carefully. Then read and approach the question the same way you would any other question. Ask yourself what you are supposed to be looking for. Then look for details in the question that help you find the answer.

Strategies for the Multiple-Choice Questions

You will do better on the multiple-choice questions if you have a strategy—a plan of attack. In this section, you review a systematic approach to the multiple-choice questions. Then you practice the strategy.

1. **Preview the multiple-choice subtest.** As you quickly skim the test, take note of those questions that seem easier (that is, questions that you think you can answer without too much thought) and consider postponing those that seem more difficult.

2. **Start with those questions that you have deemed to be easier.** Don't waste time at this point with those questions that require more thought. Be sure you get credit for the items you know well.

3. **Go through the test again, now tackling the questions you left for last.** Sometimes, the simple fact that you have answered some questions already makes you feel more confident and relaxed, and answers occur to you more easily. Sometimes, too, an answer to one question provides a clue to the answer of another.

4. **Read the question stem carefully** (the *stem* is the question part). Underline or circle important words that might help you understand the question more clearly. (By the way, it's perfectly acceptable to make marks in your test booklet. It is not graded, although it is collected at the end of the exam time.)

5. **If possible, don't look at the answer choices provided until you think of an answer.** Then analyze the responses available and choose the one that most closely matches the answer you thought of.

6. **Read all the answer choices.** Be on the lookout for *distracters* or *decoys*. These are answer choices that appear correct in some way but are not as good as the credited response.

7. **Identify any modifiers or qualifiers.** Watch for absolute words, such as *always, never, none, all,* and *only*. These words indicate that the answer is an undisputed fact. Such modifiers *usually*—but not always—signal an incorrect response. Indefinite modifiers such as *usually, often, generally, may,* and *seldom* are more likely to signal a correct response because they allow for exceptions.

8. **Use the process of elimination.** If you are not sure of a correct answer, can you be sure that at least one choice is incorrect? If so, cross out that choice on your test booklet. This gives you better odds of making a correct guess if you are forced into that position.

9. **If you are not sure of an answer, guess!** There is no penalty for incorrect responses on the CSET, so it is in your best interests to answer each question even if you are not sure.

10. **Mark your bubble sheet carefully.** If you are skipping around, it is easy to make a mistake. Double-check the number on the bubble sheet and make sure it matches the number of the question you are answering. In addition, be sure to fill in the bubbles completely. Do not make any stray marks on the answer sheet because a computer scores the multiple-choice responses that you record.

11. **Watch the time!** The testing session is five hours. If you are taking only one or two subtests, you don't really have to worry about the time—five hours should be more than enough. But if you are taking all four subtests during one testing session, you have to be very aware of the time.

12. **If you have enough time, check your answers**. Don't be afraid to change your answer if you have analyzed the question and determined that your first answer was wrong.

A Few More Tips

- Don't forget that your goal is to *pass* the CSET: English. You don't have to get the highest score in CSET history. Tests like this one are designed for you not to know all the answers, especially in the multiple-choice format. Expect that you will encounter several difficult questions and don't waste energy worrying about your score as you work.

- Don't be intimidated by difficult words or unfamiliar passages. Use the context of the question as an aid in inferring the answer on difficult test questions.

- You don't have to do the multiple-choice questions in order. You can skip around, doing the easiest questions first. Just take care that you fill in the corresponding answer bubble on the answer sheet.

- Feel free to write in your test booklet if it is helpful to you. Underline or circle key words, and put an X by any items you skipped. On the harder questions, draw a line through answer choices you're able to eliminate so you won't waste time reading them again. Just be sure to mark your final choice on the answer sheet.

- Remember that there are no patterns in the credited responses. For example, you might have three Bs in a row as correct answers. This, in itself, is not a reason to change answers.

- Read all the answer choices before choosing the answer you think is correct.

- Make sure that you answer each question. If you have left blanks, time is almost up, and you have no idea about some questions, guess!

Preview and Practice: Apply the Strategies

1. Read the passage below from "The Law of Life," a short story by Jack London; then answer the question that follows.

He placed a stick carefully upon the fire and resumed his meditations. It was the same everywhere, with all things. The mosquitoes vanished with the first frost. The little tree squirrel crawled away to die. When age settled upon the rabbit it became slow and heavy and could no longer outfoot its enemies. Even the big bald-face grew clumsy and blind and quarrelsome, in the end to be dragged down by a handful of yelping huskies. He remembered how he had abandoned his own father on an upper reach of the Klondike one winter, the winter before the missionary came with his talk books and his box of medicines. Many a time had Koskoosh smacked his lips over the recollection of that box, though now his mouth refused to moisten. The "painkiller" had been especially good. But the missionary was a bother after all, for he brought no meat into the camp, and he ate heartily, and the hunters grumbled. But he chilled his lungs on the divide by the Mayo, and the dogs afterward nosed the stones away and fought over his bones.

The main point of Koskoosh's meditations is that

A. Klondike winters are harsh.
B. Missionaries are a bother.
C. All living things must die.
D. Everyone should contribute equally to meals.

Questions 2 and 3 are based on the following excerpt from "The Blue Hotel," a short story by Stephen Crane.

The Swede backed rapidly toward a corner of the room. His hands were out protectingly [sic] in front of his chest, but he was making an obvious struggle to control his fright. "Gentlemen," he quavered, "I suppose I am going to be killed before I can leave this house! I suppose I am going to be killed before I can leave this house!" In his eyes was the dying swan look. Through the windows could be seen the snow turning blue in the shadow of dusk. The wind tore at the house and some loose thing beat regularly against the clapboards like a spirit tapping.

2. Which of the following literary elements is used in the passage above?

   A. foreshadowing
   B. metonymy
   C. apostrophe
   D. hyperbole

3. The last sentence of the passage contains an example of

   A. metaphor.
   B. simile.
   C. alliteration.
   D. oxymoron.

4. Which of the following authors are known for their writing during the Realistic Period of American literature?

   I. William Faulkner
   II. Bret Harte
   III. Mark Twain
   IV. Henry James

   A. I and III
   B. II and III
   C. II, III, and IV
   D. I, III, and IV

5. Which of the following is the LEAST reliable Internet source of information for background for a research paper?

   A. a Website whose domain name ends in .com
   B. a Website whose domain name ends in .edu
   C. a Website whose domain name ends in .gov
   D. a Website whose domain name ends in .org

6. During the prewriting stage, you might do all of the following EXCEPT

   A. create lists.
   B. have a brainstorming session.
   C. research.
   D. edit for grammar.

7. Which of the following helps explain why second-language learners often cannot pronounce certain sounds in the target language?

   A. They lack the physical ability to form the sounds.
   B. They never heard the sounds before in their native languages.
   C. Their brains work slightly differently than those of speakers of the target language.
   D. They are afraid of making mistakes and appearing foolish.

8. The most common root words in English come from

A. Greek roots.
B. Latin roots.
 C. Anglo-Saxon roots.
D. Spanish roots.

9. The most efficient way to find specific information in a textbook is to

A. consult the table of contents.
B. check in the textbook's index.
C. read the first paragraph of each chapter.
D. skim for boldfaced terms.

10. Read the passage below; then answer the question that follows.

Bond prices fell following release of the factory order data. The yield, which moves inversely to the price, rose to 4.65 from 4.64 percent for the benchmark 10-year Treasury note late Wednesday. The dollar was mixed against other major currencies, while gold prices fell.

Which of the following best describes the language in this passage?

A. jargon
B. slang
C. doublespeak
D. ambiguity

11. Read the sentences below; then answer the question that follows.

■ The woman was wearing a lovely yellow straw hat.
■ She was also wearing a blue dress with a wide yellow belt.

Which of the following sentences combines the two sentences above using an adjectival subordinate clause?

A. The woman was wearing a lovely yellow straw hat and a blue dress with a wide yellow belt.
B. The woman in the yellow straw hat was wearing a blue dress; she also had on a wide yellow belt.
C. The woman was wearing a lovely yellow straw hat and a blue dress, which was accented with a wide yellow belt.
D. The woman in the blue dress was wearing not only a wide yellow belt but also a lovely yellow straw hat.

12. Which of the following indefinite pronouns can take either a singular or plural verb?

A. something
B. each
C. neither
D. none

Answers and Explanations

		Answer Key	
Question	*Answer*	*Content Category*	*Question Type*
1.	C	Literature and Textual Analysis	Reading Passage/Complete the Statement
2.	A	Literature and Textual Analysis	Reading Passage/Which of the Following
3.	B	Literature and Textual Analysis	Reading Passage/Complete the Statement
4.	C	Literature and Textual Analysis	Roman Numeral/Which of the Following
5.	A	Composition and Rhetoric	LEAST/NOT/EXCEPT/Which of the Following
6.	D	Composition and Rhetoric	LEAST/NOT/EXCEPT/Complete the Statement
7.	B	Language, Linguistics, and Literacy	Which of the Following
8.	C	Language, Linguistics, and Literacy	Complete the Statement
9.	B	Language, Linguistics, and Literacy	Complete the Statement
10.	A	Language, Linguistics, and Literacy	Reading Passage/Which of the Following
11.	C	Language, Linguistics, and Literacy	Reading Passage/Which of the Following
12.	D	Language, Linguistics, and Literacy	Which of the Following

1. **C.** Koskoosh's meditations are mainly about the fact that all things must die. He thinks about the short lives of mosquitoes, squirrels, rabbits, "the big bald-face," his own father, and the missionary.

2. **A.** This passage from "The Blue Hotel" provides foreshadowing for the events to come in the story.

3. **B.** The last sentence in the passage contains an example of a simile, a comparison using the word *like* or *as.* In this case, the loose thing beating regularly against the clapboards is compared to a spirit tapping.

4. **C.** The Realistic Period in American Literature is approximately 1865 to 1900. Bret Harte, Mark Twain, and Henry James were writing during this time; William Faulkner came later.

5. **A.** The least reliable Internet sources are those whose domain names end in .com because, as commercial sites, they are often trying to sell something.

6. **D.** Editing for grammar is not an appropriate activity at the prewriting stage; it is done during the revising stage.

7. **B.** Second-language learners often cannot pronounce certain sounds in the target language because they have never heard them before.

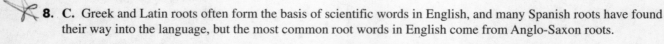

8. **C.** Greek and Latin roots often form the basis of scientific words in English, and many Spanish roots have found their way into the language, but the most common root words in English come from Anglo-Saxon roots.

9. **B.** The most efficient way to find specific information in a textbook is to check the index.

10. **A.** Jargon is the specialized language of a particular group or culture, and the passage uses the jargon of economics. Slang is informal language; doublespeak is language intended to be evasive or to conceal; ambiguity is language that has the possibility of more than one meaning.

11. **C.** The adjectival subordinate clause in this sentence is "which was accented with a wide yellow belt."

12. **D.** *None* can take either a singular or plural verb, depending on the context. Each of the other indefinite pronouns in the list always takes a singular verb.

Subtests III and IV: Constructed-Response Questions

This section provides specific examples and helpful strategies for approaching the constructed-response questions on two of the four CSET: English subtests. Constructed-response questions appear on the following CSET: English subtests:

- Subtest III: Composition and Rhetoric; Literature and Textual Analysis
- Subtest IV: Communications: Speech, Media, and Creative Performance

How to Approach the Constructed-Response Questions

The constructed-response format requires that you carefully and quickly read a short passage and then write a short-answer response to one or more questions about the passage. Let's examine a sample constructed-response question:

Directions: For this question, you will read an excerpt from a novel and then write a brief response.

Passage:

His voice faded off and Tom glanced impatiently around the garage. Then I heard footsteps on a stairs, and in a moment the thickish figure of a woman blocked out the light from the office door. She was in the middle thirties, and faintly stout, but she carried her surplus flesh sensuously as some women can. Her face, above a spotted dress of dark blue crêpe-de-chine, contained no facet or gleam of beauty, but there was an immediately perceptible vitality about her as if the nerves of her body were continually smouldering. She smiled slowly and, walking through her husband as if he were a ghost, shook hands with Tom, looking him flush in the eye. Then she wet her lips, and without turning around spoke to her husband in a soft, coarse voice:

"Get some chairs, why don't you, so somebody can sit down."

"Oh, sure," agreed Wilson hurriedly, and went toward the little office, mingling immediately with the cement color of the walls. A white ashen dust veiled his dark suit and his pale hair as it veiled everything in the vicinity—except his wife, who moved close to Tom.

Question: In Chapter 2 of *The Great Gatsby,* F. Scott Fitzerald introduces the character of Myrtle Wilson. Explain how the author uses description, dialogue, and word choice to help the reader form an impression of this woman and how she relates to her husband.

As you can see, a constructed-response question is made up of three parts: directions, a passage, and one or more questions about the passage. In the next section, you find specific strategies to use as you work on the sample constructed-response questions that appear later in this chapter and again in the practice tests in Part III.

Strategies for the Constructed-Response Questions

The following strategies help you approach the constructed-response questions more efficiently and effectively:

1. **Read the question or questions before you read the passage.** Most test-takers would read the passage first, since it appears first, but this is not the most efficient use of your time. Remember, the reason you read the passage is to get information to answer the question. If you know what the question is before you read the passage, you know what you should be looking for. Reading experts call this practice "setting a purpose for reading." Try it, and you should find that you save time and do a better job.

2. **Use *active reading strategies* when you read the passage.** While reading, take notes or mark the passage (remember that you can write on the test booklet), think about the question or questions you have to answer, and begin considering your response as you read.

3. **Reread each question and then take time to make a plan.** Do not just begin writing immediately. It's much better to jot down a few notes—a list or an informal outline—that will guide you as you write. Here's an example of some notes you might write for the previous sample question:

   Description: thickish figure, middle thirties, faintly stout, no facet or gleam of beauty

   Meaning: From an objective standpoint and according to the beauty standards of the day, Myrtle is not attractive.

   Dialogue: "Get some chairs, why don't you, so somebody can sit down."

   Meaning: Myrtle tends to boss her husband around.

   Word choice: sensuously, immediately perceptible vitality, continually smoldering, coarse voice

   Meaning: Myrtle has an animal magnetism and coarseness about her.

4. **Review the passage and question or questions.** Make sure that you have referred specifically to the passage and have addressed all parts of the question with examples and details. Add details to your outline as necessary. Here are some notes you might add to your list for the previous question:

   Description: Wilson blends into the walls.

   Meaning: He does not have the same vitality as his wife.

   Description: Myrtle moves close to Tom.

   Meaning: This suggests an intimate, illicit relationship.

5. **Review your response.** Were you clear, concise, specific, and accurate? Did you answer all parts of the question?

   Here is a sample high-scoring response to the question on *The Great Gatsby*:

   > F. Scott Fitzgerald's description of Myrtle Wilson and her relationship with her husband in Chapter 2 of <u>The Great Gatsby</u> is a masterpiece of suggestion. Fitzgerald does not have to tell the reader directly that Myrtle Wilson is a somewhat slovenly adulteress. Instead, he uses description, dialogue, and careful word choice to convey this impression. The first thing Myrtle does is block out the light with her "thickish figure" by standing in the doorway of the office. The reference to her as "faintly stout," carrying "her surplus flesh sensuously," reveals that this is a woman who does not let her imperfections stop her from enjoying sensual pleasures. Her "perceptible vitality" and her "continually smouldering" nerves give the impression of barely concealed sexuality. That sexuality, however, is not directed toward her husband. She treats her husband "as if he were a ghost," flirting with Tom as she shakes his hand. She looks Tom "flush in the eye," speaking to her husband without even looking in his direction. When she orders her husband, "in a soft,

coarse voice," to get some chairs for the guests, he obeys immediately, fading into the "cement color of the walls." As soon as her husband is out of the room, Myrtle moves close to Tom. At this point, it should come as no surprise to the reader that Myrtle is not a faithful wife to the husband she does not respect.

You may have noticed that I underlined the title of the novel. You can't italicize when you are handwriting your answers, but you can underline book titles to show that you know this convention of written English. As you'll see when we look at the content domains on which you are tested, one thing you need to do is use "a range of conventions in both spoken and written English." Look for opportunities to do so.

6. **Check to be sure you have answered all parts of multiple-part constructed-response questions.** Some questions have two or more parts rather than just one. Take care that your response addresses all parts of the question.

7. **Watch the time.** Remember that you have 5 hours of testing time to complete all the subtests for which you have signed up. If you are doing just one or two tests, time probably is not a problem. However, if you have signed up for all four tests, you need to watch the time assiduously. As explained elsewhere in this book, the constructed-response questions in Subtest III have been designed to be answered in 45–60 minutes, and there are only 2 questions. The constructed-response questions in Subtest IV have been designed to be answered in 10–15 minutes, and there are 4 questions. So you can assume that Subtest III takes about 2 hours, and Subtest IV takes about 1 hour, leaving 1 hour each for Subtests I and II. But some people might need more time than suggested to write a constructed response. I suggest that you practice your timing before the actual exam by taking the practice tests in this book and on the CSET Website. Remember, you are the one in charge of your pacing on the entire test. The four subtests of the CSET: English are not independently timed by the proctor.

Preview and Practice: Apply the Strategies

There are two types of constructed-response questions on the CSET: English—extended and short answer. This section includes a sample of each, along with sample answers and explanations. The first question requires an extended response, and the second one requires a short answer.

1. Complete the exercise that follows.

    Write a critical essay in which you analyze the passage below from *Walden* by Henry David Thoreau. Assume that you are writing for an educated audience and make sure to support your conclusions with evidence from the text. In your essay:

    ■ summarize, in your own words, Thoreau's main argument in this passage;

    ■ evaluate Thoreau's reasoning;

    ■ identify the audience for which Thoreau is most likely writing; and

    ■ describe the extent to which the passage is likely to be effective in persuading this audience, and explain why.

I have found repeatedly, of late years, that I cannot fish without falling a little in self-respect. I have tried it again and again. I have skill at it, and, like many of my fellows, a certain instinct for it, which revives from time to time; but always when I have done I feel that it would have been better if I had not fished. I think that I do not mistake. It is a faint intimation, yet so are the first streaks of morning. There is unquestionably this instinct in me which belongs to the lower orders of creation; yet with every year I am less a fisherman, though without more humanity or even wisdom; at present I am no fisherman at all. But I see that if I were to live in a wilderness I should again be tempted to become a fisher and hunter in earnest. Besides, there is something essentially unclean about this diet, and all flesh, and I began to see where housework commences, and whence the endeavor, which costs too much, to wear a tidy and respectable appearance, each day, to keep the house sweet and free from all ill odors and sights. Having been my own butcher and scullion and cook, as well as the gentleman for whom the dishes were served up, I can speak from an unusually complete experience. The practical objection to animal food in my case was its uncleanness; and, besides, when I had caught and cleaned and cooked and eaten my fish, they seemed not to have fed me essentially. It was insignificant and unnecessary, and cost more than it came to. A little bread or a few potatoes would have done as well, with less trouble and filth. Like many of my contemporaries, I had rarely for many years used animal food, or tea, or coffee, &c.; not so much because of any ill effects which I had traced to them, as because they were not agreeable to my imagination. The repugnance to animal food is not the effect of experience, but is an instinct. It appeared more beautiful to live low and fare hard in many respects; and though I never did so, I went far enough to please my imagination. I believe that every man who has ever been earnest to preserve his higher or poetic faculties in the best condition has been particularly inclined to abstain from animal food, and from much food of any kind.

2. Complete the exercise that follows.

In this soliloquy from Shakespeare's *Macbeth,* describe how the author uses various poetic devices to reveal the character of Lady Macbeth.

LADY MACBETH:

The raven himself is hoarse

That croaks the final entrance of Duncan

Under my battlements. Come, you spirits

That tend on mortal thoughts, unsex me here,

And fill me from the crown to the toe topfull

Of direst cruelty. Make thick my blood;

Stop up th' access and passage to remorse,

That no compunctious visitings of nature

Shake my fell purpose nor keep peace between

Th' effect and it. Come to my woman's breasts

And take my milk for gall, you murd'ring ministers,

Wherever in your sightless substances

You wait on nature's mischief. Come, thick night,

And pall thee in the dunnest smoke of hell,

That my keen knife see not the wound it makes,

Nor heaven peep through the blanket of the dark

To cry "Hold, hold."

Sample Responses to Constructed-Response Questions

1. Following is a sample response that would yield a score of 4:

Thoreau's main point is that a diet free from animal products is highly desirable. He begins by saying that he loses a little self-respect every time he goes fishing. He claims that even though he is good at it, he gets the feeling that it's not the best thing to be doing. He compares this "faint intimation" that fishing is ethically wrong with the faint "first streaks of morning," implying that his new attitude is like the dawn: the beginning of a new day.

He further supports his point by saying that the whole project of preparing "animal food" leads to too much work in order to keep the house "sweet and free from all odors and sights." Not only does the preparation of animal food create the need for more housework, the meal itself is inherently disappointing. He says that once he has eaten the fish, he realizes that they have not really fed him "essentially," and he claims that bread or potatoes would have been just as good for him, with less "trouble and filth." He closes his argument by claiming that abstinence from animal food—and indeed from "much food of any kind"—is practically a prerequisite for anyone who wants to keep the "higher or poetic faculties in the best condition." Thus, Thoreau equates a simple diet with the virtues of the intellectual life.

Thoreau's reasoning is basically sound. It is true that animal foods are somewhat disgusting, compared to bread and potatoes. Even people who never see the butchering phase know that animal foods require special handling. In further support of Thoreau's position, nutritionists now tell us that we can get our protein from sources other than animal products and, indeed, that certain animal foods can lead to serious medical problems. But Thoreau's arguments are not based on scientific fact; he admits that his attitude "is an instinct." Thoreau seems to be adding more evidence here to his basic argument earlier in the book that we must simplify our lives. A simple diet, simple pleasures, and a simple way of life leave more time for reflection, meditation, and enjoyment of life. However, Thoreau's claim that abstinence from animal food and "from much food of any kind" is a prerequisite to a higher intellectual life seems spurious. Too little food can be just as dangerous as too much, and for many people, animal foods are the best source of protein. We know now, although Thoreau did not, that a diet free of animal products is far from simple. It takes planning and great effort to achieve a balanced diet using vegetable sources of protein. We know now that anyone who tried to live on a diet of potatoes and bread would soon have serious health problems.

Thoreau was writing not only for his contemporaries in the 1850s but for readers who would come much later. His message is that alternative ways of living might be more rewarding than the "getting and spending" treadmill that most of us are on. When, as in this excerpt, he advises us to eat more simply, he is offering his own opinion that our lives might be richer as we leave more things alone. To the reader who is looking for a more meaningful, less distracted, way of living, Thoreau's message might be very appealing.

2. Following is a sample response that would yield a score of 3:

In this soliloquy from Macbeth, Lady Macbeth reveals that she is not quite as cold-blooded as she would have her husband believe. In an example of apostrophe, she asks for help from the spirits that "tend on mortal thoughts," thus admitting that she needs some help in order to go through with her murderous thoughts. Asking that the spirits "unsex" her here, she recognizes that it is considered unnatural for a woman to be so cruel. She asks the spirits to exchange the milk in her "woman's breast" (symbolic of nurture, life, and giving) for gall, a bitter substance. She calls upon the night to conceal itself in the "dunnest smoke of hell" so that not even her knife will be able to see what it is doing (personifying not only the night but the knife as well) and to prevent heaven from seeing her action and crying "Hold, hold."

PART II

PREPARING FOR THE CONTENT OF THE CSET: ENGLISH

This part of the book reviews the content on which you are tested on the CSET: English tests. As you take the subtests, you are expected to know these key theories, strategies, and concepts. The sections in this part are designed to help you in the following ways:

- To review English language arts content typically found on the CSET: English
- To help you assess your areas of strength and the areas you need to brush up on
- To save you time—you don't have to hunt for information in old English textbooks

It's a good idea to carefully review all the sections in this part as you review for the CSET: English. This process better prepares you to try the full-length practice tests in Part III and to pass your CSET: English exam.

Reading and Understanding Text

The Reading and Understanding Text content appears on the following CSET: English tests:

- Subtest I: Literature and Textual Analysis; Composition and Rhetoric
- Subtest III: Composition and Rhetoric; Literature and Textual Analysis

This section is organized as a brief outline of most of the content you can expect to be tested on in the literature part of each of these tests. Review this outline to refresh your memory of important details or to recognize areas that you need to study in greater depth. If parts of this outline contain unfamiliar content, investigate those areas further, perhaps by using the suggested resources listed in Part IV, "Resources."

Identifying and Interpreting Figurative Language and Other Literary Terminology

This section contains an overview of figurative language and other literary terminology to help you review for the CSET: English. You may even want to use this outline as a resource in lesson planning for your first classroom!

Allegory. A literary work in which all or most of the characters, events, and settings stand for ideas or generalizations about life. Allegories usually have a moral or a lesson.

Alliteration. The repetition of initial consonant sounds in words, as in these lines from Coleridge: "The fair breeze flew, the white foam flew, / The furrow followed free."

Allusion. A reference to a well-known person, place, or situation from history or from art, music, or another work of literature—for example, the characters Adam, Aron, and Cal in Steinbeck's *East of Eden* as allusions to Adam, Abel, and Cain in *Genesis*.

Analogy. A comparison of two things that are alike in some ways.

Anecdote. A short narrative about an interesting event, often used to make a point.

Antagonist. A person or force working against the protagonist, or central character, in a literary work.

Anthropomorphism. The assignment of human characteristics to animals, inanimate objects, or gods.

Aphorism. A wise saying, usually short and to the point, as Hippocrates' "Life is short, art is long." Also known as an epigram or maxim.

Apostrophe. A figure of speech in which a speaker addresses an absent person, an inanimate object, or an idea—for example, Byron's line "Roll on, thou deep and dark blue Ocean—roll!"

Archetype. A symbol, image, plot pattern, or character type that occurs often in literature, such as the hero on a dangerous quest.

Assonance. The repetition of the same or similar vowel sounds in stressed syllables that end with different consonant sounds, as in the first line of Poe's "Lenore": "Ah, broken is the golden bowl—the spirit flown forever!"

Atmosphere. The dominant mood or feeling of a literary work.

Ballad. A narrative song or poem.

Blank verse. Poetry or lines of dramatic verse written in unrhymed iambic pentameter.

Cadence. The rhythmic rise and fall of oral language.

Caesura. A pause or break in the meter or rhythm of a line of verse, marked in prosody by a double vertical line (||), as in this example from Tennyson: "Ring out the old, || ring in the new, / Ring, happy bells, || across the snow."

Character. A person portrayed in a literary work.

Characterization. The methods—direct and indirect—used by a writer to reveal a character's personality.

Cliché. A word or phrase that is so overused that it has lost its expressive power—for example, "I slept like a log."

Climax. The point of highest emotional intensity or suspense in a literary work.

Conflict. The struggle, internal or external, between opposing forces in a work of literature.

Connotation. The suggested or implied meaning associated with a word beyond its dictionary definition. Connotation can be positive, neutral, or negative.

Consonance. The repetition of final consonant sounds in words containing different vowels, as in "fresh cash" or "yard bird."

Couplet. A stanza made up of two rhyming lines that follow the same rhythmic pattern.

Denotation. The literal, or dictionary, meaning of a word.

Dénouement. The outcome, or resolution, of the plot.

Dialogue. Conversation between characters in a literary work.

Diction. An author's choice of words, based on their effectiveness for the author's purpose.

> **Archaic.** Old-fashioned words no longer in common use, such as *forsooth*.
>
> **Colloquialisms.** Expressions usually accepted in informal situations, such as *wicked awesome*.
>
> **Dialect.** A variety of language used by people in a particular geographic area.
>
> **Jargon.** Specialized language used in a particular profession or content area.
>
> **Profanity.** Language that shows disrespect for others or something sacred.
>
> **Slang.** Informal language used by a particular group among themselves.
>
> **Vulgarity.** Language widely consider crude, disgusting, and offensive.

Drama. A story intended to be performed before an audience by actors on a stage.

Dramatic monologue. A form of dramatic poetry in which a speaker addresses a silent listener.

Dramatic poetry. Poetry in which characters are revealed through dialogue, monologue, and description.

End rhyme. Rhyming of words at the ends of lines.

Enjambment. The continuation of a sentence from one line of a poem to another to complete meaning and grammatical structure (also called a run-on line).

Epic hero. The larger-than-life central character in an epic—a long narrative poem about events of crucial importance to the history of a culture or nation.

Epigram. A short, witty verse or saying. Also known as an aphorism or maxim.

Epigraph. A quotation from another work that suggests the main idea, or theme, of the work at hand.

Epilogue. A concluding statement or section added to a work of literature.

Epiphany. A sudden intuitive recognition of the essence or meaning of something.

Epitaph. A brief statement commemorating a dead person, often inscribed on a gravestone.

Existentialism. A philosophy that values human freedom and personal responsibility. Well-known existentialist writers include Jean-Paul Sartre, Søren Kierkegaard, Albert Camus, Friedrich Nietzsche, Franz Kafka, and Simone de Beauvoir.

Farce. A type of comedy with ridiculous characters, events, or situations.

Fiction. A narrative in which situations and characters are invented by the author.

Figurative language. Language used for descriptive effect rather than literal meaning and including at least one figure of speech.

Figure of speech. A specific kind of figurative language, such as simile, personification, metaphor, or hyperbole.

Flashback. A literary device in which the author interrupts the chronological order of a narrative to show something that happened in the past.

Flash-forward. An interruption in the chronological sequence of a narrative to leap forward in time.

Foot. The basic unit in the measurement of a line of metrical poetry. Except for a spondee, a foot usually has one stressed syllable (/) and one or more unstressed syllables (˘). There are five basic descriptions of metrical feet:

Iambic. ˘/ (unstressed, stressed)

Trochaic, /˘ (stressed, unstressed)

Anapestic. ˘˘/ (unstressed, unstressed, stressed)

Dactylic. /˘˘ (stressed, unstressed, unstressed)

Spondaic. // (stressed, stressed)

In addition, there are names for the line lengths; eight feet is the typical maximum.

One foot. Monometer

Two feet. Dimeter

Three feet. Trimeter

Four feet. Tetrameter

Five feet. Pentameter

Six feet. Hexameter

Seven feet. Septameter

Eight feet. Octameter

Foreshadowing. A literary technique in which the author uses clues to prepare readers for events that will occur later.

Free verse. Verse that contains an irregular metrical pattern and line length; also called *vers libre*.

Genre. A category or type of literature, defined by its style, form, and content. Examples of genres include poetry, drama, fiction, and nonfiction.

Hero. The chief character in a literary work, usually one with admirable qualities.

Heroic couplet. A pair of rhymed lines in iambic pentameter that work together to make a point or express an idea.

Hubris. The flaw that leads to the downfall of a tragic hero; the word comes from the Greek word *hybris,* meaning "excessive pride."

Hyperbole. A figure of speech that uses exaggeration for emphasis.

Imagery. The use of words to create pictures in the reader's mind.

Imagism. A movement in early twentieth-century poetry, which regarded the image as the essence of poetry.

Interior monologue. A literary technique that records a character's memories, opinions, and emotions.

Internal rhyme. Rhyme that occurs within a line of verse.

Inversion. Reversal of the usual word order for variety or emphasis, as in Coleridge's lines "A damsel with a dulcimer / In a vision once I saw."

Irony. The use of a word or phrase to mean the exact opposite of its literal or expected meaning. There are three types of irony:

Dramatic. The reader or the playgoer has information unknown to characters in the play.

Verbal. The writer says one thing but means something else.

Situational. An occurrence is the opposite of what was expected.

Magic realism. A literary style in which the writer combines realistic characters, events, situations, and dialogue with elements that are magical, supernatural, or fantastic.

Malapropism. A type of pun, or play on words, that results when the speaker gets two words mixed up—for example, "The flamingo dancers kept us entertained for an hour."

Maxim. A short saying that expresses a general truth or gives practical advice, usually about behavior and morality. Also called an adage or aphorism.

Memoir. A type of narrative nonfiction recounting a period in the writer's life.

Metaphor. A figure of speech in which a comparison is implied but not stated, such as "The snow was a white blanket on the meadow."

Meter. A rhythmical pattern in verse that is made up of stressed and unstressed syllables.

Metonymy. A figure of speech in which a word or phrase is substituted for another that is related—for example, the king of a country might be called "the crown."

Monologue. A long speech by a character in a literary work.

Mood. The feeling a literary work evokes in a reader, such as sadness, peace, or joy.

Moral. A lesson about right and wrong conduct taught in a fable or parable.

Motif. A significant word, phrase, idea, description, or other element repeated throughout a literary work and related to the theme. Luck is a motif in Bret Harte's "The Outcasts of Poker Flat."

Narrative. Writing or speech that tells a story.

Narrative poetry. Verse that tells a story.

Narrator. The person who tells a story. The narrator may be part of the story or an outside observer.

Onomatopoeia. The use of word or phrase that imitates or suggests the sound it describes, as in *mew, hiss, buzz,* and *plop.*

Oxymoron. A figure of speech in which opposite ideas are combined—for example, *wise fool.*

Paradox. A statement or situation that seems to be contradictory but actually makes sense—for example, "The more I learn, the more I find out I don't know."

Parallelism. The use of a series of words, phrases, or sentences that have similar grammatical form—for example, ". . . our lives, our fortunes, and our sacred honor."

Personification. A literary device in which animals, objects, forces of nature, or ideas are given human characteristics.

Plot. The sequence of events in a short story, novel, or drama.

Point of view. The perspective from which a story is told:

> **First person.** The story is told from the point of view of one character, who uses the pronouns *I* and *me.*

> **Third person**. The story is told by someone who stands outside the story.

> **Omniscient**. The narrator knows everything about the characters and events and reveals details that even the characters themselves could not reveal.

> **Limited omniscient**. The narrator knows the thoughts and feelings of one character.

Prologue. An introductory section of a play, speech, or other literary work.

Protagonist. The central character in a literary work, around whom the action revolves.

Refrain. The repetition of a line or phrase in a poem at regular intervals, usually at the end of each stanza.

Regionalism. An emphasis on themes, characters, settings, and customs of a particular geographical region.

Repetition. The recurrence of sounds, words, phrases, lines, or stanzas in a literary work or speech.

Rhetoric. Persuasive writing.

Rhetorical question. A question to which no answer is expected or the answer is obvious.

Rhyme. The repetition of the same stressed vowel sounds and any succeeding sounds in two or more rhymes.

> **End rhyme.** Occurs at the ends of lines of poetry.

> **Internal rhyme**. Occurs within a single line.

> **Slant rhyme.** Occurs when words include sounds that are similar but not identical, as in *tone* and *gone.*

Rhyme scheme. The pattern formed by end rhyme in a stanza or poem. Rhyme scheme is indicated by the assignment of a different letter of the alphabet to each new rhyme.

Rhythm. The pattern of sound created by stressed and unstressed syllables, particularly in poetry.

Setting. The time and place in which the events of a literary work occur.

Simile. A figure of speech that uses the word *like* or *as* to compare two unlike things.

Soliloquy. In drama, a long speech given by a character who is alone on stage. A soliloquy reveals the inner thoughts and emotions of that character.

Stream of consciousness. The literary representation of a character's free-flowing thought processes, memories, and emotions. This type of writing often does not use conventional sentence structure or rules of grammar.

Suspense. A feeling of curiosity or dread about what will happen next in a story.

Symbol. A person, place, thing, or event used to represent something else, such as the scarlet A representing Hester Prynne's sin of adultery in *The Scarlet Letter*.

Synecdoche. A figure of speech in which a part is used for a whole or a whole is used for a part, as in "All hands on deck."

Theme. The central understanding about life as expressed in a work of literature. A theme may be stated, or expressed directly. More commonly, the theme is implied, or revealed gradually through events, dialogue, and outcome. A literary work can have more than one theme.

Tone. The author's attitude toward his or her subject matter or audience. Tone is expressed through word choice, punctuation, sentence structure, and figures of speech. A writer's tone might be described as humorous, serious, formal, distant, friendly, or in any of a number of ways.

Transcendentalism. A literary movement and philosophical attitude that became important during the mid-nineteenth century in New England. Transcendentalists emphasized a reliance on intuition and conscience and focused on protesting the Puritan ethic and materialism. Individualism, freedom, experimentation, and spirituality are hallmarks of the movement. Noted Transcendentalists include Emerson, Thoreau, Hawthorne, Longfellow, and Holmes.

Unreliable narrator. A narrator who gives a faulty or distorted account of the events in a story. For example, a story narrated by a child might reflect a misinterpretation of adults' actions.

Identifying Patterns, Structures, and Characteristics of Literary Genres

This section helps you review the patterns, structures, and characteristics of literary genres. If some of this information is unfamiliar to you, you may want to refer to the resources listed in Part IV.

Elements of Poetry

Ballad. A short narrative poem, often written by an anonymous author, made up of short verses intended to be sung or recited.

Elegy. A poem mourning a death or other great loss.

Epic. A long narrative poem detailing a hero's deeds. Examples include *The Aeneid* by Virgil; *The Iliad* and *The Odyssey* by Homer; *Beowulf; Don Quixote* by Miguel Cervantes; *War and Peace* by Leo Tolstoy; *Faust* by John Wolfgang van Goethe; and *Hiawatha* by Henry Wadsworth Longfellow.

Haiku. A type of Japanese poem that is written in 17 syllables with 3 lines of 5, 7, and 5 syllables, respectively. Haiku presents a clear picture designed to arouse a distinct emotion. Usually, clues in the poem suggest a season of the year. The poem also suggests a specific spiritual insight.

Limerick. A humorous verse form of five anapestic lines with a rhyme scheme of *aabba.*

Lyric. A short poem expressing personal feelings and emotions.

Sonnet. A 14-line poem, usually written in iambic pentameter, with a varied rhyme scheme. There are two main types of sonnets:

Petrarchan. Opens with an octave that states a proposition and ends with a sestet that states the solution.

Shakespearean. Includes three quatrains and a couplet.

Stanza. A division of poetry named for the number of lines it contains.

Couplet. Two-line stanza

Triplet (also called **tercet**). Three-line stanza

Quatrain. Four-line stanza

Quintet. Five-line stanza

Sestet. Six-line stanza

Septet. Seven-line stanza

Octave. Eight-line stanza

Elements of Prose

In its broadest sense, the word *prose* refers to all forms of written or spoken expression that does not have a regular rhythmic pattern. This broad definition that separates prose from poetry, however, needs further limiting, since a mere collection of words thrown together, such as a set of directions or a list of ideas, is not considered prose. To be called prose, th*e* writing or oral expression must have a conscious literary purpose. This section is designed to help you review the various examples and elements of prose.

Fiction (or Narrative)

This list defines the various types of fiction that you might be tested on in the CSET: English. Remember that the definition of *fiction* is narrative writing that is drawn from the author's imagination rather than from fact or history.

Fable. A short, often humorous, tale intended to teach a moral, or lesson, about human behavior or to give advice about how to behave. The moral might be expressed explicitly at the end, or it may be left up to the reader to infer. Fables usually feature animal characters. Examples include "The Town Mouse and the Country Mouse," "The Wolf in Sheep's Clothing," and "The Tortoise and the Hare."

Fairy tale. A type of folktale that often features supernatural elements, such as magic, witches, goblins, and fairies. Many fairy tales begin with the phrase "Once upon a time." Examples include "Cinderella," "Rapunzel," and "Little Red Riding Hood."

Fantasy. A literary work that is set in an unreal world and often includes incredible characters and events. Examples include J. R. R. Tolkien's *The Lord of the Rings,* C. S. Lewis's *The Chronicles of Narnia,* and Jonathan Swift's *Gulliver's Travels.*

Folktale. An anonymous traditional story passed down orally long before it is written down. Examples include *The People Could Fly* retold by Virginia Hamilton, "Brer Rabbit Tricks Brer Fox Again," and *The Arabian Nights.*

Frame story. A story that surrounds another story or that serves to link several stories together. The frame usually precedes and follows the main, more important story. Examples include Joseph Conrad's *Heart of Darkness,* Geoffrey Chaucer's *The Canterbury Tales,* and Henry James's *The Turn of the Screw.*

Historical fiction. Narrative fiction that sets characters against the backdrop of an earlier time and often includes historically authentic people, places, or events. An example is *Lincoln* by Gore Vidal.

Horror. Fiction that is intended to scare, horrify, or unsettle the reader. Elements of fantasy and science fiction might be incorporated into this genre. Examples include Mary Shelley's *Frankenstein* and Bram Stoker's *Dracula.*

Legend. A traditional story handed down from the past, based on truth and tending to become exaggerated over time. Examples include Washington Irving's *The Legend of Sleepy Hollow* and Sir Thomas Malory's *Le Morte d'Arthur.*

Mystery. A suspenseful story in which the characters are involved in solving a puzzling crime. Examples include Edgar Allan Poe's "The Purloined Letter" and Arthur Conan Doyle's "The Adventure of the Speckled Band."

Myth. Narrative fiction involving gods and heroes or having a theme that expresses a culture's ideology. Greek myths include "Pygmalion and Galatea," "Narcissus," and "Pandora's Box." Myths are found in nearly every culture.

Novel. A book-length fictional narrative that typically has a plot, characters, setting, point of view, and theme.

Novella. A short narrative, usually less than 100 pages in length (also called a novelette). Examples include *Daisy Miller* by Henry James and *Of Mice and Men* by John Steinbeck.

Parable. A brief, simple story in prose or verse that illustrates a moral or religious lesson. Unlike a fable, it does not include anthropomorphized animals, plants, inanimate objects, or forces of nature. Examples include "The Parable of the Good Samaritan" from the *New Testament*.

Parody. A humorous imitation of a literary work that mocks the work by pointing out its shortcomings. Hamlet's love letters to Ophelia are parodies of Renaissance love poetry.

Romance. A long narrative work about the adventures and love affairs of idealized heroes who are far removed from everyday life. Examples include stories about King Arthur and the Knights of the Round Table, William Shakespeare's *Troilus and Cressida,* and *Sir Gawain and the Green Knight.*

Satire. Writing that comments, sometimes humorously, on social conventions or conditions, usually with the purpose of causing change. Examples include Jonathan Swift's essay "A Modest Proposal," Mark Twain's *Huckleberry Finn,* and Ambrose Bierce's The *Devil's Dictionary.*

Science fiction. Fiction that deals with the impact on society of current or future scientific and technological developments. Examples include Frank Herbert's *Dune,* Ursula K. Le Guin's *The Left Hand of Darkness,* and Ray Bradbury's *The Martian Chronicles.*

Short story. A brief fictional narrative that usually includes the following elements: characters, setting, plot, point of view, and theme. Examples include "A Rose for Emily" by William Faulkner, "The Gift of the Magi" by O. Henry, and "The Tell-Tale Heart" by Edgar Allan Poe.

Tragedy. A play in which the main character suffers a downfall. That character is typically of heroic or dignified stature and has a tragic flaw that leads to the downfall. An example is *Hamlet* by William Shakespeare.

Western. A novel featuring the experiences of cowboys and frontiersman in the western United States. Examples include Louis L'Amour's *How the West Was Won,* Bret Harte's "The Luck of Roaring Camp," and Elmore Leonard's *3:10 to Yuma.*

Nonfiction (or Expository)

This list defines the various types of nonfiction that you might be tested on in the CSET: English. Remember that *nonfiction* is defined as prose writing that tells about real people, events, or objects. To be called nonfiction, the writing must be about something that is true rather than imaginary.

Autobiography. A person's account of his or her own life. Examples include *The Autobiography of Benjamin Franklin, Up from Slavery* by Booker T. Washington, and *The Interesting Narrative of the Life of Olaudah Equiano.*

Biography. An account of a person's life written by another person. Examples include James Boswell's *Life of Samuel Johnson* and Carl Sandburg's *Abe Lincoln Grows Up.*

Document (letter, diary, journal). An eloquently written expository piece that becomes part of the recognized literature of an era. Documents often reveal historical facts, details about the culture, and the personality of the author. Examples include the Constitution of the United States, Samuel Pepys's diary, and *Anne Frank: The Diary of a Young Girl.*

Essay. A short piece of nonfiction on any topic. Essays can be formal or informal. Examples include "Self-Reliance" by Ralph Waldo Emerson, "Notes on Camp" by Susan Sontag, and "The Death of the Moth" by Virginia Woolf.

Historical and Cultural Contexts of Texts

Knowledge of the historical and cultural contexts of texts enables you to apply your knowledge of the various schools of writers, associate works with certain authors, identify the period within which an author wrote or a piece was written, and identify representative works from a period. This section presents a comprehensive outline of the history of English literature, including representative authors and works. If you are not familiar with parts of this outline, refer to the resources listed in Part IV.

Classicism

Greek Classical and Hellenistic periods (8th to 2nd centuries B.C.). Examples: Homer's *The Odyssey,* Sophocles's *Antigone,* and Aristophanes's *The Birds*.

Roman Classical period (1st century B.C. to 5th century A.D.). Examples: Cicero's letters to Atticus, Brutus, Quintus, and others; Virgil's *The Aeneid;* and Plutarch's *Parallel Lives*.

Renaissance

Renaissance (13th–15th centuries). A period during which learning and the arts flourished in Europe. Examples: Dante's *The Divine Comedy,* Chaucer's *Canterbury Tales,* and Malory's *Le Morte d'Arthur*.

Neoclassicism

French Neoclassical period (17th century). Examples: Racine's *Bérénice,* Moliere's *Tartuffe,* and de la Fontaine's *Adonis*.

English Neoclassical period (17th and 18th centuries). Examples: Dryden's *Absalom and Achitophel,* Swift's *Gulliver's Travels,* and Pope's *The Dunciad*.

German Neoclassical period (18th and 19th centuries). Examples: Lessing's *Zur Geschichte und Literature* (On History and Literature) von Schiller's *William Tell,* and Goethe's *The Sorrows of Young Werther*.

British Literature

Old English period (450–1066 A.D.). Example: *Beowulf*.

Middle English period (1066–1550). Examples: Chaucer's *Canterbury Tales,* More's *Utopia,* and the morality play *Everyman*.

Elizabethan period (1550–1625). Examples: Shakespeare's *King Lear* and *Twelfth Night,* Marlowe's *Doctor Faustus,* and Spenser's *Epithalamion*.

Puritan period (1625–1660). Examples: Milton's *Areopagitica,* Walton's *Life of Donne,* and Milton's *L'Allegro* and *Il Penseroso*.

Neoclassical period (1660–1780). Examples: Pepys's *Diary,* Dryden's *The Hind and the Panther,* and Swift's *Journal to Stella*.

Romantic period (1780–1840). Examples: Blake's *Songs of Innocence,* Scott's *The Lady of the Lake,* and Austen's *Sense and Sensibility*.

Victorian period (1840–1900). Examples: Dickens's "A Christmas Carol," Eliot's *Adam Bede,* and Hardy's *Jude the Obscure*.

Modernism (1900–1945). Examples: Yeats's *Cathleen ni Houlihan*, Woolf's *To the Lighthouse*, and Maugham's *Of Human Bondage.*

Postmodernism (1945–1970). Examples: Eliot's "The Waste Land," Greene's *The End of the Affair*, Thomas's *Under Milk Wood.*

American Literature

Colonial period (1630–1760). Examples: Bradford's *History of the Plymouth Plantation;* Bradstreet's *The Tenth Muse, Lately Sprung Up in American;* and Increase Mather's *A Plain Discourse Showing Who Shall and Who Shall not Enter Heaven.*

Revolutionary period (1760–1787). Examples: The Declaration of Independence, Paine's *Common Sense*, and Crèvecoeur's *Letters from an American Farmer.*

Nationalist period (1828–1836). Examples: Cooper's *Leatherstocking Tales*, which included *The Deerslayer, The Last of the Mohicans, The Pathfinder, The Pioneers,* and *The Prairie;* Emerson's *Nature;* and Poe's *The Raven and Other Poems.*

American Renaissance period (1830–1860). Examples: Melville's *Moby-Dick*, Thoreau's *Walden*, and Whitman's "Oh, Captain, My Captain!"

Modern period (1900–1950). Examples: London's *The Call of the Wild*, Wharton's *The House of Mirth*, and Hemingway's *The Sun Also Rises.*

Postmodern period (1950–1970). Examples: Mailer's *The Naked and the Dead*, Miller's *The Death of a Salesman*, and Kerouac's *On the Road.*

Contemporary (1970–present). Examples: Walker's *The Color Purple*, Frazier's *Cold Mountain*, and Tyler's *Breathing Lessons.*

Composition and Rhetoric

The Composition and Rhetoric content appears on the following CSET: English tests:

- Subtest I: Literature and Textual Analysis; Composition and Rhetoric
- Subtest III: Composition and Rhetoric; Literature and Textual Analysis

This section is organized as a brief outline of most of the content you can expect to be tested on in the composition and rhetoric part of each of these tests. Review this outline to refresh your memory of important details or to recognize areas that you need to study in greater depth. If parts of this outline contain unfamiliar content, investigate those areas further, perhaps by using the suggested resources listed in Part IV.

Elements of Teaching Writing

According to the NCTE (National Council of Teachers of English), writing is a skill that can be taught, and teachers can help students improve their writing abilities. In order to teach students how to write, you need to know certain basic elements, such as the stages of the writing process, various writing activities that help students become better writers, source materials that students can use for inspiration and information, and ways to cite sources.

Stages of the Writing Process

Writing is a multistep process. This is not to say that it involves a set of formulaic steps that must be done in a certain order. The writer can move easily from one step to another, backtracking and jumping ahead as necessary. Good writers shift between different stages according to the circumstances. For example, during the revision stage, the writer might realize that more brainstorming (a prewriting step) would be helpful. The stages of the writing process are as follows:

1. **Prewriting (also called *planning* or *rehearsal*).** In this stage of the writing process, the student gathers and selects ideas. English teachers can aid in the process in several ways: by encouraging students to create lists, conduct research, brainstorm, discuss ideas, collect memorabilia or clips from other texts, and *free-write* (write freely without worrying about grammar and other matters of mechanics).

2. **Drafting.** In this stage, students begin writing, connecting, and developing ideas. Depending on the purpose for writing and the audience of the piece, there may be few drafts or many.

3. **Revising.** This stage of the writing process involves rewriting, or *re-seeing*. At this point, the writer looks at the piece again, either alone or with the help of a teacher or capable peer. The writer strives to ensure that the reader is able to make meaning of the piece of writing. In the revising stage, the writer examines sentence structure, word choice, voice, and organization of the piece.

4. **Editing.** This stage involves checking for style and conventions—spelling, grammar, usage, and punctuation. At this point in the writing process, the writer ensures that errors in conventions will not be intrusive when others read the piece of writing.

5. **Publishing.** The going public stage. A writer can share his or her writing with a larger audience in many ways. Teachers can help by encouraging students to publish their work in newsletters, online publications, performance, brochures, magazines, school newspapers, yearbooks, and bulletin boards.

6. **Evaluating.** In this stage, the writer reviews his or her work and self-evaluates, and the audience evaluates the effectiveness of the writing.

Writing Activities

Like any other skill, writing requires practice—and lots of it. Teachers help students become better writers by providing many opportunities for practice, both in class and out of class, and for many purposes and audiences. Examples of the types of writing you might assign include the following:

- Personal writing
- Workplace writing
- Subject writing
- Creative writing
- Persuasive writing
- Scholarly writing

Encourage students to express their innermost thoughts, feelings, and responses in journals, diaries, logs, personal narratives, and personal essays. Give students practice in workplace writing by having them prepare cover letters, business letters, job applications, and résumés. Examples of subject writing include interviews, accounts, profiles, and descriptions. Creative writing options allow students to play with language, express emotions, tell stories, create poetry, and develop drama. Students can learn to persuade others as they write editorials, commentaries, and advertisements. Students also need practice in scholarly writing, such as essays, research papers, and bibliographies.

In Subtest I of the CSET: English, you are asked a series of multiple-choice questions based on these concepts. In Subtest III, you are asked to demonstrate your own ability to produce various types of writing.

Types of Source Material for Writing

To help students develop ideas, find information, and check facts, teachers need to be familiar with various types of source material, such as the following:

Reference works. Dictionaries, encyclopedias, writers' reference handbooks, books of lists, almanacs, thesauruses, books of quotations, and so on.

Internet. Each of the types of reference works above is available online. In addition, writers can use search engines or portals (sites that list many resources and websites) to gather ideas and information.

Student-created sources. Students might get ideas from their own journals, oral histories, note cards, graphic organizers, and personal dictionaries of words to know or spell.

Other sources. Film, art, media, and so on.

Evaluating Source Materials

Students must learn to evaluate sources carefully to ensure that each source is worthwhile, reliable, and credible. The following general guidelines should help students determine whether print (such as journal articles) and nonprint sources (such as Internet sources) are reliable:

Check the basic information about the source, such as the author, year published, and publisher. Review this initial information to check for credibility, evidence of bias, conflict or interest or other agendas, and accuracy. Is your source reviewed by peers or edited by others? Have other works by this author proven to be credible and accurate?

If your source initially seems reliable, take time to read a portion of the material. Use the following questions to guide your next level of review: Is the writing style factual, credible, and free of errors in conventions? Are you the intended audience, or is this piece written for a purpose different from yours? Is the coverage of the content thorough and accurate for your purposes? Have other people read the source and found it credible, accurate, and helpful?

MLA and APA Citations

The MLA (Modern Language Association) style is most commonly used to cite sources within the liberal arts and humanities. The APA (American Psychological Association) style is most commonly used to cite sources within the social sciences. Study the following citations for a book in both formats.

> **MLA:** McMurtry, Larry. <u>Buffalo Girls.</u> New York: Simon and Schuster, 1960.
>
> **APA:** McMurtry, Larry (1960). *Buffalo Girls*. New York: Simon and Schuster.

As you can see, the MLA and the APA use slightly different formats to cite sources. Each format has its own rules for citing books, journals, and periodicals; in-text citations; and more. Middle- and secondary-school students must learn how to use each format and the proper way to cite the words or ideas of others. Refer to the following Websites for more detailed information about MLA and APA formats:

- www.mla.org
- www.apa.org

Students must be taught how to cite sources responsibly, thus avoiding plagiarism. They need to learn how to paraphrase material they have read, cite a source, and quote a source directly.

Understanding and Evaluating Rhetorical Features in Writing

Rhetoric is the art of prose composition. The term *rhetorical features* refers to all those elements that comprise an oral or written text and contribute to the voice of the piece. They include the organizational pattern chosen by the writer to develop ideas (such as analogy, cause and effect, compare and contrast, and illustration). They also include the specific features of various kinds of writing. For example, the rhetorical features of a short story are necessarily different from the rhetorical features of a business document. You can expect to be tested on these concepts in the Composition and Rhetoric sections of Subtest I and Subtest III.

Audience and Purpose

Effective writers know that writing for a specific audience and a specific purpose will have a direct impact on the style of their writing. Imagine that you're writing a personal letter to a favorite uncle. Then imagine the differences between that letter and a letter that you are writing to a prospective employer. Your audience determines the words you choose, the style of writing you employ, and the formality of your letter. English teachers can provide students with many opportunities to practice writing for different purposes and for specific audiences. Here are just a few prompts to help your future students think about audience and purpose as they write:

- In addition to the teacher, who is the intended or imaginary audience of the piece of writing?
- How knowledgeable is the audience? What kinds of information do you have to provide so your audience will understand your writing?
- In order to communicate most effectively, what voice should the writer use? For example, is this a formal piece, or would an informal voice that included dialect or other informal language be more appropriate?
- In what ways might this piece of writing be useful outside of the classroom? Would it be helpful in some other context, such as for a local nonprofit agency or to persuade readers to get involved in a community project?
- What is the purpose of this writing assignment? For example, is it to persuade, to entertain, to inform?

Organization of the Writing

To communicate effectively, students have to organize their writing. Here are several general methods of organization:

Cause and effect. The writer shows how events and their results are related.

Chronological order. The writer shows steps in a process or order of time.

Classification. The writer explains the relationships between concepts or terms.

Climax. The writer states the details first and places the topic sentence at the end.

Comparison. The writer shows similarities and differences between two or more subjects.

Illustration. The writer states the topic sentence first followed by details.

Location. The writer describes a person, place, or thing, organizing the description in a logical manner.

Rhetorical Features

Here is a partial list of rhetorical features that affect the voice of a piece:

Style is the unique way in which a writer uses words, phrases, and sentences to express ideas. Style is thought of as the ways by which one writer's work is distinguished from the work of others.

Tone is the writer's attitude toward his or her audience. The tone of a piece can be described as formal or informal, humorous or serious, satiric or sympathetic, or any number of other ways.

Point of view is the perspective from which a piece is written. First-person point of view is told from the view of one of the characters. Third-person point of view is told by someone outside the story. Third-person point of view can be told from three different perspectives: omniscient (the narrator shares the thoughts and feeling of all the characters), limited omniscient (the narrator shares the thoughts and feelings of only one character), or camera view (the narrator records the action from his or her point of view, unaware of any of the other characters' thoughts or feelings, as if taking a film of the event).

Sarcasm is the use of cutting wit to mock someone.

Counterpoint is the use of contrasting ideas to communicate a message.

Praise is the use of positive messages to recognize or influence others.

Presentation Strategies

In the final stage of the composition and rhetoric processes, students present their ideas to an audience. Students can do this in many ways. Here are a few common ways you can help your students make effective presentations in your English classroom:

- Creating booklets, brochures, family scrapbooks, or personal Websites
- Making a speech, participating in a debate, or giving a PowerPoint presentation
- Performing speeches, plays, videos, or readers' theater productions
- Publishing a school newspaper, student magazine, or portfolio of work
- Submitting work for publication beyond the classroom in a literary magazine for young adults, in the local newspaper, in a professional publication for writers, in a contest, or for an online publication

The Language, Linguistics, and Literacy content appears on the following CSET: English test:

- Subtest III: Language, Linguistics, and Literacy

This section is organized as a concise outline of the major content assessed on this test. Review this outline to refresh your memory of the content. If portions of content are not familiar to you, study further by completing the full-length practice tests in Part III of this book and by using the suggested resources in Part IV.

Principles of Language Acquisition and Development

Linguistics is the formal study of the structures and processes of a language. Linguists describe language acquisition and language in general. Key areas of study in this field include the following:

Morphology. The study of the structure of words

Phonetics. The study of the sounds of language and their physical properties

Phonology. The analysis of how sounds function in a language or dialect

Pragmatics. The role of context in the interpretation of meaning

Semantics. The study of meaning in language

Syntax. The study of the structure of sentences

Social, Cultural, and Historical Influences

Language acquisition and development can be understood through several frameworks, including the following:

Sociolinguistics. The study of language as it relates to society, including race, class, gender, and age.

Ethnolinguistics. The study of language as it relates to culture, frequently associated with minority linguistic groups within the larger culture.

Psycholinguistics. The study of language as it relates to the psychological and neurobiological factors that enable humans to learn language.

Historical and political influences on language acquisition. Some experts regard every language as a dialect of an older communication form. For example, the Romance languages (French, Spanish, Portuguese, Italian, and so on) are dialects of Latin. Political relationships also affect views of language as either a dialect or a new entity. For example, English is seen as having two main dialects—British English and American English. The United States and Great Britain are close political allies.

The Nature and Role of Dialects

A **dialect** is a variation of a language, spoken by people inhabiting a particular geographical area. With its own grammar and vocabulary, it is a complete system of verbal (and sometimes written) communication. Dialects, especially those spoken by large numbers of people, can have subdialects.

Standard dialects are supported by institutions, such as governments and schools. In English, for example, standard dialects include Standard American English, Standard Indian English, and Standard British English. Subdialects of Standard American English include African American English Vernacular (also known as Black English Vernacular or Ebonics), Southern American English, Hawaiian English, Spanglish, and Appalachian English.

In the English classroom, students need to be familiar with various dialects in order to better understand literature, composition, and rhetoric. *The Adventures of Huckleberry Finn* is but one example of a book in which students read Southern American English. Students learn to write in Standard American English and in other dialects they may speak or try to imitate. For certain audiences, such as peers, dramatic performances, and debates, they need to use appropriate dialects.

Overview of the English Language

This section lists basic facts about the English language. If, as you review this list, you find areas that seem unfamiliar, refer to the resources listed in Part IV.

Linguistic Change

English is derived from Anglo-Saxon, which is a dialect of West Germanic, although English today contains vocabulary words with roots from many languages, including Chinese, Hebrew, and Russian. The most common root words are of Anglo-Saxon descent, although more than half of the words in English either come from the French or have a French cognate (a word with a common origin). Scientific words in English often have Greek or Latin roots. The Spanish language is found in many English words, especially in terms originating in the southwestern United States.

Etymology and the Process of Word Formation

Etymology is the study of the history and origin of words. Some words are derived from other words and other languages. Key parts of words and origins of words include

- Language origin of word (for example, *excel* is derived from the Latin *excellere,* meaning "be eminent")
- Affixes, prefixes, and suffixes
- Compound words
- Slang words that become common language
- Common words that become slang (for example, *slammer* is slang for *prison* or *jail*)
- Portmanteau words, which are words that have been melded together, such as *smog = smoke + fog*
- Taboo words that become euphemisms

Syntax and Sentence Structure

The word *syntax* refers to the arrangement and relationship of words in phrases and sentences. This section lists basic facts about sentences.

Sentence Meaning and Purpose

A **declarative** sentence makes a statement and tells about a person, place, thing, or idea.

>   *Example:* The bird drank from the water fountain.

An **interrogative** sentence asks a question.

>   *Example:* Have you signed up for the test yet?

An **imperative** sentence issues a command.

>   *Example*: Please take the dog out for a walk.

An **exclamatory** sentence communicates strong ideas or feelings.

> *Example:* You scared me!

A **conditional** sentence expresses wishes or conditions contrary to fact.

> *Example:* If you build it, they will come.

Sentence Structure

A **simple** sentence can have a single subject or a compound subject and a single predicate or a compound predicate. What makes it a simple sentence is the fact that it has only *one* independent clause, and it has *no* dependent clauses. A simple sentence can have one or more phrases.

> **Single subject, single predicate.** Angela dances.
> **Compound subject, single predicate.** Angela and Jerome dance.
> **Compound subject, compound predicate.** Angela and Jerome dance and win contests.
> **Independent clause with two phrases.** Angela dances with Jerome on Saturday nights.

A **compound** sentence is made up of two independent clauses. The clauses must be joined by a semicolon or by a comma and a coordinating conjunction.

> Perry wants to stay in shape, so he rides his bicycle for exercise.
> Perry wants to stay in shape; he rides his bicycle for exercise.

A **complex** sentence has one independent clause and one or more dependent clauses.

> If you want to stay healthy [dependent clause], you must choose your food carefully [independent clause].

A **compound/complex** sentence has two or more independent clauses and one or more dependent clauses.

> When Sara turned seven [dependent clause], her mother planned a birthday party for her [independent clause], and Sara invited everyone in her class [independent clause].

Effective Sentences

Effective sentences are clear and concise. In addition, effective sentences might include imagery, precise language, and rhythm. Ineffective sentences often have one or more of the following problems:

- Unnatural language, such as clichés and inappropriate jargon
- Nonstandard language or unparallel construction
- Errors such as disagreement between pronoun and referent
- Short, stilted sentences; run-on sentences; or sentence fragments

Elements of English

This section provides a brief overview of nouns, verbs, pronouns, modifiers, phrases and clauses, punctuation, and semantics.

Nouns

Common nouns do not name specific people, places, or things. Common nouns are not capitalized.

> *Examples:* woman, lion, sedan

Proper nouns name particular people, places, or things. Proper nouns are capitalized.

> *Examples:* Queen Elizabeth, Aspen, Lake Geneva

Concrete nouns name things that are tangible (they can be seen, heard, touched, smelled, or tasted). They can be proper or common.

> *Examples:* bear, Gold Miner Restaurant, basketball

Abstract nouns name ideas, conditions, or feelings (in other words, things that are not concrete).

> *Examples:* peace, memory, euphoria

Collective nouns name groups or units.

> *Examples:* army, family, club

Number of Nouns

Nouns can be either **singular** or **plural** in number. Examples of singular nouns include earthquake, citizen, and city. Examples of plural nouns include earthquakes, citizens, and cities.

Gender of Nouns

Nouns are considered to have a gender or to be neutral (neuter) or indefinite in gender:

> **Masculine**. father, uncle, brother, stag
>
> **Feminine**. mother, aunt, sister, doe
>
> **Neutral**. floor, desk, computer
>
> **Indefinite**. politician, doctor, principal

Case of Nouns

Nouns also are considered to be one of three cases:

- A **nominative case noun** can be the subject of a clause or the predicate noun when it follows a linking verb.
- A **possessive case noun** shows possession or ownership.
- An **objective case noun** can be a direct object, an indirect object, or an object of a preposition.

Verbs

Transitive verbs take direct objects—words or word groups that complete the meaning of a verb by naming a receiver of the action.

> *Example:* Daniel [subject] threw [transitive verb] the ball [direct object].

Intransitive verbs take no objects or complements.

> *Example:* The cat *napped.*

Linking or connecting verbs connect the subject and the subject complement (an adjective, noun, or noun equivalent).

> *Example:* Erin *is* happy.

An **auxiliary or helping verb** comes before another verb.

Example: She *has* done well on the exam.

Verb Tenses

Present tense is used to describe situations that exist in the present time.

Example: Courtenay and Meredith *are enjoying* their dessert.

Past tense is used to tell about what happened in the past.

Example: Yesterday, the cafeteria *offered* frozen yogurt for dessert.

Future tense is used to express action that will take place in the future.

Example: Tomorrow, Jasmine *will bring* her lunch from home.

Present perfect tense is used when the action began in the past but continues into the present.

Example: Ted *has ordered* the same thing for lunch every day this month.

Past perfect tense is used to express action that began in the past and happened prior to another past action.

Example: Ellen said that she *had been* to Lake Tahoe many times.

Future perfect tense is used to express action that will begin in the future and will be completed in the future.

Example: By this time next year, Steven *will have completed* all the course work for his credential.

Verbals versus Verbs

An **infinitive** is made up of *to* and the base form of a verb, such as *to see* or *to leave.* It can function as an adjective, adverb, or noun.

A **participle** is a verb form that usually ends in *-ing* or *-ed.* Participles operate as adjectives but also maintain some characteristics of verbs. You might think of a participle as a verbal adjective. Examples include *singing* waiter and *baked* goods.

A **gerund** is made up of a present participle (a verbal ending in *-ing*) and always functions as a noun.

Example: Swimming is Alice's favorite form of exercise.

Pronouns

There are three types of pronouns:

> **Simple**. I, you, he, she, it, we, they, who, what
> **Compound**. itself, myself, anybody, someone, everything
> **Phrasal**. each other, one another

Pronoun Antecedents

An **antecedent** is the noun to which a pronoun refers. Each pronoun must agree with its antecedent in person and number.

Example: The *girls* are going to the mall this afternoon. *They* need to buy new tennis shoes.

Classes of Pronouns

Personal pronouns refer to individuals or sets of individuals.

> *Example:* Miss Greene changed *her* mind about the homework assignment.

Relative pronouns relate adjective clauses to the nouns or pronouns they modify.

> *Example:* The noise *that* frightened you was made by the boy *who* lives in the green house.

Indefinite pronouns usually refer to unnamed or unknown people or things.

> *Example:* Is *anybody* home?

Interrogative pronouns ask questions.

> *Example: Which* of these jackets is yours?

Demonstrative pronouns (*this, that, these, those*) point out people, places, or things without naming them.

> *Example:* I'll take *this* basket and *those* apples.

Reflexive pronouns refer to the subject of a sentence or clause.

> *Example:* I can do *it* myself.

Intensive pronouns are used to draw attention to a noun. They have the same form as reflexive pronouns.

> *Example:* I *myself* will pay the bill.

Reciprocal pronouns indicate an interchange of the action started by the verb. There are only two in English: *each other* for an interaction involving two and *one another* for an interaction involving three or more.

> *Example:* After the debate, the two opponents shook hands with *each other.*

Cases of Pronouns

Pronouns also are considered to be one of three cases:

- A **nominative case pronoun** can be the subject of a clause or the predicate noun when it follows a linking verb. Examples are *I, you, he, she, it, we,* and *they.*
- A **possessive case pronoun** shows possession or ownership. Examples are *my, mine, your, yours, his, hers, its, ours, their,* and *theirs.*
- An **objective case pronoun** can be a direct object, an indirect object, or an object of a preposition. Examples are *me, you, him, her, it, us,* and *them.*

Modifiers

Modifiers are words, clauses, or phrases that limit or describe other words or groups of words.

Adjectives describe or modify nouns or pronouns.

> *Examples:* small, yellow, young, sleek, the

Adverbs describe or modify verbs, adjectives, or other adverbs. They answer the questions *when, where, how,* and *to what degree.*

> *Examples:* later, here, quickly, very

Phrases and Clauses

Phrases are groups of related words that function as a single part of speech, such as a verb, verbal, prepositional, appositive, or absolute. For example, *at the bus stop* is a prepositional phrase.

Clauses are groups of related words that have both a subject and a predicate. For example, *We can go to the movies if Janice gets back on time* contains the independent clause *We can go to the movies* and the dependent clause *if Janice gets back on time.*

Punctuation

Various forms of punctuation are available for usage in English, and guidelines abound for using punctuation correctly. Here is a brief overview of punctuation rules.

A **comma** is used between two independent clauses, to separate adjectives, to separate contrasted elements, to set off appositives, to separate items in a list, to enclose explanatory words, after an introductory phrase, after an introductory clause, to set off a nonrestrictive phrase, to ensure clarity, in numbers, to set off titles, in a direct address, to set off dialogue, to set off items in an address, and to set off dates.

A **period** is used at the end of a sentence, after an initial or abbreviation, or as a decimal point.

A **question mark** is used at the end of a direct question and to show uncertainty.

An **exclamation point** is used to express strong feeling.

An **apostrophe** is used in contractions; to form singular and plural possessives; and to form plurals of letters, numbers, and words named as words.

A **dash** is used for emphasis, to set off interrupted speech, to set off an introductory series, and to indicate a sudden break.

Parentheses are used to set off explanatory information and to set off full sentences.

Brackets are used to set off added words, editorial corrections, and clarifying information.

A **hyphen** is used between numbers, between fractions, to form compound adjectives, to attach some prefixes and suffixes, and to create new words.

Semantics

Semantics is the study of the meaning in language.

Ambiguity occurs when there are two or more possible meanings to a word or phrase.

Example: Joanne told Michelle that she needed to study harder.

A **euphemism** is a bland, inoffensive word or phrase used to replace a word or expression that may suggest something unpleasant.

Example: Maureen excused herself from the table to go to the *ladies' room.*

Doublespeak is language that is intended to be evasive or to conceal the truth. The term came into use in the 1950s and is similar to *newspeak,* a term coined by George Orwell in his novel *1984.* Doublespeak is related to euphemism but is distinguished by its use by government, military, and business organizations.

Example: Ethnic cleansing is doublespeak for *genocide.*

Jargon is the specialized language of a particular group or culture. Education-related jargon includes words such as *rubric, decoding skills, phonemic awareness,* and *benchmark.*

Communications

The Communications content appears on the following CSET: English tests:

- Subtest IV: Communications: Speech, Media, and Creative Performance

This section is organized as a brief glossary of some of the terms you might encounter in this subtest. This list is not meant to be exhaustive; instead, it is meant to suggest topics you might wish to study further. Review this glossary to refresh your memory of these terms. If some of these terms are unfamiliar to you, investigate those areas.

Oral Performance Forms

Debate. A speech form in which two sides take opposite positions on a question and take turns arguing their view. Lincoln-Douglas debates are a special type of debate commonly held for high school competitions, in which each side is only one person rather than a team of two. Debates are strictly timed.

Expository speech. A speech with the purpose of informing the audience about a topic.

Extemporaneous speech. Like an impromptu speech, but the speaker is often given a little time to prepare.

Impromptu speech. A speech given on the spur of the moment with very little preparation.

Interpretive performance. The performance of a work of literature with the purpose of communicating its emotional meaning.

Persuasive speech. A speech with the purpose of influencing the audience members' opinions.

Performance Skills

Body language. The way one uses the body to communicate. For example, a speaker who holds his arms stiffly at his side, rather than making natural-looking gestures, appears uncomfortable and will make the audience uncomfortable.

Diction. The choice and use of words in speech.

Enunciation. The way one pronounces words.

Eye contact. The practice of looking into the eyes of individual audience members. A good speaker will pick a friendly face and maintain eye contact for a brief time before moving on to another, trying to include members from all sections of the audience at various intervals.

Response to audience. The way in which a speaker picks up on audience mood and adjusts performance or speech accordingly.

Vocal pitch. The degree of highness or lowness of a speaker's voice.

Vocal range. A measure of how far a speaker's voice carries.

Vocal rate. The speed at which one speaks.

Volume. The degree of loudness of a speaker's voice.

Persuasive Techniques Used by the Media

Bandwagon. The suggestion that one should buy something or think a certain way because "everyone else" is doing so.

Either-or fallacy. The idea that one has only two choices, when in fact there may be many choices.

Emotionalism/slanted language. The use of emotion-packed words to get a desired response.

Implied benefit. The suggestion that more than what is being sold will be delivered; for example, the idea that by using a certain product, one will have a better love life or a different lifestyle.

Overgeneralization. Sweeping statements about a situation or product.

Plain folks. The suggestion that since "we are all alike," you should buy a product or adopt a certain attitude because the speaker does; for example, "As a busy high-school student, I don't have time to deal with acne, so I use XYZ acne medication, and you should, too."

Red herring. The practice of citing a minor detail as a major bonus; for example, "This is the only brand of socks that comes in a choice of 28 different colors."

Snob appeal. The suggestion that all the rich/cool/smart/stylish people are doing/buying/believing something, so you should, too; for example, a famous actor uses a certain brand of perfume, so you should, too.

Testimonial. The use of a well-known person to recommend a product or way of thinking.

Drama Terms

Blocking. The physical arrangement of actors on a stage or film set.

Costume. Clothing worn by actors on a stage or film set.

Dramatic arc. Rising and falling action in a play.

Improvisation. The act of creating and performing spontaneously or without preparation.

Lighting. The way lights are used to emphasize or de-emphasize parts of a stage.

Props. Portable objects used on the set of a play or film.

Set. A collection of scenery, stage furniture, and so on, used for a scene in a play or film.

Sound. Music, speech, and sound effects accompanying a play, film, or broadcast.

Tempo. The speed at which events occur in a play or other performance.

PART III

FULL-LENGTH PRACTICE TESTS

This part allows you to practice taking the CSET: English tests that you are required to pass in order to get your license to teach English in California. Two complete practice tests are in this section. Each practice test covers the following subtests:

Subtest 1: Literature and Textual Analysis; Composition and Rhetoric

Subtest II: Language, Linguistics, and Literacy

Subtest III: Composition and Rhetoric; Literature and Textual Analysis

Subtest IV: Communications: Speech, Media, and Creative Performance

Taking the practice tests gives you a feel for the format of the test and helps you determine which content areas you should brush up on. Be aware of your pacing as you take these full-length practice tests. Remember, the test session is five hours. You can take one or more of the subtests during this time. The CSET: English is designed in such a way that all subtests may be completed with a single five-hour test session. As you take these practice tests, you can determine whether you want to sign up for all four at the same time or sign up for multiple testing sessions.

Each test is followed by a detailed answer key. After you complete the practice tests, score your answers. Then use the explanations to determine the content areas in which you need more study time.

So get comfortable. Find a quiet place where you will not be interrupted. Get your pencils ready, take a look at the clock, and get started on your first practice test.

(Remove this sheet and use it to mark your answers to the multiple-choice questions.)

Answer Sheet

1	Ⓐ Ⓑ Ⓒ Ⓓ		26	Ⓐ Ⓑ Ⓒ Ⓓ
2	Ⓐ Ⓑ Ⓒ Ⓓ		27	Ⓐ Ⓑ Ⓒ Ⓓ
3	Ⓐ Ⓑ Ⓒ Ⓓ		28	Ⓐ Ⓑ Ⓒ Ⓓ
4	Ⓐ Ⓑ Ⓒ Ⓓ		29	Ⓐ Ⓑ Ⓒ Ⓓ
5	Ⓐ Ⓑ Ⓒ Ⓓ		30	Ⓐ Ⓑ Ⓒ Ⓓ
6	Ⓐ Ⓑ Ⓒ Ⓓ		31	Ⓐ Ⓑ Ⓒ Ⓓ
7	Ⓐ Ⓑ Ⓒ Ⓓ		32	Ⓐ Ⓑ Ⓒ Ⓓ
8	Ⓐ Ⓑ Ⓒ Ⓓ		33	Ⓐ Ⓑ Ⓒ Ⓓ
9	Ⓐ Ⓑ Ⓒ Ⓓ		34	Ⓐ Ⓑ Ⓒ Ⓓ
10	Ⓐ Ⓑ Ⓒ Ⓓ		35	Ⓐ Ⓑ Ⓒ Ⓓ
11	Ⓐ Ⓑ Ⓒ Ⓓ		36	Ⓐ Ⓑ Ⓒ Ⓓ
12	Ⓐ Ⓑ Ⓒ Ⓓ		37	Ⓐ Ⓑ Ⓒ Ⓓ
13	Ⓐ Ⓑ Ⓒ Ⓓ		38	Ⓐ Ⓑ Ⓒ Ⓓ
14	Ⓐ Ⓑ Ⓒ Ⓓ		39	Ⓐ Ⓑ Ⓒ Ⓓ
15	Ⓐ Ⓑ Ⓒ Ⓓ		40	Ⓐ Ⓑ Ⓒ Ⓓ
16	Ⓐ Ⓑ Ⓒ Ⓓ		41	Ⓐ Ⓑ Ⓒ Ⓓ
17	Ⓐ Ⓑ Ⓒ Ⓓ		42	Ⓐ Ⓑ Ⓒ Ⓓ
18	Ⓐ Ⓑ Ⓒ Ⓓ		43	Ⓐ Ⓑ Ⓒ Ⓓ
19	Ⓐ Ⓑ Ⓒ Ⓓ		44	Ⓐ Ⓑ Ⓒ Ⓓ
20	Ⓐ Ⓑ Ⓒ Ⓓ		45	Ⓐ Ⓑ Ⓒ Ⓓ
21	Ⓐ Ⓑ Ⓒ Ⓓ		46	Ⓐ Ⓑ Ⓒ Ⓓ
22	Ⓐ Ⓑ Ⓒ Ⓓ		47	Ⓐ Ⓑ Ⓒ Ⓓ
23	Ⓐ Ⓑ Ⓒ Ⓓ		48	Ⓐ Ⓑ Ⓒ Ⓓ
24	Ⓐ Ⓑ Ⓒ Ⓓ		49	Ⓐ Ⓑ Ⓒ Ⓓ
25	Ⓐ Ⓑ Ⓒ Ⓓ		50	Ⓐ Ⓑ Ⓒ Ⓓ

CUT HERE

Practice Test 1

Subtest I: Literature and Textual Analysis; Composition and Rhetoric

Part 1: Content Domains for Subject Matter Understanding and Skill in English

Following is a list of the areas on which you will be tested. This information is also available at the CSET Website. It is reproduced here for your convenience.

Literature and Textual Analysis (SMR Domain 1)

Candidates demonstrate knowledge of the foundations and contexts of the literature and textual analysis contained in the *English-Language Arts Content Standards for California Public Schools Kindergarten Through Grade Twelve* (1999) at a post secondary level of rigor. Candidates have both broad and deep conceptual knowledge of the subject matter. The candidate's preparation should include breadth of knowledge in literature, literary analysis and criticism, as well as nonliterary test analysis. Literary analysis presumes in-depth exploration of the relationship between form and content. The curriculum should embrace representative selections from different literary traditions and major works from diverse cultures. Advanced study of multicultural writers is also fundamental preparation for teaching these works. Shakespeare remains integral to the secondary school curriculum; advanced study of his work is, therefore, essential to future secondary teachers. Candidates must be enthusiastic readers and writers, who know and apply effective reading strategies and compose thoughtful well-crafted responses to literary and nonliterary tests. Candidates will be able to:

0001 Literary Analysis (SMR 1.1)

a. Recognize, compare, and evaluate different literary traditions to include:
   - American (inclusive of cultural pluralism)
   - British (inclusive of cultural pluralism)
   - World literature and literature in translation (inclusive of cross-cultural literature)
   - Mythology and oral tradition

b. Trace development of major literary movements in historical periods (e.g., Homeric Greece, medieval, neoclassic, romantic, modern).

c. Describe the salient features of adolescent/young adult literature.

d. Analyze and interpret major works by representative writers in historical, aesthetic, political, and philosophical contexts.

(*English-Language Arts Content Standards for California Public Schools*, Grade 6, Reading: 2.4; Grades 11–12, Reading: 2.2, 3.5–7)

0002 Literary Elements (SMR 1.2)

a. Distinguish salient features of genres (e.g., short stories, non-fiction, drama, poetry, novel).

b. Define and analyze basic elements of literature (e.g., plot, setting, character, point of view, theme, narrative structure, figurative language, tone, diction, style).

    c. Articulate the relationship between the expressed purposes and the characteristics of different forms of dramatic literature (e.g., comedy, tragedy, drama, dramatic monologue).

    d. Develop critical thinking and analytic skill through close reading of texts.

(*English-Language Arts Content Standards for California Public Schools,* Grade 6, Reading: 1.1–2, 2.1, 2.4, 2.6, 2.8, 3.0; Grade 7, Reading: 1.1, 2.4, 3.1–5; Grade 8, Reading: 1.1, 2.7, 3.0; Grades 9–10, Reading: 1.1, 2.8, 3.1–4, 3.7–10; Grades 11–12, Reading: 2.2, 3.1–4)

0003 Literary Criticism (SMR 1.3)

    a. Research and apply criticism of major texts and authors using print and/or electronic resources.

    b. Research and apply various approaches to interpreting literature (e.g., aesthetic, historical, political, philosophical).

(*English-Language Arts Content Standards for California Public Schools,* Grade 6, Reading: 2.1–2, 2.6–8, 3.6; Grade 7, Reading: 2.1, 2.4, 2.6, 3.0; Grade 8, Reading: 2.2, 2.6, 3.0; Grades 9–10, Reading: 2.2, 2.4, 2.8, 3.5–7, 3.11–12, Writing: 1.6–7; Grades 11–12, Reading: 2.2, 2.4, 3.8–9, Writing: 1.6–7)

0004 Analysis of Non-Literary Texts (SMR 1.4)

    a. Compare various features of print and visual media (e.g., film, television, Internet).

    b. Evaluate structure and content of a variety of consumer, workplace, and public documents.

    c. Interpret individual works in their cultural, social, and political contexts.

(*English-Language Arts Content Standards for California Public Schools,* Grade 6, Reading: 2.0, 3.0; Grade 7, Reading: 2.1–5, 2.2, 3.0; Grade 8, Reading: 2.1–7, 3.0; Grades 9–10, Reading: 2.1, 2.2, 2.4–7, 3.0; Grades 11–12, Reading: 2.1–3, 2.6, 3.0)

Composition and Rhetoric (SMR Domain 3)

Candidates demonstrate knowledge of the foundations and contexts of the composition and rhetoric contained in the *English-Language Arts Content Standards for California Public Schools* (1997) as outlined in the *Reading/Language Arts Framework for California Public Schools: Kindergarten Through Grade Twelve* (1999) at a post-secondary level of rigor. Candidates have both broad and deep conceptual knowledge of the subject matter. Candidates face dynamic challenges in the domains of oral and written communication. They must make appropriate use of current text-production technologies and develop sensitivity to patterns of communication used by different social and cultural groups. Candidates are competent writers and speakers who are able to communicate appropriately in various rhetorical contexts, using effective text structures, word choice, sentence options, standard usage conventions, and advanced research methods as needed. The subject matter preparation program provides opportunities for candidates to develop skills and confidence in public speaking. Candidates will be able to:

0005 Written Composing Processes (Individual and Collaborative) (SMR 3.1)

    a. Reflect on and describe their own writing processes.

    b. Investigate and apply alternative methods of prewriting, drafting, responding, revising, editing, and evaluating.

    c. Employ such strategies as graphic organizers, outlines, notes, charts, summaries, or précis to clarify and record meaning.

    d. Integrate a variety of software applications (e.g., databases, graphics, spreadsheets) to produce print documents and multi-media presentations.

(*English-Language Arts Content Standards for California Public Schools,* Grade 6, Reading: 2.1–2, 2.4, Writing: 1.4–6; Grade 7, Reading: 2.3–4, Writing: 1.3–4, 1.6–7; Grade 8, Reading: 2.4, Writing: 1.1, 1.4–1.6, Listening and Speaking: 1.4; Grades 9–10, Reading: 2.4, Writing: 1.8–9; Grades 11–12, Writing: 1.4, 1.7–9, Listening and Speaking: 2.4)

0006 Rhetorical Features of Literary and Non-Literary, Oral and Written Texts (SMR 3.2)

a. Recognize and use a variety of writing applications (e.g., short story, biographical, autobiographical, expository, persuasive, business and technical documents, historical investigation).

b. Demonstrate awareness of audience, purpose, and context.

c. Recognize and use various text structures (e.g., narrative and non-narrative organizational patterns).

d. Apply a variety of methods to develop ideas within an essay (e.g., analogy, cause and effect, compare and contrast, definition, illustration, description, hypothesis).

e. Apply critical thinking strategies to evaluate methods of persuasion, including but not limited to:

- Types of appeal (e.g., appeal to reason, emotion, morality)
- Types of persuasive speech (e.g., propositions of fact, value, problem, policy)
- Logical fallacies (e.g., bandwagon, red herring, glittering generalities, ad hominem)
- Advertising techniques (e.g., Maslow's hierarchy of needs)
- Logical argument (e.g., inductive/deductive reasoning, syllogisms, analogies)
- Classical argument (e.g., claim, qualifiers, rules of evidence, warrant)

(*English-Language Arts Content Standards for California Public Schools,* Grade 6, Reading: 2.1–2, 2.4, 2.6, 2.8, Writing: 1.1–3, 1.6, 2.1–5, Listening and Speaking: 1.8–9; Grade 7, Reading: 1.3, 2.2–3, Writing: 1.1–3, 1.7, 2.1–5, Listening and Speaking: 1.1, 1.3; Grade 8, Reading: 1.3, 2.2, Writing: 1.1–3, 1.5, 2.1–6, Listening and Speaking: 1.8; Grades 9–10, Writing: 1.1–2, 1.4, 1.9, 2.1–6, Listening and Speaking: 1.5, 1.10, 1.13; Grades 11–12, Reading: 1.3, 2.2, 2.4–6, Writing: 1.1–5, 1.9, 2.1–6, Listening and Speaking: 1.4, 1.12–13)

0007 Rhetorical Effects of Grammatical Elements (SMR 3.3)

a. Employ precise and extensive vocabulary and effective diction to control voice, style, and tone.

b. Use clause joining techniques (e.g., coordinators, subordinators, punctuation) to express logical connections between ideas.

c. Identify and use clausal and phrasal modifiers to control flow, pace, and emphasis (e.g., adjective clauses, appositives, participle and verbal phrases, absolutes).

d. Identify and use devices to control focus in sentence and paragraph (e.g., active and passive voice, expletives, concrete subjects, transitional phrases).

e. Maintain coherence through use of cohesive devices.

(*English-Language Arts Content Standards for California Public Schools,* Grade 6, Reading: 1.1, Writing: 1.2, 1.6, Written and Oral English Language Conventions: 1.1–5; Grade 7, Writing: 1.1, 1.7, Written and Oral English Language Conventions: 1.1–7; Grade 8, Writing: 1.2, 1.6, Written and Oral English Language Conventions: 1.1–6, Listening and Speaking: 1.5–6; Grades 9–10, Writing: 1.1–2, 1.6, 1.9, Written and Oral English Language Conventions: 1.1–5; Grades 11–12, Reading: 2.1–2, Writing: 1.2–5, 1.9, Written and Oral English Language Conventions: 1.1–3, Listening and Speaking: 1.5)

0008 Conventions of Oral and Written Language (SMR 3.4)

a. Apply knowledge of linguistic structure to identify and use the conventions of Standard Edited English.

b. Recognize, understand, and use a range of conventions in both spoken and written English, including:

- Conventions of effective sentence structure (e.g., clear pronoun reference, parallel structure, appropriate verb tense)
- Preferred usage (e.g., verb/subject agreement, pronoun agreement, idioms)
- Conventions of pronunciation and intonation
- Conventional forms of spelling
- Capitalization and punctuation

(*English-Language Arts Content Standards for California Public Schools,* Grade 6, Reading: 1.1, Written and Oral English Language Conventions: 1.1–5; Grade 7, Written and Oral English Language Conventions: 1.1–7; Grade 8, Writing: 1.2, Written and Oral English Language Conventions: 1.1–6, Listening and Speaking: 1.6; Grades 9–10, Writing: 1.9, Written and Oral English Language Conventions: 1.9; Grades 11–12, Writing: 1.4, Written and Oral English Language Conventions: 1.1–3, Listening and Speaking: 1.8)

0009 Research Strategies (SMR 3.5)

a. Develop and apply research questions.

b. Demonstrate methods of inquiry and investigation.

c. Identify and use multiple resources (e.g., oral, print, electronic; primary and secondary), and critically evaluate the quality of the sources.

d. Interpret and apply findings.

e. Use professional conventions and ethical standards of citation and attribution.

f. Demonstrate effective presentation methods, including multi-media formats.

(*English-Language Arts Content Standards for California Public Schools,* Grade 6, Reading: 1.1, 2.1, 2.3, 2.6–8, Writing: 1.4–5, Listening and Speaking: 1.1–2, 1.6–7, 2.1, 2.3; Grade 7, Reading: 2.2, 2.6, Writing: 1.4–5, Listening and Speaking: 1.2, 1.6–7, 2.1, 2.3; Grade 8, Reading: 2.2, 2.7, Writing: 1.3–6, Listening and Speaking: 1.2–3, 1.6–8, 2.3; Grades 9–10, Reading: 2.2–5, 2.8, Writing: 1.3–8, Listening and Speaking: 1.7, 2.2; Grades 11–12, Writing: 1.4, 1.6–8, Listening and Speaking: 2.4)

Subtest I: Literature and Textual Analysis; Composition and Rhetoric

Directions: Each of the questions or statements below is followed by four suggested answers or completions. Select the one that is best in each case.

1. In which period in British literature were the following works written?

Christopher Marlowe's *Doctor Faustus*

Sir Philip Sidney's *Arcadia*

William Shakespeare's *Romeo and Juliet*

Edmund Spenser's *The Faerie Queene*

   A. Old English Period
   B. Middle English Period
   C. the Renaissance
   D. the Augustinian Age

2. Literary works by regional American writers such as Willa Cather, William Faulkner, Bret Harte, and Sara Orne Jewett generally tend to share which of the following characteristics?

   A. an emphasis on the importance of the individual and all the experiences and emotions that the individual might feel
   B. the attitude that the individual is like an animal in the natural world, helpless over the environmental forces and internal drives that drive his or her fate
   C. disjointed narratives that include shifting points of view, changes in chronology, flashbacks, and flash forwards
   D. accurate depiction of the habits, speech, history, manners, folklore, or beliefs of a particular geographical area

Questions 3–4 are about the following excerpt from a Robert Frost poem:

When I see birches bend to left and right

Across the lines of straighter darker trees,

I like to think some boy's been swinging them.

But swinging doesn't bend them down to stay.

3. Which of the following is the correct title of the poem from which this excerpt is taken?

   A. "Bending Birches"
   B. "Birches"
   C. "Thoughts on Birches"
   D. "Birches in Winter"

4. Which of the following describes the versification of the lines above?

   I. anapestic trimeter
   II. unrhymed iambic pentameter
   III. blank verse
   IV. free verse

   A. I and III
   B. III and IV
   C. II and III
   D. All of the above

GO ON TO THE NEXT PAGE

Questions 5–7 are based on this excerpt from *I Know Why the Caged Bird Sings* by Maya Angelou.

For nearly a year, I sopped around the house, the Store, the school and the church, like an old biscuit, dirty and inedible. Then I met, or rather got to know, the lady who threw me my first lifeline.

Mrs. Bertha Flowers was the aristocrat of Black Stamps. She had the grace of control to appear warm in the coldest weather, and on the Arkansas summer days it seemed she had a private breeze which swirled around, cooling her. She was thin without the taut look of wiry people, and her printed voile dresses and flowered hats were as right for her as denim overalls for a farmer. She was our side's answer to the richest white woman in town.

5. Which of the following is an example of a simile?

   A. "I sopped around . . . like an old biscuit, dirty and inedible."
   B. "the lady who threw me my first lifeline"
   C. "she had a private breeze which swirled around"
   D. "our side's answer to the richest white woman in town"

6. Which is an example of a metaphor?

   A. "For nearly a year, I sopped around"
   B. "threw me my first lifeline"
   C. "Mrs. Bertha Flowers was the aristocrat of Black Stamps."
   D. "her printed voile dresses and flowered hats were as right for her as denim overalls for a farmer."

7. What can the reader expect to find next in this narrative?

   A. further description of Mrs. Bertha Flowers's physical appearance
   B. some description of Mrs. Bertha Flowers's behavior
   C. an explanation of how Mrs. Bertha Flowers helped the narrator
   D. All of the above

Questions 8–12 are based on the following poem, "Piazza Piece," by John Crowe Ransom.

—I am a gentleman in a dustcoat trying

To make you hear. Your ears are soft and small

And listen to an old man not at all.

They want the young men's whispering and sighing.

But see the roses on your trellis dying

And hear the spectral singing of the moon;

For I must have my lovely lady soon.

I am a gentleman in a dustcoat trying.

—I am a lady young in beauty waiting

Until my truelove comes, and then we kiss.

But what gray man among the vines is this

Whose words are dry and faint as in a dream?

Back from my trellis, Sir, before I scream!

I am a lady young in beauty waiting.

8. This poem is an example of a(n):

   A. Petrarchan sonnet.
   B. Shakespearean sonnet.
   C. elegy.
   D. concrete poem.

9. The gentleman in the dustcoat is:

   A. an older suitor of the young lady.
   B. a servant in the young lady's home.
   C. Death, come to take the lady.
   D. the young lady's "truelove," visiting from the future.

10. The meter of this poem is:

    A. dactylic tetrameter.
    B. spondaic heptameter.
    C. anapestic trimeter.
    D. iambic pentameter.

11. The rhyme scheme of this poem is:

    A. *ababcdcd dcedce.*
    B. *abcdefg hijklm.*
    C. *abbaacca dcceed.*
    D. *abbabccb defdef.*

12. Internal clues suggest that the setting of this poem is:

    A. the Old South.
    B. New England.
    C. California.
    D. New York City.

13. Literary works by romantic writers such as William Wordsworth, Samuel Taylor Coleridge, Thomas Gray, and Robert Burns generally tend to share which of the following characteristics?

    A. an emphasis on intellectualism and logical thought, along with a sense of neatness, balance, dignity, and discipline
    B. a rejection of older standards of morality, faith, and spiritual values; a sense that the only constant is change
    C. a celebration of nature rather than civilization and an emphasis on emotion and imagination rather than reason
    D. a sense that human beings are powerless over their fates, responding to external forces and internal drives beyond their control

14. Which of the following best describes Edgar Allan Poe's view concerning poetry, as expressed in his essay "The Poetic Principle"?

    A. Poetry must offer lessons in truth.
    B. Poetry must allow the reader to enjoy the contemplation of the beautiful.
    C. The best subject for a poem is something supernatural or weird.
    D. A good poem should teach a moral lesson.

Read this excerpt from the film script for *Ikiru*, Akira Kurosawa's 1952 film. Then answer Questions 15–17.

WATANABE: Here, Ono, take care of this.

He hands him a document on which is written: "PETITION FOR RECLAIMING DRAINAGE AREA— KUROE-CHO WOMEN'S ASSOCIATION." There is a notice attached which says: "This Petition to be forwarded to the Public Works Section." WATANABE *tears off the notice.*

ONO: But this petition should go—

WATANABE: No, unless we do something about it, nothing will ever be done. Everyone will have to cooperate, the Public Works Section, the Parks Section, the Sewage Section—all must cooperate. Now call me a car. I must make an inspection, and prepare a report today.

ONO: But this will be difficult.

WATANABE: No, it won't, not if you are determined.

GO ON TO THE NEXT PAGE

15. This excerpt best illustrates Akira Kurosawa's message that the best use of one's life is:

  A. in social action, particularly action that leaves the world a better place.

  B. in making sure people cooperate with one another.

  C. in reclaiming drainage areas for other public uses.

  D. in taking a stand against the bureaucracy of civil service jobs.

16. Watanabe's lines suggest that:

  A. he likes to order people around.

  B. he has been frustrated by bureaucratic red tape in the past.

  C. he has no hope of accomplishing his goal.

  D. he usually takes orders from Ono.

17. Ono's lines suggest that:

  A. he likes to follow established procedures and avoid problems.

  B. he takes the initiative at work and gets things done.

  C. he is concerned about the project being promoted by the women's association.

  D. he has great respect for Watanabe's opinions.

Questions 18–20 are based on the following poem:

On the plum tree glows

One blossom, now another

Warmth, too, is growing.

18. This poem is an example of a(n):

  A. limerick.

  B. tanka.

  C. haiku.

  D. epic.

19. The mood of the poem can best be described as:

  A. mournful.

  B. angry.

  C. astonished.

  D. joyful.

20. The reader can deduce that the time of year is:

  A. winter.

  B. spring.

  C. summer.

  D. fall.

Questions 21–23 are based on the following excerpt from Shakespeare's *The Merchant of Venice*.

LORENZO: How sweet the moonlight sleeps upon this bank!

Here will we sit and let the sounds of music

Creep in our ears; soft stillness and the night

Become the touches of sweet harmony.

Sit, Jessica. Look how the floor of heaven

Is thick inlaid with patens of bright gold.

There's not the smallest orb which thou behold'st

But in his motion like an angel sings,

Still quiring to the young-eyed cherubins;

Such harmony is in immortal souls,

But whilst this muddy vesture of decay

Doth grossly close it in, we cannot hear it.

21. This passage most clearly reflects the Elizabethan world view that:

  A. human beings are insignificant compared with the forces of nature.

  B. the universe is a unified whole in which everything has its place.

  C. scientific knowledge is the only means by which we can appreciate the universe.

  D. the forces of the universe conspire against humanity, preventing happiness

22. The lines "There's not the smallest orb which thou behold'st / But in his motion like an angel sings," contain an example of:

   A. a simile.

   B. a metaphor.

   C. alliteration.

   D. hyperbole.

23. The phrase "muddy vesture of decay" refers to:

   A. the earth.

   B. death.

   C. the human body.

   D. human civilization.

Questions 24–25 are based on the following excerpt from "How Grandmother Spider Named the Clans."

After Tawa, the Sky God, and Grandmother Spider had made Earth and all of the things upon it, Tawa went back up into the heavens. Grandmother Spider remained with the animals and all of the people there in the four great caves of the underworld. It was left to Grandmother Spider to put things on Earth into order. So Grandmother Spider gathered all of the living creatures around her. She began to separate the people into the different Indian nations, telling them how it would be from then on for them. So it was that she made the Ute and the Zuni and the Comanche and the Pueblo people and the Hopi and all of the others. She named them and from then on they knew their names. So too she gave all of the animals their names so that they also would know who they were.

24. This passage is part of a story known as a(n):

   A. trickster story.

   B. epic.

   C. parable.

   D. creation myth.

25. Based on the fact that she named the people and the animals, Grandmother Spider can be compared to the Biblical character of:

   A. Eve.

   B. Adam.

   C. Noah.

   D. Abraham.

26. Which of the following descriptions applies to adolescent/young adult literature?

   I.   subject matter that appeals to an audience age 12–18

   II.   themes that young adults might find interesting

   III.   often part of a series

   IV.   written for, published for, or marketed to young adults

   A. I and IV

   B. II and III

   C. I, II, and IV

   D. I, II, III, and IV

27. What is the main difference between comedy and tragedy?

   A. Tragedy has no funny scenes.

   B. Comedy has no sad scenes.

   C. Comedy has a happy ending.

   D. No one dies in a comedy.

28. Actors on stage reveal their characters' innermost thoughts in a long speech called a(n):

   A. soliloquy.

   B. aside.

   C. epilogue.

   D. dialogue.

GO ON TO THE NEXT PAGE

29. Which of the following descriptions can be applied to all of the following poems?

"My Last Duchess" by Robert Browning

"The Love Song of J. Alfred Prufrock" by T. S. Eliot

"Ulysses" by Alfred, Lord Tennyson

"Dover Beach" by Matthew Arnold

   I.   lyric

  II.   ballad

 III.   epic poem

 IV.   dramatic monologue

  A. I and II

  B. I and III

  C. II and III

  D. I and IV

Questions 30 and 31 are based on this poem by Lu Yu, a Chinese poet of the twelfth century.

Gazing after Her Husband

I saw you go beyond the river to guard over the frontier,

For men ought to dedicate their bodies to the country.

I can neither bend the bow nor ride untamed horses.

Therefore, my lover, how could I follow your example?

I climb the hill with my head raised, gazing at the northwest clouds.

Though my features have changed, still my heart is constant.

All night the winter moon shines on my tear-marked face,

But to you, my lover, I send my heart of iron.

30. Which of the following best describes the mood of the poem?

  A. The speaker's grief over her husband's absence makes her resent the military leaders.

  B. The speaker's love for her husband is diminishing as time passes.

  C. Although she misses her husband, the speaker supports him and sends her love.

  D. The speaker resents her husband for leaving her to fight in the war.

31. Which line reveals that the poem is set in the distant past?

  A. "For men ought to dedicate their bodies to the country."

  B. "I can neither bend the bow nor ride untamed horses."

  C. "I climb the hill with my head raised, gazing at the northwest clouds."

  D. "All night the winter moon shines on my tear-marked face..."

32. To gain a greater appreciation of *Anne Frank: The Diary of a Young Girl,* which of the following types of criticism would best be applied?

  A. formalist criticism

  B. psychological criticism

  C. new criticism

  D. historical criticism

33. Which of the following best describes a primary aim of deconstructionist criticism?

  A. to challenge the idea that authors can control the meaning of the texts they create

  B. to explore the effects of modern psychology on literature

  C. to determine how elements of form—such as style, structure, tone, and imagery—affect a work

  D. to focus on the biographical facts of an author's life as a means of illuminating the text

34. Read this quotation from Edmund Wilson's *Axel's Castle,* and answer the question that follows:

If we do not ordinarily think of Yeats as primarily a Symbolist poet, it is because, in taking Symbolism to Ireland, he fed it with new resources and gave it a special accent which lead us to think of his poetry from the point of view of its national qualities rather than from the point of view of its relation to the rest of European literature.

Which of the following choices best describes this approach to literary criticism?

A. mythological criticism
B. gender criticism
C. historical criticism
D. psychological criticism

35. Which sentence is most likely to appear in an essay that employs gender criticism?

A. It is interesting that none of the characters in Shakespeare's *Othello* ever thinks to question the right of a husband to murder a wife suspected of adultery.

B. The realization that the plague was having such a devastating effect on Europe at the time helps the reader understand why the friar's messenger was unable to deliver this message to Romeo.

C. Scholars have questioned the motivation behind Hamlet's anguish over his mother's hasty marriage—was he being protective of his father or simply jealous of his mother's new husband?

D. It is clear that Shakespeare was trying to flatter his new patron, James I, by emphasizing the longevity of the Scottish line, all the way back to Banquo.

36. A researcher wants to locate the specific words or phrases in a text. Which is the best form of the text for the researcher to use?

A. printed version
B. electronic version
C. televised version of a reading of the text
D. All of the above

Read the excerpt below. It is from Senator Kennedy's eulogy at the funeral of his brother Robert F. Kennedy on June 8, 1968. **Questions 37–40** are based on this excerpt.

Some believe there is nothing one man or one woman can do against the enormous array of the world's ills. Yet many of the world's great movements, of thought and action, have flowed from the work of a single man. A young monk began the Protestant Reformation, a young general extended an empire from Macedonia to the borders of the earth, and a young woman reclaimed the territory of France. It was a young Italian explorer who discovered the New World, and a thirty-two-year-old Thomas Jefferson who proclaimed that all men are created equal.

These men moved the world, and so can we all. Few will have the greatness to bend history itself, but each of us can work to change a small portion of events, and in the total of all those acts will be written the history of this generation. It is from numberless diverse acts of courage and belief that human history is shaped. Each time a man stands up for an ideal, or acts to improve the lot of others, or strikes out against injustice, he sends forth a tiny ripple of hope, and crossing each other from a million different centers of energy and daring, those ripples build a current that can sweep down the mightiest walls of oppression and resistance.

GO ON TO THE NEXT PAGE

37. Which of the following is the main claim being advanced in the excerpt?

- **A.** It takes millions of people to have any effect on the world.
- **B.** One person alone cannot do much to improve the world.
- **C.** The world suffers from oppression and resistance.
- **D.** Each person can play a role in improving the world.

38. The second paragraph includes an example of:

- **A.** hyperbole.
- **B.** simile.
- **C.** metaphor.
- **D.** personification.

39. This excerpt is especially poignant because:

- **A.** Robert Kennedy had been favored to win the nomination as the Democratic candidate for President.
- **B.** Ted Kennedy had lost two brothers to assassins.
- **C.** Robert Kennedy had been regarded as an important figure in the Civil Rights Movement.
- **D.** All of the above

40. In the first paragraph, the main way Senator Ted Kennedy develops his argument is through the use of:

- **A.** a series of specific examples.
- **B.** references to unnamed, mysterious heroes.
- **C.** comparison and contrast.
- **D.** an embedded quote.

41. Which of the following activities would be useful during the revision stage of the writing process?

- **A.** prewriting
- **B.** drafting
- **C.** teacher editing
- **D.** peer conferencing

42. What is another word for a writing scoring guide?

- **A.** frame story
- **B.** rubric
- **C.** graphic organizer
- **D.** chart

43. Which of the following are appropriate ways to open a business letter?

- I. Dear Sir or Madam:
- II. Dear Mr. Henderson,
- III. Dear Ms. Wilson:
- IV. Hi, Miss Johnson,

- **A.** I and II
- **B.** II and III
- **C.** I and III
- **D.** I and IV

44. Read this excerpt from a 1968 speech by labor leader Cesar Chavez and answer the question that follows.

Our struggle is not easy. Those who oppose our cause are rich and powerful and they have many allies in high places. We are poor. Our allies are few. But we have something the rich do not own. We have our own bodies and spirits and the justice of our cause as our weapons.

What method has Chavez used to develop his idea?

- **A.** compare and contrast
- **B.** cause and effect
- **C.** analogy
- **D.** definition

45. This excerpt is from a 1984 speech by Mario Cuomo, in which he challenges President Ronald Reagan. What strategy is Cuomo using?

A shining city is perhaps all the president sees from the portico of the White House and the veranda of his ranch, where everyone seems to be doing well. But there's another city. There's another part of the "shining city": the part where some people can't pay their mortgages and most young people can't afford one, where students can't afford the education they need and middle-class parents watch the dream they hold for their children evaporate. In this part of the city there are more poor than ever, more families in trouble. More and more people who need help but can't find it. Even worse, there are elderly people who tremble in the basements of the houses there.

    A. appeal to authority
    B. appeal to emotion
    C. extended metaphor
    D. appeal to reason

46. A writer wants to convey an informal tone in a story. Which of the following sentences best contributes to that tone?

    A. Maggie, unsure of herself in this unfamiliar situation, looked to her sister for behavioral clues.
    B. Fidgeting and uncomfortable, Maggie avoided eye contact with everyone but her sister.
    C. Once again out of her element, Maggie relied on her sister for a good example.
    D. Maggie hardly knew what to do, so she just copied her sister, as usual.

47. Consider the following sentences:

David spent many hours practicing basketball. David was not a good basketball player.

Which revision makes the most sense?

    A. Although David spent many hours practicing basketball, he was not a good player.
    B. David spent many hours practicing basketball, so he was not a good player.
    C. David spent many hours practicing basketball; therefore, he was not a good player.
    D. Since David spent many hours practicing basketball, he was not a good player.

48. Consider the following sentence:

Shortly after he joined the union, Larry appears at a meeting and makes a speech.

Which of the following errors appears in the sentence above?

    A. lack of agreement between pronoun and antecedent
    B. dangling modifier
    C. inconsistent use of verb tense
    D. incorrect use of punctuation

49. Consider the following sentence:

After decorating the house, setting the table, and having prepared the feast, Melanie was ready for her guests.

Which of the following is the best improvement of the sentence above?

    A. After having decorated the house, setting the table, and having prepared the feast, Melanie was ready for her guests.
    B. After decorating the house, setting the table, and preparing the feast, Melanie was ready for her guests.
    C. Having decorated the house, Melanie set the table and prepared the feast, she was ready for her guests.
    D. After having decorated the house, having set the table, and having prepared the feast, Melanie was ready for her guests.

50. When evaluating the dependability of an Internet source for a research paper, which of the following criteria should you consider?

    I. author
    II. accuracy
    III. purpose of the site
    IV. access

    A. I
    B. I and II
    C. I, II, and III
    D. I, II, III, and IV

Annotated Responses for CSET: English Subtest I

Literature and Textual Analysis

The parenthetical information about SMR codes in the following answers refers to the standards being tested. For further clarification of these codes, see the information reprinted from the CSET Website at the beginning of this practice test.

1. **C.** (SMR Code: 1.1 a) The four authors listed all wrote during the Renaissance, a period in English literature usually considered to have begun a little before 1500 and lasting until about 1642. The Old English and Middle English periods were earlier, and the Augustinian Age was later.

2. **D.** (SMR Code 1.1 a) Regionalism is a quality in literature that is the result of fidelity to a particular geographical area. Regional writers take care to accurately represent the habits, customs, speech patterns, and other details of the setting. Choice A describes Romanticism; choice B describes Naturalism; and choice C describes Modernism.

3. **B.** (SMR Code 1.1 a) This excerpt is the first four lines of Robert Frost's famous poem "Birches."

4. **C.** (SMR Code 1.2 a) The definition of blank verse is unrhymed iambic pentameter, or five feet of an unstressed syllable followed by a stressed syllable. Robert Frost often used this form in his poetry. Blank verse is generally accepted as the form best adapted to dramatic verse in English. The form was developed to perfection by Shakespeare and Milton. Choice A is three feet of two unaccented syllables followed by an unaccented one, and choice D refers to poetry written in an irregular metrical pattern and varying line lengths.

5. **A.** (SMR Code 1.2 a) A simile is a comparison using the word *like* or *as*. Here, the author is using the word *like* to compare herself and her actions to "an old biscuit, dirty and inedible."

6. **B.** (SMR Code: 1.2 a) A metaphor is a comparison made without the use of the word *like* or *as*. Here, the author is comparing an action taken by Mrs. Bertha Flowers to the act of throwing a lifeline to a drowning person.

7. **D.** (SMR Code 1.2 d) The reader can expect to read more about Mrs. Bertha Flowers's physical appearance and behavior; the reader can also expect to read an explanation of how she helped the narrator— that is, some elaboration about the "lifeline" she threw to the narrator.

8. **A.** (SMR Code 1.2 a) This poem is an example of a Petrarchan sonnet, also called the Italian sonnet. It is distinguished by its division into an octave and a sestet. The Petrarchan sonnet usually has a rhyme scheme of *abba abba, cdc, cdc,* or *cde dce,* but this can vary somewhat, as it does in this poem. The Shakespearean sonnet, on the other hand, is made up of three quatrains (each with its own rhyme pattern) and a rhymed couplet. An elegy is a sustained and formal poem expressing the poet's thoughts on death or about a serious theme. A concrete poem is one with a distinctive shape that matches the subject matter in some way.

9. **C.** (SMR Code 1.1 d) The gentleman in the dustcoat is Death, come to take the lady. This is made clear by the fact that the roses on the trellis are dying as he approaches. The dustcoat worn by the character suggests the dust from which we all come and to which we will return. The reference to the "spectral" singing of the moon further underscores this interpretation. In the second stanza, the word *kiss* suggests the clichéd expression "kiss of death." The young lady's reference to him as "gray" and his words as "dry and faint" further suggest his alienation from life.

10. **D.** (SMR Code 1.2 a) Although the lines do not all scan perfectly, the general meter of "Piazza Piece" is iambic pentameter. This is the meter customarily (but not always) used in sonnets.

11. **C.** (SMR Code: 1.2 a) The rhyme scheme of "Piazza Piece" is *abbaacca deeffd.* That is, in the first stanza lines 1, 4, 5, and 8 rhyme; lines 2 and 3 rhyme; and lines 6 and 7 rhyme. In the second stanza, lines 1 and 6 rhyme, 2 and 3 rhyme, and 4 and 5 rhyme.

12. **A.** (SMR Code 1.1 d) The internal clues include the use of the word *piazza*, a term that is generally associated with Southern houses. Furthermore, the speaker of the poem is very courteous, reminding the reader of the image of Southern gentility. Even though he is determined in his mission, he is polite about it—he is patiently waiting for the lady to notice him. The young lady's words, "Back from my trellis, Sir, before I scream," suggest her upbringing as an aristocratic lady of the South. Rose-covered trellises, too, belong to that overall picture.

13. C. (SMR Code 1.1 b) A celebration of nature rather than civilization and an emphasis on emotion and imagination rather than reason are characteristics of Romanticism.

14. B. (SMR Code 1.3 a) In "The Poetic Principle," Poe elaborated on the idea that poetry must allow the reader to enjoy the contemplation of the beautiful. Poe specifically said that lessons about truth (choice A) and morals (choice D) could certainly be introduced into a poem, but that their role was less important than the beauty, which is the real essence of the poem. Elements of the supernatural and the weird (choice C), although apparent in Poe's poetry, are not mentioned in "The Poetic Principle."

15. A. (SMR Code 1.4 c) The excerpt shows that Watanabe is willing to go against the usual protocol in order to complete a reclamation project being promoted by a women's association. This suggests Kurosawa's message that the best use of one's life is in social action, particularly action that leaves the world a better place. Choices B, C, and D are too small, too insignificant, and too limited in scope to be considered as the best use of one's life.

16. B. (SMR Code: 1.4 c) Watanabe's lines suggest that he has some experience with red tape. Otherwise, he wouldn't know that "nothing will ever be done" unless he takes some initiative. Even though Watanabe gives orders to Ono, there is no suggestion that he likes to order people around (choice A). It is clear that he hopes to accomplish his goal, eliminating choice C. And choice D is clearly incorrect, since Watanabe is the one telling Ono what to do.

17. A. (SMR Code 1.2 d) It is clear that Ono likes to follow established procedures and avoid problems, since he objects when Watanabe goes against the usual practice. Choice B is obviously incorrect, as Ono seems to be stopped by the idea that a project might be difficult. You can eliminate choice C because Ono seems more concerned about procedure than results. As for choice D, there is no evidence that Ono has great respect for Watanabe's opinions; in fact, the opposite seems to be true.

18. C. (SMR Code 1.2 a) This poem is an example of a haiku, a seventeen-syllable poem evocative of a mood and usually suggesting a certain time of year. The first line of a haiku has five syllables; the second line has seven; and the third line has five. The poem does not fit the definition of a limerick (five anapestic lines of which the first, second, and fifth rhyme and have three feet; the third and fourth lines, consisting of two feet, rhyme), a tanka (a type of Japanese poetry similar to the haiku, consisting of 31 syllables, arranged in five lines, each of seven syllables, except the first and third, which each have five syllables), or an epic (a long narrative poem in elevated style).

19. D. (SMR Code 1.2 b) The mood can best be described as joyful. Certainly, no one would be mournful (choice A), angry (choice B), or astonished (choice C) at the arrival of spring, which is described in the poem.

20. B. (SMR Code 1.2 d) The time of year is obviously spring, for the plum tree is glowing with blossoms, and warmth is growing. Winter, summer, and fall would show different stages of the natural cycle.

21. B. (SMR Code: 1.1 d) The Elizabethans saw the universe as a unified whole in which everything has its place, from a hierarchical ordering of heavenly bodies to a hierarchical ordering in society.

22. A. (SMR Code 1.2 a) The lines contain a simile, a comparison using the word *like* or *as.* In this case, the motion of "the smallest orb" is compared to the singing of an angel. Alliteration (choice C) is the repetition of initial identical consonant sounds or any vowel sounds in nearby words or syllables. Hyperbole (choice D) is a figure of speech in which conscious exaggeration is used to heighten effect or produce comic effect.

23. C. (SMR Code 1.1 d) "Muddy vesture of decay" refers to the human body, which is holding the immortal soul, closing it in. The word "muddy" might tempt you to choose A, the earth, but a close reading of the text reveals that the phrase has another meaning.

24. D. (SMR Code 1.1 a) This passage is part of a creation myth. Creation myths are stories designed to explain the origins of the earth and everything on it.

25. B. (SMR Code 1.1 a) According to the Biblical account in Genesis, it was Adam who named the animals; therefore, Grandmother Spider can be compared to Adam.

26. D. (SMR Code: 1.1 c) The characteristics of adolescent/young adult literature are that it has subject matter that appeals to an audience 12–18; it has themes that young adults (defined as those aged 12–18) might find interesting; and it is often part of a series.

27. **C.** (SMR Code 1.2 c) The main difference between comedy and tragedy is that comedy has a happy ending, whereas tragedy does not.

28. **A.** (SMR Code 1.2.c) Actors reveal their characters' innermost thoughts through use of a soliloquy. An aside is also used to reveal a character's inner thoughts, but an aside is a short comment rather than a long speech. An epilogue is a concluding statement, or the final remarks of an actor addressed to the audience at the end of a play. Dialogue is conversation between two characters.

29. **D.** (SMR Code 1.2 c) The four poems listed are all examples of dramatic monologues, or lyric poems revealing the inner character of the speaker. In a dramatic monologue, the speaker addresses an identifiable but silent listener in a dramatic moment in the speaker's life. The words of the speaker provide deep insight into his or her character.

30. **C.** (SMR Code 1.2 b) The poem expresses the speaker's longing for her husband, who has left to fight a war. Although she misses him, she supports him and sends her love. There is no evidence to support any of the other choices.

31. **B.** (SMR Code: 1.1 d) The reference to the bow and riding "untamed horses" call up images that would not be seen in a modern war.

32. **D.** (SMR Code 1.3 a) Historical criticism, which considers a literary work in its historical perspective, is clearly useful in gaining an appreciation of Anne Frank's story.

33. **A.** (SMR Code 1.3 b) Deconstructionists recognize that a word such as "flower" or "house" conjures up different mental images for different people. Therefore, because literature is made up of words, it has no fixed, single meaning. According to a deconstructionist critic, not even the author of a work can control the meaning of the texts he or she writes. Choice B describes psychological criticism; choice C describes formalist criticism; and choice D describes biographical criticism.

34. **C.** (SMR Code 1.3 b) This quote is best described as historical criticism because it considers the place Yeats has in the history of European literature.

35. **A.** (SMR Code 1.3 b) Gender criticism considers how sexual identity influences the creation as well as the interpretation of literary works. Most gender criticism is feminist and written from the point of view that patriarchal attitudes have colored many literary texts. Choices B and D are examples of historical criticism; choice C is an example of psychological criticism.

36. **B.** (SMR Code: 1.4 a) Locating specific words or phrases in a traditional printed text can be extremely time-consuming, even with a good index. If the text is available on the Internet or in another electronic version, this task is greatly simplified, as the researcher can easily use an Internet search engine to locate the word or phrase in the text.

37. **D.** (SMR Code 1.4 b) The examples Kennedy uses in his speech all support the assertion that each person can play a role in improving the world. He actually says the opposite of choices A and B. And while he does refer to the "walls of oppression and resistance," this is not the point of his speech.

38. **C.** (SMR Code 1.4 b) In comparing the effect of an act of courage to a "tiny ripple of hope" that eventually forms part of a "current," Kennedy is using a metaphor.

39. **D.** (SMR Code 1.4 c) The passage is poignant for all the reasons given.

Composition and Rhetoric

40. **A.** (SMR Code 3.2 c) Kennedy develops his argument through the use of a series of specific examples. Without naming the individuals, he touts the accomplishments of Martin Luther, Alexander the Great, St. Joan of Arc, and Christopher Columbus. He also mentions Thomas Jefferson. Although Kennedy does use unnamed heroes and an embedded quote to make his point, neither of these is the main method in his argument.

41. D. (SMR Code: 3.1 a) Prewriting and drafting occur early in the writing process, and teacher editing occurs after. During the revision process, which can take place at any point in the writing process, peer conferencing is a useful activity. For example, students may revise outlines to modify the topic covered, or they may revise prewriting exercises to explore different approaches. Peer conferencing can be a useful addition to the revision process at any of these stages.

42. B. (SMR Code 3.1 b) A writing scoring guide is called a rubric. A rubric clearly spells out for the student the standards by which his or her writing will be judged. A rubric also describes the kind of paper that will earn a superior grade, an above-average grade, an average grade, a below-average grade, and a failing grade.

43. C. (SMR Code 3.2 a) Business letters are opened with a formal greeting, such as "Dear Sir or Madam" or "Dear Mr. Maloney." The greeting is always followed by a colon. Using a comma after a greeting in a business letter is considered too informal.

44. A. (SMR Code 3.2 d) Chavez is using the method of compare and contrast to develop his idea. He compares those who oppose his cause (the rich and powerful, with many allies) with those who are fighting for his cause (the poor, with few allies).

45. B. (SMR Code 3.2 e) This paragraph is clearly an appeal to emotion. Cuomo wants his listeners to feel sorry for the poverty-stricken people who can't afford basic necessities, and he uses graphic descriptions of their suffering to arouse this emotion. An appeal to authority or to reason would not have the desired effect. He wants to generate anger toward the policies of President Reagan, and his emotional appeal is quite effective.

46. D. (SMR Code: 3.3 a) The only choice that has an informal tone is D.

47. A. (SMR Code 3.3 b) Choice A is the only one that makes logical sense. Choices B, C, and D suggest that practicing basketball is the cause of David's not being a good player.

48. C. (SMR Code 3.4 b) The sentence demonstrates an inconsistent use of verb tense. The subordinate clause that opens the sentence has a verb in the past tense; the independent clause that follows has two verbs in the present tense. The sentence should be rewritten so that all verbs are in the same tense.

49. B. (SMR Code 3.4 b) The error in the sentence is that it lacks parallel structure. The word *having* is unnecessary, and the phrase *having prepared* should be changed to *preparing* to be parallel in structure to *decorating* and *setting*.

50. D. (SMR Code 3.5 c) All the listed criteria—author, accuracy, purpose of the site, and access—should be considered when evaluating the dependability of an Internet source.

(Remove this sheet and use it to mark your answers to the multiple-choice questions.)

Answer Sheet

1 Ⓐ Ⓑ Ⓒ Ⓓ	26 Ⓐ Ⓑ Ⓒ Ⓓ
2 Ⓐ Ⓑ Ⓒ Ⓓ	27 Ⓐ Ⓑ Ⓒ Ⓓ
3 Ⓐ Ⓑ Ⓒ Ⓓ	28 Ⓐ Ⓑ Ⓒ Ⓓ
4 Ⓐ Ⓑ Ⓒ Ⓓ	29 Ⓐ Ⓑ Ⓒ Ⓓ
5 Ⓐ Ⓑ Ⓒ Ⓓ	30 Ⓐ Ⓑ Ⓒ Ⓓ
6 Ⓐ Ⓑ Ⓒ Ⓓ	31 Ⓐ Ⓑ Ⓒ Ⓓ
7 Ⓐ Ⓑ Ⓒ Ⓓ	32 Ⓐ Ⓑ Ⓒ Ⓓ
8 Ⓐ Ⓑ Ⓒ Ⓓ	33 Ⓐ Ⓑ Ⓒ Ⓓ
9 Ⓐ Ⓑ Ⓒ Ⓓ	34 Ⓐ Ⓑ Ⓒ Ⓓ
10 Ⓐ Ⓑ Ⓒ Ⓓ	35 Ⓐ Ⓑ Ⓒ Ⓓ
11 Ⓐ Ⓑ Ⓒ Ⓓ	36 Ⓐ Ⓑ Ⓒ Ⓓ
12 Ⓐ Ⓑ Ⓒ Ⓓ	37 Ⓐ Ⓑ Ⓒ Ⓓ
13 Ⓐ Ⓑ Ⓒ Ⓓ	38 Ⓐ Ⓑ Ⓒ Ⓓ
14 Ⓐ Ⓑ Ⓒ Ⓓ	39 Ⓐ Ⓑ Ⓒ Ⓓ
15 Ⓐ Ⓑ Ⓒ Ⓓ	40 Ⓐ Ⓑ Ⓒ Ⓓ
16 Ⓐ Ⓑ Ⓒ Ⓓ	41 Ⓐ Ⓑ Ⓒ Ⓓ
17 Ⓐ Ⓑ Ⓒ Ⓓ	42 Ⓐ Ⓑ Ⓒ Ⓓ
18 Ⓐ Ⓑ Ⓒ Ⓓ	43 Ⓐ Ⓑ Ⓒ Ⓓ
19 Ⓐ Ⓑ Ⓒ Ⓓ	44 Ⓐ Ⓑ Ⓒ Ⓓ
20 Ⓐ Ⓑ Ⓒ Ⓓ	45 Ⓐ Ⓑ Ⓒ Ⓓ
21 Ⓐ Ⓑ Ⓒ Ⓓ	46 Ⓐ Ⓑ Ⓒ Ⓓ
22 Ⓐ Ⓑ Ⓒ Ⓓ	47 Ⓐ Ⓑ Ⓒ Ⓓ
23 Ⓐ Ⓑ Ⓒ Ⓓ	48 Ⓐ Ⓑ Ⓒ Ⓓ
24 Ⓐ Ⓑ Ⓒ Ⓓ	49 Ⓐ Ⓑ Ⓒ Ⓓ
25 Ⓐ Ⓑ Ⓒ Ⓓ	50 Ⓐ Ⓑ Ⓒ Ⓓ

CUT HERE

CUT HERE

Subtest II: Language, Linguistics, and Literacy

Content Domains for Subject Matter Understanding and Skill in English

Here is a list of the areas on which you will be tested. This information is also available at the CSET Website. It is reproduced here for your convenience.

Language, Linguistics, and Literacy (SMR Domain 2)

Candidates demonstrate knowledge of the foundations and contexts of the language, linguistics, and literacy contained in the *English-Language Arts Content Standards for California Public Schools Kindergarten Through Grade Twelve* (1999) at a post secondary level of rigor. Candidates have both broad and deep conceptual knowledge of the subject matter. Many California students, coming from a variety of linguistic and sociocultural backgrounds, face specific challenges in mastering the English language. The diversity of this population requires the candidate to understand the principles of language acquisition and development. Candidates must become knowledgeable about the nature of human language, language variation, and historical and cultural perspectives on the development of English. In addition, candidates must acquire a complex understanding of the development of English literacy among both native and non-native speakers. Candidates will be able to:

0001 Human Language Structures (SMR 2.1)

a. Recognize the nature of human language, differences among languages, the universality of linguistic structures, and changes across time, locale, and communities.

b. Demonstrate knowledge of word analysis, including sound patterns (phonology) and inflection, derivation, compounding, roots and affixes (morphology).

c. Demonstrate knowledge of sentence structures (syntax), word and sentence meanings (semantics), and language function in communicative context (pragmatics).

d. Use appropriate print and electronic sources to research etymologies; recognize conventions of English orthography and changes in word meaning and pronunciation.

(*English-Language Arts Content: Standards for California Public Schools,* Grade 6, Reading: 1.1–5; Grades 7–8, Reading: 1.2; Grades 9–10, Reading: 1.1–3)

0002 Acquisition and Development of Language and Literacy (SMR 2.2)

a. Explain the influences of cognitive, affective, and sociocultural factors on language acquisition and development.

b. Explain the influence of a first language on second language development.

c. Describe methods and techniques for developing academic literacy (e.g., tapping prior knowledge through semantic mapping, word analogies, cohesion analysis).

(*English-Language Arts Content Standards for California Public Schools,* Grades 6–12, Reading: 1.0)

0003 Literacy Studies (SMR 2.3)

a. Recognize the written and oral conventions of Standard English, and analyze the social implications of mastering them.

b. Describe and explain cognitive elements of reading and writing processes (e.g., decoding and encoding, construction of meaning, recognizing and using text conventions of different genres).

c. Explain metacognitive strategies for making sense of text (e.g., pre-reading activities, predicting, questioning, word analysis, concept formation).

(*English-Language Arts Content Standards for California Public Schools,* Grades 6–12, Reading: 1.0)

0004 Grammatical Structures of English (SMR 2.4)

a. Identify methods of sentence construction (e.g., sentence combining with coordinators and subordinators; sentence embedding and expanding with clausal and phrasal modifiers).

b. Analyze parts of speech and their distinctive structures and functions (e.g., noun phrases including count and nonount nouns and the determiner system; prepositions, adjectives, and adverbs; word transformations).

c. Describe the forms and functions of the English verb system (e.g. modals, verb complements, verbal phrases).

(*English-Language Arts Content Standards for California Pubic Schools,* Grade 8, Reading: 1.2)

Subtest II: Language, Linguistics, and Literacy

Directions: Each of the questions or statements below is followed by four suggested answers or completions. Select the one that is best in each case.

1. A phoneme is:

   A. a short word with just one vowel sound.
   B. a single syllable in a spoken language.
   C. a single basic sound unit in a language.
   D. the smallest meaningful unit in a language.

2. Morphology is a branch of linguistics that:

   A. deals with the internal structure and forms of words.
   B. analyzes the historical development of words and grammar.
   C. studies the ways in which children acquire language ability.
   D. compares various dialectical forms of a language.

3. According to current linguistic theories, which of the following is the best definition of a word's meaning?

   A. the way it's used in a particular situation
   B. its corresponding idea or image in the mind
   C. the object to which it refers (its *referent*)
   D. its definition as found in a dictionary

4. Read the passage below. Then answer the question that follows.

   Ferdinand de Saussure revolutionized the study of linguistics in the early years of the twentieth century. At that time, most linguists saw language as a collection of speech sounds, words, and grammatical endings. Saussure, on the other hand, saw language as a structured system of elements. In this system, the place of each element is defined chiefly by the way in which it relates to other elements.

   Which word best describes Saussure's approach to linguistics?

   A. atomistic
   B. generative
   C. transformational
   D. structuralist

5. Which of the following examples prove that language changes over time?

   I. The language of Chaucer's time is almost incomprehensible to readers today.
   II. In Chinese, verbs have no tense markers.
   III. The use of the subjunctive mood has largely disappeared in English.
   IV. The statement "I logged onto the Web with my laptop" would have made no sense 20 years ago.

   A. I and II
   B. I and III
   C. III and IV
   D. I, III, and IV

GO ON TO THE NEXT PAGE

Questions 6–8 are based on the following phonetic description:

eks' pli kə bəl

6. Which word is represented above?

A. explicate
B. explicable
C. explication
D. expedite

7. Which of the following words has the same root as the word above?

A. explicit
B. exponential
C. exploration
D. exploitative

8. Which is another acceptable pronunciation of the word?

A. eks pli kə' bəl
B. eks pli kə bəl'
C. ik splik' ə bəl
D. iks plə kə bəl'

9. Which of the following words are adjectives?

I. joyful
II. joyfully
III. joylessness
IV. joyous

A. I and II
B. I, II, and III
C. I, III, and IV
D. I and IV

10. Which of the following are compound words?

I. baseball
II. brother-in-law
III. red dress
IV. high school

A. I and II
B. I, II, and III
C. I, II, and IV
D. I and IV

11. Use the diagram below to answer the question that follows.

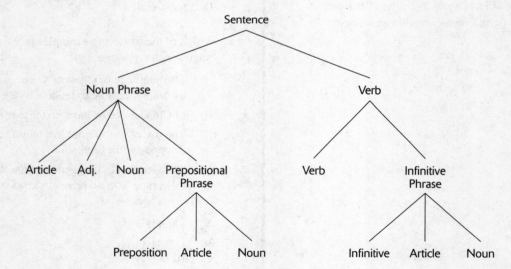

The diagram represents the structure of which of the following sentences?

A. The creative child in the sandbox wanted to make a sandcastle.
B. The stray dog in the park seemed to be afraid of everyone and everything.
C. A sunny day on the weekend is a good opportunity to go for a walk.
D. The guests of the bride should sit on the left side of the church.

12. Which of the following best defines the word *semantics?*

    A. the study of the internal structure of words

    B. the study of how words combine to form grammatical sentences

    C. the study of meaning in language, both oral and contextual

    D. the study of word meanings and how words combine to form the meaning of sentences

13. Which pronunciation of this sentence implies that Darla was telling a joke when she said she was happy to see David?

    A. Darla said she was happy to see David, and then *Carla* made a joke.

    B. Darla said she was *happy* to see David, and then Carla made a joke.

    C. Darla said she was happy to see *David,* and then Carla made a joke.

    D. Darla said she was happy to see David, and then Carla made a *joke.*

14. In Shakespeare's *Julius Caesar,* when Mark Antony says, "Brutus is an honorable man," the reader understands that he means just the opposite. This demonstrates:

    A. pragmatic competence.

    B. deep structure.

    C. surface structure.

    D. syntactical knowledge.

15. Which of the following is an example of a compound sentence?

    A. Andy ate his dinner while Shirley did her homework.

    B. Andy ate his dinner, and Shirley did her homework.

    C. Andy and Shirley did their homework and ate dinner.

    D. Andy ate his dinner and did his homework, while Shirley did the same.

16. The best place to research the etymology of the word *thermometer* is in:

    A. an almanac.

    B. a thesaurus.

    C. a dictionary.

    D. an encyclopedia.

17. Which of the following words is an exception to a basic rule of orthography?

    A. receive

    B. believe

    C. weigh

    D. conscience

18. Which of the following shows the British spelling of the word?

    A. color

    B. colour

    C. colore

    D. collor

19. What is the most probable cause of the Great Vowel Shift in London and then throughout England from 1400 to 1600?

    A. the invention of the printing press, which led to greater stabilization in spelling

    B. the flowering of the Renaissance and the renewal in interest in ancient Greek and Roman civilizations

    C. streams of young immigrants coming to England, introducing various dialects into the speech

    D. higher rates of literacy among the lower classes

20. What was the effect of the Great Vowel Shift on English orthography?

    A. All words that had "ay" sounds were now spelled with "ee."

    B. The diphthong with the sound "oi" as in "boil" was changed from an "oy" spelling.

    C. The silent "e" in words like "olde" was dropped.

    D. The most common spellings of many words no longer corresponded to their sounds.

GO ON TO THE NEXT PAGE

21. Which of the following best describes the way in which children acquire language?

    A. a series of imitative stages proceeding in a rough, overlapping sequence with possible regressions

    B. a series of imitative stages in which each advance is built on the previous one and proceeding in a necessary order

    C. a random sequence of development in which the stages are not distinct

    D. a logical process under adult supervision, instruction, and correction by which a child learns to express his or her thoughts

22. Which is the best description of Noam Chomsky's ideas about language acquisition and development?

    A. Children learn language by being corrected when they say something wrong and rewarded when they say something right.

    B. Human beings are genetically endowed with language ability, which can be called Universal Grammar (UG) or the Language Acquisition Device (LAD).

    C. Language learning results only from general cognitive abilities and the way the learner interacts with other learners and the surrounding community.

    D. The acquisition of complex syntactic constructions always follows the same order, beginning with babbling and ending with pragmatic competence.

23. What is the primary way in which adults acquire new words and expressions?

    A. through formal study under the guidance of a teacher

    B. through casual explanations from friends and associates

    C. through exposure to their use

    D. by using a dictionary or thesaurus while they read

24. Which of the following best describes the Acquisition/Learning Hypothesis in Stephen Krashen's theory about second-language performance?

    A. Students cannot acquire a second language unless they spend a great deal of time memorizing its grammar rules.

    B. A second language can be acquired subconsciously, the way children acquire a first language; or it can be learned consciously, through formal instruction.

    C. The more vocabulary words in a second language that a person acquires, the easier it will be for that person to learn that second language.

    D. The optimum time for a student to acquire a second language is when he or she is learning the grammar rules of the first language.

25. Read the passage and answer the question that follows.

    Learners who have high motivation, self-confidence, a good self-image, and a low level of anxiety are more likely to do well in second language acquisition. On the other hand, low motivation, low self-esteem, and a high level of anxiety can combine to form a mental block impeding language acquisition.

    This passage explains:

    A. Cartesian linguistics

    B. Dell Hyme's Theory of Communicative Competence

    C. Eric Lenneberg's Critical Period Hypothesis

    D. Stephen Krashen's Affective Filter Hypothesis

26. Having been told that her use of the pronoun *who* was incorrect earlier, a woman speaks to a caller on the phone, asking, "Whom shall I say is calling?" This illustrates which of the following types of linguistic behavior?

   A. hypercorrection
   B. negative transfer
   C. borrowing
   D. code-switching

27. A teacher writes the phrase "super heroes" on the board and asks students to list and then categorize all the words that come to mind based on this phrase. The teacher is using which of the following techniques to help develop the students' academic literacy?

   A. word analogies
   B. cohesion analysis
   C. semantic mapping
   D. freewriting

28. Which of the following is most likely to improve a reader's comprehension of a difficult text?

   A. stopping from time to time to look up any unfamiliar words
   B. reading the text aloud
   C. taking notes while reading and reviewing the notes later
   D. reading each paragraph at least twice

29. Unsure of the meaning of a certain passage, a student turns to other passages in the same essay for clarification. This is an example of:

   A. semantic mapping.
   B. cohesion analysis.
   C. rereading.
   D. repetition.

30. A person engages in code-switching when he or she:

   A. paraphrases a difficult text into a simpler language to help in understanding and in explaining it to others.
   B. uses graphic organizers after reading a text to represent the main ideas and themes in a more visual way.
   C. uses information or skills related to one topic to assist learning in another, such as using knowledge of the Revolutionary War to understand the Civil War.
   D. interacts with strangers and business associates in the Standard English dialect, and uses a different dialect when interacting with friends in a social environment.

31. A reader uses decoding skills when he or she:

   A. makes an outline of difficult text for study later.
   B. sounds out an unfamiliar word by applying phonics and syllabication skills.
   C. looks up the meaning of an unfamiliar word in a dictionary.
   D. discusses a difficult passage with a peer.

32. A student's first language is Spanish, which uses double negatives. That student assumes that double negatives are also acceptable in English. This is an example of:

   A. positive transfer.
   B. faulty reasoning.
   C. negative transfer.
   D. borrowing.

33. A teacher explains that a story is set in the South in 1860 and asks students to relate to the class what they know about that setting. Which of the following best describes what the teacher is doing?

   A. explaining the literary term "setting"
   B. arousing curiosity
   C. reviewing history
   D. activating prior knowledge

GO ON TO THE NEXT PAGE

34. Which of the following techniques are part of the process of word analysis that a student might employ to decode an unfamiliar word?

    I.   breaking the word into syllables

    II. sounding out the word phonetically

    III. skipping over the word, planning to come back to it later

    IV. considering whether the root word looks familiar

    A. I and II

    B. I, II, and III

    C. II, III, and IV

    D. I, II, and IV

35. At what points in reading a story does the technique of predicting aid in comprehension?

    I.   after reading the title and looking at the art, if any

    II. at various points in the text

    III. after finishing the story

    IV. when rereading the story

    A. I and II

    B. I, II, and III

    C. I, II, and IV

    D. II and IV

Questions 36 and 37 are based on these two sentences.

Wallace Stevens is my favorite poet.

He wrote "The Emperor of Ice Cream."

36. Which of the following sentences uses an embedded appositional phrase to combine the two sentences?

    A. Wallace Stevens, who is my favorite poet, wrote "The Emperor of Ice Cream."

    B. Wallace Stevens, my favorite poet, wrote "The Emperor of Ice Cream."

    C. Wallace Stevens, who wrote "The Emperor of Ice Cream," is my favorite poet.

    D. Wallace Stevens wrote "The Emperor of Ice Cream"; he is my favorite poet.

37. Which of the following sentences combines the sentences and expands them with a clausal modifier?

    A. Wallace Stevens, my favorite poet, wrote "The Emperor of Ice Cream," which has two stanzas of eight lines each.

    B. Wallace Stevens is my favorite poet; in his poem "The Emperor of Ice Cream," he uses the alliterative line "In kitchen cups concupiscent curds."

    C. Wallace Stevens, my favorite poet, wrote "The Emperor of Ice Cream," a rather startling poem.

    D. Have you ever read "The Emperor of Ice Cream," a poem by Wallace Stevens, my favorite poet?

38. Which of these sentences includes a subordinate clause?

    A. Amy declined Ben's invitation; she was extremely tired.

    B. Amy was extremely tired, so she declined Ben's invitation.

    C. Amy, extremely tired, declined Ben's invitation.

    D. Because Amy was extremely tired, she declined Ben's invitation.

39. Read these two sentences; then answer the question that follows.

Sara was the smallest person on the team.

She was the fastest runner.

Which of these sentences combines the two sentences above with a coordinator?

    A. Although Sara was the smallest person on the team, she was the fastest runner.

    B. Despite being the smallest person on the team, Sara was the fastest runner.

    C. Sara was the smallest person on the team, but she was the fastest runner.

    D. Sara, the smallest person on the team, was the fastest runner.

40. Identify the underlined part of this sentence.

Diane, <u>whom you met earlier this year</u>, has just written an exciting book.

    A.   an adjectival clause
    B.   an adverbial clause
    C.   an adjectival phrase
    D.   a coordinate clause

41. Which sentence includes an underlined word that functions as a noncount noun?

    A.   The past few <u>days</u> have just been gorgeous!
    B.   This <u>weather</u> is very surprising for this time of year.
    C.   I guess I won't be needing this <u>raincoat</u> for a while.
    D.   Let's go out for a <u>walk</u> on the beach.

42. Which sentence has a noun phrase used as a direct object?

    A.   Erin has a new catcher's mitt.
    B.   Erin's mitt fits her well.
    C.   Erin is an excellent catcher.
    D.   Erin enjoys softball.

43. Which of the following words are noun determiners?

    I.   careful
    II.   first
    III.   the
    IV.   your

    A.   I and II
    B.   II and III
    C.   I, III, and III
    D.   III and IV

44. Which of the following sentences contains an underlined word that functions as an adverb?

    A.   Thoreau wished to live <u>deliberately</u>, so he went out into the woods.
    B.   He built a <u>small</u> cabin for himself.
    C.   He entertained many visitors, but he didn't like it <u>when</u> they stayed too long.
    D.   He enjoyed the solitude and <u>simplicity</u> of his life in the woods.

45. Which of the following sentences contains an underlined phrase that functions as an adjective?

    A.   The movie <u>that we saw last night</u> was more than two hours long.
    B.   We sat <u>on the couch</u> and ate popcorn while we watched it.
    C.   The director <u>of the movie</u> was Martin Scorsese.
    D.   Many people were pleased <u>when he finally won an Oscar</u>.

46. What is the function of a modal auxiliary?

    A.   It indicates the tense of a verb.
    B.   It indicates a necessity, possibility, capability, willingness, or the like.
    C.   It indicates whether a clause functions in a coordinating or subordinating manner.
    D.   It indicates whether a clause works as an adjective or an adverb.

47. Which of the following sentences has a verbal phrase that acts as a noun?

    A.   Getting to school on time was Cynthia's objective.
    B.   Cynthia got to school just in the nick of time.
    C.   Cynthia had not been late once.
    D.   If Cynthia were late to school, the consequences would be dire.

48. What is the function of the underlined word in this sentence?

Isabel gave the <u>mouse</u> a cookie.

    A.   direct object
    B.   indirect object
    C.   appositive
    D.   subject

GO ON TO THE NEXT PAGE

49. What is the function of the underlined verbal phrase in this sentence?

Danielle does not enjoy <u>shopping at the mall.</u>

  A. direct object
  B. indirect object
  C. prepositional phrase
  D. adverbial clause

50. Which words can be understood as coming between a verb and an indirect object?

  I.   over
  II. to
  III. through
  IV. for

  A. I and II
  B. II and III
  C. III and IV
  D. II and IV

Annotated Responses for CSET: English Subtest II

Language, Linguistics, and Literacy

Human Language Structures

1. **C.** (SMR Code: 2.1) A phoneme is a speech sound that is psychologically a single unit, in contrast with other such sound units, as the phoneme /p/. Even though this sound can have slight variations, depending on its position in a word, it is considered a single phoneme. Consider the variations in the pronunciation of the phoneme /p/ in the words *pin* (with a perceptible puff of breath before the vowel), the unaspirated *p* after the *s* in a word like *spin,* and the *p* pronounced with a final closure of the lips in a word like *slip.* Despite these positional variations, the average English speaker perceives the sound as a single phoneme.

2. **A.** (SMR Code: 2.1) Based on the Greek root word *morph,* meaning "form," morphology is the study of the forms of words, from their internal structure to the relationships among words. Morphology is particularly concerned with those changes in the form of an individual word that modify that word's meaning, such as inflectional endings (for example, the *-s* added to *food,* which turns it into the plural *foods*), prefixes (for example, the *un-* prefixed to *stoppable,* which gives it the meaning of "not stoppable"), as well as internal changes (for example, the change of vowel in *sank* which marks it as the past of *sink*).

3. **A.** (SMR Code: 2.1) To define any given word, you have to know how it is being used in a particular situation. The word *right,* to give just one example, needs context before it can be defined. It can be used as an adjective, an adverb, a noun, or a verb. Notice how its meaning changes in each of these examples: *I have my rights. He has the right stuff. Turn to the right. I sleep on my right side. She went right to the end of the pier. His political leanings are to the right. Superman rights wrongs. Is everything all right?*

4. **D.** (SMR Code: 2.1) The atomistic approach perceives a language as primarily a collection of objects, such as speech sounds, words, and grammatical endings. Saussure's approach emphasized the structural nature of language. *Generative* and *transformational* are descriptions applied to grammar.

5. **D.** (SMR Code: 2.1) The facts that Chaucer's writing is difficult for contemporary readers, that the subjunctive mood has very limited uses today, and words like *Web* and *laptop* have very specialized meanings today all point to the fact that language changes over time. Item II, that Chinese verbs do not indicate tense, is irrelevant.

6. **B.** (SMR Code: 2.1) Clearly, B is the choice here. The phonetic description does not apply to the other words.

7. **A.** (SMR Code: 2.1) The root is the Latin *explicare,* "to unfold."

8. **C.** (SMR Code: 2.1) This is a good example of the way language changes. Older dictionaries show an accented first syllable as the only acceptable pronunciation, but because of widespread use of the word with the second syllable accented, this second pronunciation has gained acceptance.

9. **D.** (SMR Code: 2.1) *Joyful* and *joyous* are adjective forms of the word. The suffix *-ly* is an adverb-forming ending, and the suffix *-ness* is a noun-forming ending.

10. **C.** (SMR Code: 2.1) Compound words are those in which two or more words combine to form a new word. Compound words can be closed up, as in *baseball;* hyphenated, as in *brother-in-law;* or two words, as in *high school.* Often, compound words that started out as two separate words move together as hyphenated compounds before finally ending up as a single word. *Red dress* is not a compound word, for the word *red* is simply modifying *dress.* However, a word like *red tape, red-eye,* or *redhead* would be a compound word.

11. **A.** (SMR Code: 2.1) The diagram corresponds to choice A. The noun phrase is "The creative child," the prepositional phrase is "in the sandbox," the verb phrase consists of the verb "wanted" and the infinitive phrase "to make a sandcastle."

12. **C.** (SMR Code: 2.1) Semantics is the study of meaning in language. Choice A refers to morphology, the study of the internal structure of words. Choice B refers to syntax, and Choice D is a combination of syntax and morphology.

13. **A.** (SMR Code: 2.1) The emphasis in Choice A suggests that Darla was making a joke when she spoke, and then Carla made another joke.

14. **A.** (SMR Code: 2.1) Pragmatics is the study of the way language is used and how it context affects its meaning. A listener or reader who has pragmatic competence would realize that Antony is being sarcastic in this context and really means to imply that Brutus is not an honorable man. We can eliminate the other choices by defining them and comparing their definitions to the question. The deep structure of a sentence or other linguistic expression is its theoretical underlying meaning that can be expressed in any number of forms. For example, the sentences "John opened the door" and "The door was opened by John" are roughly the same thing and use similar words. Some linguists, particularly Noam Chomsky, say that this similarity can be explained by the so-called deep structure, the unobservable common source, that underlies both sentences. Choice D refers to the way the sentence is put together, rather than its meaning in context.

15. **B.** (SMR Code: 2.1) A compound sentence is one that has two or more independent clauses joined by a coordinating conjunction or by a semicolon. Choice A is a complex sentence, or an independent clause and one or more subordinate or dependent clauses. Choice C is a simple sentence with a compound subject and a compound predicate. Choice D is a complex sentence, in which the independent clause has a compound predicate.

16. **C.** (SMR Code: 2.1) The only reference source mentioned that includes etymology, or word origins, is a dictionary. Not all dictionaries include etymologies.

17. **D.** (SMR Code: 2.1) The basic rule of orthography demonstrated by choices A, B, and C is "*i* before *e* except after *c,* or when sounded as *ay,* as in *neighbor* and *weigh.*" Choice D breaks the rule, with the letter combination *ie* following *c.*

18. **B.** (SMR Code: 2.1) Many American spellings differ from English spellings. The original settlers to New England switched over to Noah Webster's spelling rules, omitting the *u* in words ending in *our* (for example, *vigor/vigour, honor/honour*) and also promoted single consonants instead of double consonants in second syllables (for example, *traveler/traveller*). Other Americanized spellings include changing *-ise* endings to *-ize* (*standardize/standardise*)

19. **C.** (SMR Code: 2.1) No one is sure what caused the Great Vowel Shift, a phenomenon that was first identified and studied by the Danish linguist Otto Jesperson, during the late nineteenth and early twentieth centuries. But some theories suggest that the mass migrations to England after the Black Death led to different accents that were later standardized over time.

20. **D.** (SMR Code: 2.1) It is the Great Vowel Shift that has made English such a challenging language to spell, for spellings that matched sound in one century had no relation to the sound in the next century.

Acquisition and Development of Language and Literacy

21. **A.** (SMR Code: 2.2) The fact that children acquire language at different rates and in slightly different stages points to choice A as the correct answer. We can eliminate choice B because the order of steps is not necessarily the same for each child. Choice C is incorrect because the stages do have some qualities that distinguish them from each other, with most children beginning with babbling. Choice D can be eliminated because in the early stages of language acquisition, the child would not even understand any instruction and correction by an adult.

22. **B.** (SMR Code: 2.2) This is one of the most well-known of Chomsky's theories. Chomsky reasons that certain rules of grammar are too complex for children to figure out, yet children manage to use language in a grammatical sense. This skill must be innate, he reasons, because it cannot have been learned.

23. **C.** (SMR Code: 2.2) Adults expand their linguistic ability in much the same way that children do—that is, by being exposed to language. Even in an academic setting, as described in choice A, the meaning of a new term or phrase is usually communicated by the way the writer or speaker uses it, rather than by direct explanation. Choice B is incorrect because it is rarely necessary for an adult to interrupt a conversation to ask for an explanation of an unfamiliar term. Choice D, while one way to learn new words, is not the most effective way.

24. **B.** (SMR Code: 2.2) The Acquisition-Learning distinction is the basis of all the hypotheses in Krashen's theory of second language acquisition. Krashen says that there are two independent systems for learning a second language. The "acquired system" is similar to the process children go through as they acquire their first language, and is largely subconscious. The "learned system" is a conscious process that includes learning grammar rules through formal instruction. Krashen believes that "acquisition" is more important than "learning."

25. **D.** (SMR Code: 2.2) This is one of the five main hypotheses proposed by Krashen. He believes that these "affective variables" help, but do not cause, the acquisition of a second language. In other words, positive affect is necessary for acquisition to take place, but it is not sufficient on its own.

26. **A.** (SMR Code: 2.2) Another example of hypercorrection might be something like this: "Let's keep this between you and I." The speaker of such a sentence might been told that saying "Him and me went to the movies" is incorrect, and it should be "he and I." Then, hypercorrecting (overcorrecting), the speaker avoids using the objective case *me* even in situations where it is necessary.

27. **C.** (SMR Code: 2.2) Semantic mapping might also include the use of graphic organizers, such as starburst diagrams, clusters, and Venn diagrams.

28. **C.** (SMR Code: 2.2) Although choices A, B, and D might help some readers understand a difficult text, choice C is most likely to improve comprehension. Taking notes forces the reader to paraphrase, which necessitates careful reading and interpreting; reviewing notes later fixes the information in the reader's mind.

29. **B.** (SMR Code: 2.2) Cohesion analysis involves determining how all the parts of a work come together to create an effect or communicate a message. This technique comes in handy when a reader is faced with a difficult section or passage. He or she might read ahead or review other parts of the work, looking for clarification. Although cohesion analysis might involve rereading (choice C), it also involves reading ahead.

30. **D.** (SMR Code: 2.2) Code-switching might also be used by a speaker for rhetorical effect, such as a politician who mixes formal speech-making style with down-home dialect in order to increase a feeling of camaraderie with the audience.

Literacy Studies

31. **B.** (SMR Code: 2.3) Other decoding methods include considering the root word in an unfamiliar word, analyzing the use of prefixes or suffixes, using clues in accompanying art, and considering context.

32. **C.** (SMR Code: 2.3) Negative transfer is using skills from a previously learned behavior or subject but applying them incorrectly to the new subject. A child who assumes the past tense of *take* is *taked,* based on knowledge of the past tense of *bake,* is using negative transfer.

33. **D.** (SMR Code: 2.3) Activating prior knowledge is one way to get students involved in reading and comprehending something new. Although choices A, B, and C are involved in the activity, they are byproducts, rather than goals, of activating prior knowledge.

34. **D.** (SMR Code: 2.3) Item III is the only one that would be completely unhelpful to the student who wants to decode an unfamiliar word.

35. **A.** (SMR Code: 2.3) After the student has finished reading the story, the technique of predicting is impossible. Hence, items I and II are the only choices where predicting can have a role.

Grammatical Structures of English

36. **B.** (SMR Code: 2.4) In choice B, "my favorite poet" is the embedded appositional phrase. Choice A has an embedded appositional clause, as does choice C. Choice D has no appositional elements.

37. **A.** (SMR Code: 2.4) In choice A, the clausal modifier is "which has two stanzas of eight lines each." This clause modifies "The Emperor of Ice Cream." Choices B, C, and D do not have clausal modifiers, although choices C and D do contain phrasal modifiers. Note that to qualify as a clause, a group of words must have a verb.

38. **D.** (SMR Code: 2.4) Only choice B has a subordinate clause, which is "Because Amy was extremely tired." Choice A is made up of two independent clauses joined by a semicolon. Choice C is made up of two independent clauses, joined by a comma and a coordinating conjunction. Choice C is an independent clause with a phrasal modifier.

39. **C.** (SMR Code: 2.4) The coordinator in choice C is the conjunction *but.* Choice A joins the sentences with a subordinating conjunction, *although,* and choice B uses the subordinator *despite.* Choice D combines the sentences by using a phrasal modifier.

40. **A.** (SMR Code: 2.4) The underlined part, an adjectival clause, describes Diane. It is not an adverbial clause because it does not function as an adverb (describing a verb, an adjective, or another adverb). It is not an adjectival phrase because it has a verb in it. And it is not a coordinate clause, but rather a subordinate clause.

41. **B.** (SMR Code: 2.4) A nouncount noun is one that has only a singular form. You cannot add a number to the front or an *s* to the end of a nouncount noun. A few other examples of noncount nouns are *furniture, happiness, lightning, advice, popcorn,* and *software.* Some nouns can be both count and noncount, depending on context. An example would be the word *time.*

42. **A.** (SMR Code: 2.4) The noun phrase used as a direct object is "a new catcher's mitt."

43. **D.** (SMR Code: 2.4) The words *the* and *your* are noun determiners because they indicate that a noun follows. Other noun determiners include *a, an, my, his, her,* and *their.*

44. **A.** (SMR Code: 2.4) The *-ly* ending is an adverb indicator. Remember that an adverb answers the question *how, when, where, why, under what conditions,* or *with what result.*

45. **C.** (SMR Code: 2.4) Remember that an adjective describes a noun or pronoun, answering the question *what kind, which one,* or *how many.* In choice A, the underlined section functions as an adjective, but it is a clause because it has a verb. In choice B, the underlined section functions as an adverb, modifying the verb *sat* and answering the question *where.* In choice D, the underlined section is an adverbial clause.

46. **B.** (SMR Code: 2.4) Examples of modal auxiliaries include the helping verbs *can, could, may, might, must, ought, shall, should, will,* and *would.*

47. **A.** (SMR Code: 2.4) The verbal phrase is "getting to school on time," and it functions as the subject of the sentence.

48. **B.** (SMR Code: 2.4) An indirect object tells to whom (or what) or for whom (or what) an action was done.

49. **A.** (SMR Code: 2.4) The verbal phrase acts as the direct object of the verb *does enjoy,* and it answers the question *what.*

50. **D.** (SMR Code: 2.4) As suggested in the explanation for question 48, if you can mentally insert the word *to* or *for* in front of a noun or pronoun, it is an indirect object. For example, *Old Mother Hubbard gave (to) the poor dog a bone* or *Nigel bought (for) us all a round of drinks.*

Subtest III: Composition and Rhetoric; Literature and Textual Analysis

Content Domains for Subject Matter Understanding and Skill in English

Here is a list of the areas on which you will be tested. This information is also available at the CSET Website. It is reproduced here for your convenience.

Composition and Rhetoric (SMR Domain 3)

Candidates demonstrate knowledge of the foundations and contexts of the composition and rhetoric contained in the *English-Language Arts Content Standards for California Public Schools* (1997) as outlined in the *Reading/Language Arts Framework for California Public Schools: Kindergarten Through Grade Twelve* (1999) at a post secondary level of rigor. Candidates have both broad and deep conceptual knowledge of the subject matter. Candidates face dynamic challenges in the domains of oral and written communication. They must make appropriate use of current text-production technologies and develop sensitivity to patterns of communication used by different social and cultural groups. Candidates are competent writers and speakers who can communicate appropriately in various rhetorical contexts, using effective text structures, word choice, sentence options, standard usage conventions, and advanced research methods as needed. The subject matter preparation program provides opportunities for candidates to develop skills and confidence in public speaking. Candidates will be able to:

0001 Written Composing Processes (Individual and Collaborative) (SMR 3.1)

a. Reflect on and describe their own writing processes.

b. Investigate and apply alternative methods of prewriting, drafting, responding, revising, editing, and evaluating.

c. Employ such strategies as graphic organizers, outlines, notes, charts, summaries, or précis to clarify and record meaning.

d. Integrate a variety of software applications (e.g., databases, graphics, spreadsheets) to produce print documents and multi-media presentations.

(*English-Language Arts Content: Standards for California Public Schools*, Grade 6, Reading: 2.1–2, 2.4, Writing: 1.4–6; Grade 7, Reading: 2.3–4, Writing: 1.3–4, 1.6–7; Grade 8, Reading: 2.4, Writing: 1.1, 1.4–6; Listening and Speaking: 1.4; Grades 9–10, Reading: 2.4, Writing: 1.8–9; Grades 11–12, Writing: 1.4, 1.7–9, Listening and Speaking: 2.4)

0002 Rhetorical Features of Literary and Non-Literary, Oral and Written Texts (SMR 3.2)

a. Recognize and use a variety of writing applications (e.g., short story, biographical, autobiographical, expository, persuasive, business and technical documents, historical investigation).

b. Demonstrate awareness of audience, purpose, and context.

c. Recognize and use various text structures (e.g., narrative and non-narrative organizational patterns).

d. Apply a variety of methods to develop ideas within an essay (e.g., analogy, cause and effect, compare and contrast, definition, illustration, description, hypothesis).

e. Apply critical thinking strategies to evaluate methods of persuasion, including but not limited to:

  ■ Types of appeal (e.g., appeal to reason, emotion, morality)

  ■ Types of persuasive speech (e.g., propositions of fact, value, problem, policy)

  ■ Logical fallacies (e.g., bandwagon, red herring, glittering generalities, ad hominem)

- Advertising techniques (e.g., Maslow's hierarchy of needs)
- Logical argument (e.g., inductive/deductive reasoning, syllogisms, analogies)
- Classical argument (e.g., claim, qualifiers, rules of evidence, warrant)

(*English-Language Arts Content Standards for California Public Schools,* Grades 6, Reading: 2.1–2, 2.4, 2.6. 2.8, Writing: 1.1–3, 1.6, 2.1–5, Listening and Speaking: 1.8–9; Grade 7, Reading: 1.3, 2.2–3, Writing: 1.1–3, 1.7, 2.1–5, Listening and Speaking: 1.1, 1.3; Grade 8, Reading: 1.3, 2.2, Writing: 1.1–3, 1.5, 2.1–6, Listening and Speaking: 1.8; Grades 9–10, Writing: 1.1–2, 1.4, 1.9, 2.1–6, Listening and Speaking: 1.5, 1.10, 1.13; Grades 11–12, Reading: 1.3, 2.2, 2.4–6, Writing: 1.1–5, 1.9, 2.1–6, Listening and Speaking: 1.4, 1.12–13)

0003 Rhetorical Effects of Grammatical Elements (SMR 3.3)

a. Employ precise and extensive vocabulary and effective diction to control voice, style, and tone.

b. Use clause joining techniques (e.g., coordinators, subordinators, punctuation) to express logical connections between ideas.

c. Identify and use clausal and phrasal modifiers to control flow, pace, and emphasis (e.g., adjective clauses, appositives, participles and verbal phrases, absolutes).

d. Identify and use devices to control focus in sentence and paragraph (e.g., active and passive voice, expletives, concrete subjects, transitional phrases).

e. Maintain coherence through use of cohesive devices.

(*English-Language Arts Content Standards for California Public Schools,* Grade 6, Reading: 1.1, Writing: 1.2, 1.6, Written and Oral English Language Conventions: 1.1–5; Grade 7, Writing: 1.1, 1.7, Written and Oral English Language Conventions: 1.1–7; Grade 8, Writing: 1.2, 1.6, Written and Oral English Language Conventions: 1.1–6, Listening and Speaking: 1.5–6; Grades 9–10, Writing: 1.1–2, 1.6, 1.9, Written and Oral English Language Conventions: 1.1–5; Grades 11–12, Reading: 2.1–2, Writing: 1.2–5, 1.9, Written and Oral English Language Conventions: 1.1–3, Listening and Speaking: 1.5)

0004 Conventions of Oral and Written Language (SMR 3.4)

a. Apply knowledge of linguistic structure to identify and use the conventions of Standard Edited English.

b. Recognize, understand, and use a range of conventions in both spoken and written English, including:

- Conventions of effective sentence structure (e.g., clear pronoun reference, parallel structure, appropriate verb tense)
- Preferred usage (e.g., verb/subject agreement, pronoun agreement, idioms)
- Conventions of pronunciation and intonation
- Conventional forms of spelling
- Capitalization and punctuation

(*English-Language Arts Content Standards for California Pubic Schools,* Grade 6, Reading: 1.1, Written and Oral English Language Conventions: 1.1–5; Grade 7, Written and Oral English Language Conventions: 1.1–7; Grade 8, Writing: 1.2, Written and Oral English Language Conventions: 1.1–6, Listening and Speaking: 1.6; Grades 9–10, Writing: 1.9, Written and Oral English Language Conventions: 1.9; Grades 11–12, Writing: 1.4, Written and Oral English Language Conventions: 1.1–3, Listening and Speaking: 1.8)

0005 Research Strategies (SMR 3.5)

a. Develop and apply research questions.

b. Demonstrate methods of inquiry and investigation.

c. Identify and use multiple resources (e.g., oral, print, electronic; primary and secondary) and critically evaluate the quality of the sources.

d. Interpret and apply findings.

e. Use professional conventions and ethical standards of citation and attribution.

f. Demonstrate effective presentation methods, including multi-media formats.

(*English-Language Arts Content Standards for California Pubic Schools,* Grade 6, Reading: 1.1, 2.1, 2.3, 2.6–8, Writing: 1.4–5, Listening and Speaking: 1.1–2, 1.6–7, 2.1, 2.3; Grade 7, Reading: 2.2, 2.6, Writing: 1.4–5, Listening and Speaking: 1.2, 1.6–7, 2.1, 2.3; Grade 8, Reading: 2.2, 2.7, Writing: 1.3–6, Listening and Speaking: 1.2–3, 1.6–8, 2.3; Grades 9–10, Reading: 2.2–5, 2.8, Writing: 1.3–8, Listening and Speaking: 1.7, 2.2; Grades 11–12, Writing: 1.4, 1.6–8, Listening and Speaking: 2.4)

Literature and Textual Analysis (SMR Domain 1)

Candidates demonstrate knowledge of the foundations and contexts of the literature and textual analysis contained in the *English-Language Arts Content Standards for California Public Schools* (1997) as outlined in the *Reading/Language Arts Framework for California Public Schools: Kindergarten Through Grade Twelve* (1999) at a post secondary level of rigor. Candidates have both broad and deep conceptual knowledge of the subject matter. The candidate's preparation should include breadth of knowledge in literature, literary analysis and criticism, as well as non-literary text analysis. Literary analysis presumes in-depth exploration of the relationship between form and content. The curriculum should embrace representative selections form different literary traditions and major works from diverse cultures. Advanced study of multicultural writers is also fundamental preparation for teaching these works. Shakespeare remains integral to the secondary school curriculum; advanced study of his work is, therefore, essential to future secondary teachers. Candidates must be enthusiastic readers and writers, who know and apply effective reading strategies and compose thoughtful, well-crafted responses to literary and non-literary texts. Candidates will be able to:

0006 Literary Analysis (SMR 1.1)

a. Recognize, compare, and evaluate different literary traditions to include:

- American (inclusive of cultural pluralism)
- British (inclusive of cultural pluralism)
- World literature and literature in translation (inclusive of cross-cultural literature)
- Mythology and oral tradition

b. Trace development of major literary movements in historical periods (e.g., Homeric Greece, medieval, neoclassic, romantic, modern).

c. Describe the salient features of adolescent/young adult literature.

d. Analyze and interpret major works by representative writers in historical, aesthetic, political, and philosophical contexts.

(*English-Language Arts Content Standards for California Public Schools,* Grade 6, Reading: 2.4; Grades 11–12, Reading: 2.2, 3.5–7)

0007 Literary Elements (SMR 1.2)

a. Distinguish salient features of genres (e.g., short stories, non-fiction, drama, poetry, novel).

b. Define and analyze basic elements of literature (e.g., plot, setting, character, point of view, theme, narrative structure, figurative language, tone, diction, style).

c. Articulate the relationship between the expressed purposes and the characteristics of different forms of dramatic literature (e.g., comedy, tragedy, drama, dramatic monologue).

d. Develop critical thinking and analytic skill through close reading of texts.

(*English-Language Arts Content Standards for California Public Schools,* Grade 6, Reading: 1.1–2, 2.1, 2.4, 2.6, 2.8, 3.0; Grade 7, Reading: 1.1, 2.4, 3.1–5; Grade 8, Reading: 1.1, 2.7, 3.0; Grades 9–10, Reading: 1.1, 2.8, 3.1–4, 3.7–10; Grades 11–12, Reading: 2.2, 3.1–4)

0008 Literary Criticism (SMR 1.3)

a. Research and apply criticism of major texts and authors using print and/or electronic resources.

b. Research and apply various approaches to interpreting literature (e.g., aesthetic, historical, political, philosophical).

(*English-Language Arts Content Standards for California Public Schools,* Grade 6, Reading: 2.1–2, 2.6–8, 3.6; Grade 7, Reading: 2.1, 2.4, 2.6, 3.0; Grade 8, Reading: 2.2, 2.6, 3.0; Grades 9–10, Reading: 2.2, 2.4, 2.8, 3.5–7, 3.11–12; Writing: 1.6–7; Grades 11–12, Reading: 2.2, 2.4, 3.8–9, Writing: 1.6–7)

0009 Analysis of Non-Literary Texts (SMR 1.4)

a. Compare various features of print and visual media (e.g., film, television, Internet).

b. Evaluate structure and content of a variety of consumer, workplace, and public documents.

c. Interpret individual works in their cultural, social, and political contexts.

(*English-Language Arts Content Standards for California Public Schools,* Grade 6, Reading: 2.0, 3.0; Grade 7, Reading: 2.1–5, 2.2, 3.0; Grade 8, Reading: 2.1–7, 3.0; Grades 9–10, Reading: 2.1, 2.2, 2.4–7, 3.0; Grades 11–12, Reading: 2.1–3, 2.6, 3.0)

Subtest III: Composition and Rhetoric; Literature and Textual Analysis

Directions: Below is a set of constructed-response questions that are similar to the questions you will see on Subtest III of CSET: English. You are encouraged to respond to the questions without looking at the responses provided in the next section. Record your responses on the test booklets that follow the questions and compare them with the provided responses.

1. Complete the exercise that follows.

Write a critical essay in which you compare, analyze, and evaluate the following selections, supporting your points with specific evidence from the texts. Assume that you are writing for an educated audience knowledgeable about literary criticism. In your essay:

- identify a significant theme that the two texts share;
- compare and contrast the two writers' perspectives on the theme you have identified;
- examine how the two writers use literary techniques, including genre features, literary elements, and rhetorical devices, to express their perspectives on this theme; and
- draw a conclusion that explains how the literary techniques you have identified affect the ideas conveyed in the texts.

Selection I: "To Be or Not to Be" from Act III, Scene 1 of Shakespeare's *Hamlet* (1603)

To be, or not to be—that is the question:

Whether 'tis nobler in the mind to suffer

The slings and arrows of outrageous fortune

Or to take arms against a sea of troubles

And by opposing end them. To die, to sleep

No more, and by a sleep to say we end

The heartache, and the thousand natural shocks

That flesh is heir to. 'Tis a consummation

Devoutly to be wished. To die, to sleep,

To sleep—perchance to dream—ay, there's the rub,

For in that sleep of death what dreams may come

When we have shuffled off this mortal coil

Must give us pause. There's the respect

That makes calamity of so long life.

GO ON TO THE NEXT PAGE

For who would bear the whips and scorns of time,

Th' oppressor's wrong, the proud man's contumely,

The pangs of despised love, the law's delay,

The insolence of office, and the spurns

That patient merit of th' unworthy takes,

When he himself might his quietus[1] make

With a bare bodkin?[2] Who would fardels[3] bear,

To grunt and sweat under a weary life.

But that the dread of something after death,

The undiscovered country, from whose bourn[4]

No traveler returns, puzzles the will,

And makes us rather bear those ills we have

Than fly to others that we know not of?

Thus conscience does make cowards of us all,

And thus the native hue of resolution

Is sicklied o'er with the pale cast of thought,

And enterprises of great pitch and moment

With this regard their currents turn awry

And lose the name of action.

[1]*quietus:* settlement (literally: release ["quit"] from debt

[2]*bodkin:* short dagger

[3]*fardels:* burdens

[4]*bourn:* region

Selection II: Excerpt from "The Awakening" (1899), a short story by Kate Chopin

Despondency had come upon her there in the wakeful night, and had never lifted. There was no one thing in the world that she desired. There was no human being whom she wanted near her except Robert; and she even realized that the day would come when he, too, and the thought of him would melt out of her existence, leaving her alone. The children appeared before her like antagonists who had overcome her; who had overpowered and sought to drag her into the soul's slavery for the rest of her days. But she knew a way to elude them. She was not thinking of these things when she walked down to the beach.

The water of the Gulf stretched out before her, gleaming with the million lights of the sun. The voice of the sea is seductive, never ceasing, whispering, clamoring, murmuring, inviting the soul to wander in abysses of solitude. All along the white beach, up and down, there was no living thing in sight. A bird with a broken wing was beating the air above, reeling, fluttering, circling disabled down, down to the water.

Edna had found her old bathing suit still hanging, faded, upon its accustomed peg.

She put it on, leaving her clothing in the bath-house. But when she was there beside the sea, absolutely alone, she cast the unpleasant, pricking garments from her, and for the first time in her life she stood naked in the open air, at the mercy of the sun, the breeze that beat upon her, and the waves that invited her.

How strange and awful it seemed to stand naked under the sky! how delicious! She felt like some new-born creature, opening its eyes in a familiar world that it had never known.

The foamy wavelets curled up to her white feet, and coiled like serpents about her ankles. She walked out. The water was chill, but she walked on. The water was deep, but she lifted her white body and reached out with a long, sweeping stroke. The touch of the sea is sensuous, enfolding the body in its soft, close embrace.

She went on and on. She remembered the night she swam far out, and recalled the terror that seized her at the fear of being unable to regain the shore. She did not look back now, but went on and on, thinking of the blue-grass meadow that she had traversed when a little child, believing that it had no beginning and no end.

Her arms and legs were growing tired.

GO ON TO THE NEXT PAGE

She thought of Léonce and the children. They were a part of her life. But they need not have thought that they could possess her, body and soul. How Mademoiselle Reisz would have laughed, perhaps sneered, if she knew! "And you call yourself an artist! What pretensions, Madame! The artist must possess the courageous soul that dares and defies."

Exhaustion was pressing upon and overpowering her.

"Good-by—because I love you." He did not know; he did not understand. He would never understand. Perhaps Doctor Mandelet would have understood if she had seen him—but it was too late; the shore was far behind her, and her strength was gone.

She looked into the distance, and the old terror flamed up for an instant, then sank again. Edna heard her father's voice and her sister Margaret's. She heard the barking of an old dog that was chained to the sycamore tree. The spurs of the cavalry officer clanged as he walked across the porch. There was the hum of bees, and the musky odor of pinks filled the air.

2. Complete the exercise that follows.

Write a critical essay in which you analyze the speech below. It was given by Rose Schneiderman, a union activist, at a memorial gathering after the deaths of 146 workers—3 men and 143 women and girls—in the Triangle Shirtwaist Fire in New York City on March 25, 1911. Here's some background on that fire: Five hundred employees were on duty that day. As they tried to escape the fire that had broken out, they found that exit doors had been locked. There was only one accessible fire escape, but it collapsed under all the weight of the panicked workers. There were no sprinklers inside. When the fire trucks finally got there, they found that their ladders were too short to reach the top three floors of the ten-story building, where the fire was raging. Later, the owners of the factory were found not guilty of manslaughter, which outraged the public. Demands were made for safety reforms in the workplace, and some of these demands were met. But many people felt that this was too little, too late. One of those who felt this way was Rose Schneiderman, a labor activist. A memorial was held for the victims at the Metropolitan Opera House, and Rose Schneiderman was one of the speakers.

As you respond to her speech, assume that you are writing for an educated audience and make sure to support your conclusions with evidence from the text. In your essay:

- summarize, in your own words, the author's main point in this passage;
- evaluate the author's style;
- identify the audience for which the author is most likely writing; and
- describe the extent to which the passage is likely to be effective in persuading the audience, and explain why.

I would be a traitor to these poor burned bodies if I came here to talk good fellowship. We have tried you good people of the public, and we have found you wanting. This is not the first time girls have been burned alive in the city. Every week I must learn of the untimely death of one of my sister workers. Every year thousands of us are maimed. The life of men and women is so cheap and property is so sacred. There are so many of us for one job it matters little if 143 are burned to death.

We have tried you, citizens; we are trying you now, and you have a couple of dollars for the sorrowing mothers and daughters and sisters by way of a charity gift. But every time the workers come out in the only way they know to protest against conditions which are unbearable, the strong hand of the law is allowed to press down heavily upon us.

Public officials have only words of warning to us—warning that we must be intensely orderly and must be intensely peaceable, and they have the workhouse just back of all their warnings. The strong hand of the law beats us back when we rise into the conditions that make life bearable.

I can't talk fellowship to you who are gathered here. Too much blood has been spilled. I know from my experience it is up to the working people to save themselves. The only way they can save themselves is by a strong working-class movement.

GO ON TO THE NEXT PAGE

Written Response Document for CSET: English Subtest III

For both questions 1 and 2, you will record your written response to each question on a four-page response document. The length of your response to each question is limited to the lined space available in the response document. Samples of the response documents are provided on the following pages.

Written Response Booklet A

Written Response Booklet A continued

_____

_____

_____

_____

_____

_____

_____

_____

_____

_____

_____

_____

_____

_____

_____

_____

_____

_____

_____

_____

_____

Written Response Booklet A continued

Written Response Booklet A continued

Written Response Booklet B

Written Response Booklet B continued

Written Response Booklet B continued

Written Response Booklet B continued

Examples of Responses to Sample Constructed-Response Questions for CSET: English Subtest III

Composition and Rhetoric; Literature and Textual Analysis

Question #1 (Score Point 4 Response)

Both Shakespeare, in this soliloquy from <u>Hamlet</u>, and Kate Chopin, in this excerpt from her story "The Awakening," are writing about fundamental questions concerning life and death. Is there a point at which emotional anguish and inner turmoil might be so overwhelming that one would be justified in taking one's own life? The two writers wrestle with the question and come to different conclusions.

The indecisive Hamlet weighs the pros and cons of suicide in a tone that suggests a longing for the peace of death, declaring that it is a "consummation / Devoutly to be wished." Almost immediately, however, he struggles with the "dread of something after death" that might present further ills "that we know not of." All Hamlet can do is debate the issue, coming to no conclusion.

In "The Awakening," on the other hand, Kate Chopin gives us a character whose decisive action allows no time for debate. Without much forethought, Edna plunges into the sea and swims so far out that she cannot possibly return. Ironically, moments before, she had "felt like some newborn creature, opening its eyes in a familiar world that it had never known." Unlike Hamlet, who feared that "undiscovered country," Edna prefers it over the turmoil of her life. Even this short excerpt reveals much information about that turmoil. Edna loves a man who is not her husband, but this is not the real reason for her unhappiness. The real reason is that she has lost all desire for the things of the world, except Robert, but she realizes that the day will come when she will not even care for him. She also feels that her husband and children have put too many demands on her, wanting to "possess her, body and soul." Sadly, her solitary swim is the one moment of real freedom in her life.

Both writers consider the element of courage. Shakespeare's character claims that "conscience does make cowards of us all," implying that it takes courage to go through with such a drastic act. Chopin's character refers to the "courageous soul that dares and defies." But is it courage that has enabled Edna to perform this act? She seems more seduced by the sea than in full control of her actions. As she stands at the water's edge, the "foamy wavelets . . . coiled like serpents about her ankles," reminding the reader of Eve's temptation. Earlier, she had noticed that the "voice of the sea is seductive": now, she feels that "the touch of the sea is sensuous." It seems that Edna has given herself up to the sea in a weak moment. Lacking the courage to look at her life and make it better, she instead embraces death.

The main difference in the two approaches to the theme is in the degree to which the intellect plays a part. Hamlet is all thought, no action. Edna is all action, little thought. As Hamlet weighs the consequences of each choice, it is clear that he is losing momentum, finally "sicklied o'er with the pale cast of thought." But Edna never loses momentum. All her senses are engaged in her final act. At the water's edge, Edna's senses of sight and hearing are stimulated: the water gleams "with the million lights of the sun"; she hears the voice of the sea "whispering, clamoring, murmuring." She feels a breeze on her skin; then she feels the chill of the water. In her last moments, she hears the voices of her father and her sister, the barking of a dog, the hum of bees. She also smells the "musky odor of pinks." All this imagery, with its emphasis on sensory experience, is in stark contrast to the more intellectual feel of Hamlet's soliloquy, a fitting effect, considering the differences between the two characters.

Question #1 (Score Point 3 Response)

In Shakespeare's "To Be or Not to Be" soliloquy from <u>Hamlet</u> and in the excerpt from Kate Chopin's story "The Awakening," the authors explore the theme of suicide. In <u>Hamlet</u>, the character is undecided about the issue. He wonders which is the nobler path: to go on suffering in a difficult life or to end the pain by taking his own life. In "The Awakening," the character just goes ahead and does it, without too much thought beforehand. It is clear that Hamlet is a more cerebral character than Edna. He is so caught up in his thought processes that he becomes almost paralyzed when it comes to taking any action. Edna, on the other hand, does not seem to think the issue through. She acts almost on a whim. One minute she's walking down to the beach; the next minute she's swimming out too far on purpose.

Shakespeare shows Hamlet's indecisiveness by interrupting each thought he has with its opposite. He opens with the choice: "To be, or not to be." Then he elaborates by touting the advantages of dying, saying it is one way to end our "heartache" and the "thousand natural shocks / That flesh is heir to." That long sleep sounds so peaceful, until Hamlet brings up the possibility that the dreams that "may come" might not be so wonderful. He brings up the fact that we do not know what awaits us after death. Will we face an even worse existence? These considerations have stopped him from taking his own life.

Kate Chopin, on the other hand, creates a character who perhaps does not think enough. Edna acts on her feelings; she is not bogged down by second thoughts. She seems to enjoy "the touch of the sea," which enfolds her body "in its soft, close embrace." She keeps swimming out deeper and deeper, until she is so far from shore that she cannot come back. Even at the end, she is enjoying her senses, hearing her father's and sister's voices, the barking of a dog, boots on a porch, the hum of bees, and even smelling the odor of flowers.

Shakespeare's series of questions and their possible answers in blank verse are the perfect format to express Hamlet's confusion, hesitation, and indecisiveness. There are so many answers to choose from, and he cannot pick just one, so he does nothing. In Kate Chopin's narrative, however, the character is not troubled by many choices. She feels "like some new-born creature," who reaches out with a "long, sweeping stroke." The only choice open to her, as she sees it, is to surrender to the sea, and she does not hesitate.

Question #1 (Score Point 2 Response)

The speaker in the Shakespeare piece and the character in "The Awakening" are very different from each other. For one thing, Hamlet is a man from a long time ago, whereas Edna is a woman from relatively recent times. Still, they do have some things in common. Both of them are grappling with the question of suicide.

For Hamlet, it seems to be an intellectual question, not a real possibility. He seems to think of suicide as an attractive alternative to life's sufferings, but he comes up with all kinds of doubts as to whether it's a good idea. For Edna, on the other hand, it is a real possibility that does not even require debate. She never asks herself what alternatives she has. She's unhappy, so she just ends her life. What a loser! And what a selfish solution—she doesn't seem to think about how it will affect her children and her husband.

Shakespeare uses a soliloquy in the middle of a play to explore the theme. Hamlet speaks in blank verse, balancing each point he makes with a counterpoint. For example, he wonders why anyone should "bear the whips and scorns of time, /Th' oppressor's wrong, the proud man's contumely, / The pangs of love" when he can end it all with a "bare bodkin." Then, in the next breath, he reminds us that it might be worse in that "undiscovered country" after death.

Kate Chopin's character has no such argument with herself. Without so much as a second thought, she starts swimming out, far from shore. She has a brief moment of "the old terror," but it quickly goes away as she dies in what seems almost a pleasant experience.

I think that Hamlet's attitude is much healthier. He might be unable to act, but at least he's still alive and can try to work out his problems the next day. For Edna, it's all over.

Question #1 (Score Point 1 Response)

At first glance, these two pieces do not seem to have much in common. The poem uses a lot of old-fashioned words like " 'tis," "perchance," "ay," and "o'er." It also uses some very difficult or obsolete words like "quietus," "bodkin," "fardels," and "bourn." Yes, it's true that these words are footnoted, but that only makes it more complicated. The story is easier to understand, but it has some unnecessary details, such as the bird with the broken wing. What does that have to do with the plot?

In the poem, the speaker is asking himself a lot of questions that are hard to understand. At one point he seems to say that dying is the same as sleeping no more. Later, he says that dying is the same as sleeping, but we don't know what kinds of dreams we'll have. No wonder the reader gets confused—it seems like the speaker is confused. The speaker seems to be interested in the idea of suicide, but just can't decide if it's a good idea or a bad idea. It seems so obvious that it's a bad idea—you just want to shake some sense into him!

The story is told from the third-person limited omniscient point of view. That is, the author gets into the mind of the main character, to whom she refers by using third-person pronouns. From this point of view, the reader learns that Edna is a very unhappy woman. She has lost interest in life. When the idea of suicide occurs to her, she does not even fight it. It's almost as if she's hypnotized, the way she just walks into the water and starts swimming. What was she thinking? Or was she thinking at all?

Question #2 (Score Point 4 Response)

This speech was given by Rose Schneiderman at a memorial gathering for the victims of the Triangle Shirtwaist Fire of 1911. We can assume that the members of the audience included people who cared about the victims, such as family members and friends. Internal evidence from the speech (such as the reference to "couple of dollars for the sorrowing mothers and daughters and sisters by way of a charity gift") suggests that representatives of the Triangle Shirtwaist Company were also there.

The author says that the tragedy could have been avoided if working conditions had been better. She reminds the audience that such a tragedy has occurred before. She says that at least one of her "sister workers" is killed every week due to fire in the workplace. She says that thousands more are maimed each year. She blames this situation on unbearable working conditions. She says that every time the workers protest, they are opposed by the "strong hand of the law." All these facts lead up to the author's main point that the situation will never improve unless and until the workers unite and demand better conditions.

The author's style is straightforward. She is angry about what has happened, and she is not afraid to express her anger. She refuses to "talk good fellowship" to members of the public who had the power and opportunity to improve conditions for the workers but failed to do so. She uses phrases such as "poor burned bodies," "burned alive," and "too much blood" to provide graphic images that people will remember.

When she says to the audience that she has "found you wanting," she is placing the blame where it belongs. No doubt some of the listeners in that room were squirming in their seats as she spoke. When she says "it is up to the working people to save themselves," her purpose is to get the survivors to unionize. She realizes, even if they don't, that the workers must act as one to demand safe working conditions.

Some members of the audience might have found this speech inappropriate at a memorial service. After all, they might say, the focus should be on the victims of the fire and should offer some comfort to the grieving families. The memorial service, some might feel, is not the place to lobby for the unions. I believe, however, that this speech was appropriate for the time and place. The women who died in the fire cannot be brought back, obviously, but better working conditions can help prevent such a tragedy from occurring again. I think Rose Schneiderman did the right thing by talking about unionizing at this gathering.

Question #2 (Score Point 3 Response)

In her speech at a memorial gathering, Rose Schneiderman gets right to the point about what happened. She immediately blames "you good people of the public" for the terrible accident that claimed the lives of 146 workers in a garment factory in 1911. She obviously does not care if she hurts anyone's feelings. She knows that the greed of the owners of the Triangle Shirtwaist Company is a direct cause of the tragedy. If they had spent some money on fire safety, many deaths could have been avoided.

Her style is simple and direct. She refers to the "poor burned bodies" of girls who have been "burned alive." She says something like this happens every week, on a smaller scale. She reminds the audience that even though the workers have protested their unsafe conditions in the past, nothing has been done. In fact, she says, "the strong hand of the law" has always kept the workers in their place. Even though "a couple of dollars . . . by way of a charity gift" has been offered to the grieving families, it is far from enough. Schneiderman's indignation at the working conditions endured by these workers is apparent in every sentence of her speech.

The audience to whom Schneiderman is speaking was no doubt composed of survivors of the fire, friends and relatives of the victims, representatives of the Triangle Shirtwaist Company, and other interested members of the public. Schneiderman's purpose obviously is to do more than merely mourn for the victims. She wants to get people riled up enough to want to do something about it. She wants the workers to unionize so that their rights to a safe working environment and fair pay will be acknowledged.

Because of the passionate way in which Schneiderman expresses herself, I am sure that she motivated many audience members to either join a union or support those who did.

Question #2 (Score Point 2 Response)

In her speech at the memorial gathering for victims of the Triangle Shirtwaist Fire, Rose Schneiderman manages to offend every member of the audience. They had come to the gathering to honor the victims of the fire, not to be preached at by a union organizer.

Can you imagine what it must have been like for the mother, sister, or father of one of the victims to hear about "these poor burned bodies"? Yes, it was a fire that killed the victims, but phrases such as "burned alive" and "burned to death" do little to offer comfort to the grieving families.

Rose Schneiderman is obviously very focused on her mission, which is to build up the unions. She makes the point that it is up to the workers to demand safe working environments. She also knows that one worker making a demand will not be respected. Only when all workers unite in their demands will management listen. She makes her point, but this is not the proper place to do it.

It is my opinion that this speech is not likely to be effective in persuading the audience. The reason for this is that the members of the audience would have been too grief-stricken to think about unionizing just then.

Question #2 (Score Point 1 Response)

There was a terrible fire on March 15, 1911, at the Triangle Shirtwaist Factory in New York City. I think shirtwaists are a type of dress. About 500 people worked there, and they all tried to escape when the fire broke out. Because the exit doors were blocked, and there were no sprinklers, many of them were doomed. There was probably a lot of fabric in the sewing rooms, which just added fuel to the fire.

There was one accessible fire escape, but it collapsed when it got overloaded. In all, 146 people died in the fire—3 men and 143 women and girls. When the company was found not guilty of manslaughter, the public was outraged. Demands for reform were made, and some reforms were put into place. But it wasn't really enough. Garment factories were still dangerous places, and Rose Schneiderman wanted to do something about it.

There was a memorial gathering for the victims some time later. Rose Schneiderman got up to speak. She didn't really eulogize the victims, as one might have expected. Instead, the ranted on and on about how terrible the factory owners are. She also criticized the "strong hand of the law," as if the law had anything to do with the fire.

There's a time and a place for everything, and Rose Schneiderman obviously didn't know when union talk would be appropriate. She had a right to talk about unions, of course—just not at a memorial gathering.

Scoring Information for CSET: English Subtest III

The following information is available at the CSET Website. It is reproduced here for your convenience.

There are two constructed-response questions in Subtest III of CSET: English. Each of these constructed-response questions is designed so that a response can be completed within approximately 45–60 minutes. Responses to the constructed-response questions are scored by qualified California educators using focused holistic scoring. Scorers will judge the overall effectiveness of your responses while focusing on the performance characteristics that have been identified as important for this subtest (see below). Each response will be assigned a score based on an approved scoring scale (see page 117).

Your performance on the subtest will be evaluated against a standard determined by the California Commission on Teacher Credentialing based on professional judgments and recommendations of California educators.

Performance Characteristics for CSET: English Subtest III

The following performance characteristics will guide the scoring of responses to the constructed-response questions on CSET: English Subtest III.

Purpose	The extent to which the response addresses the constructed-response assignment's charge in relation to relevant CSET subject matter requirements.
Subject Matter Knowledge	The application of accurate subject matter knowledge as described in the relevant CSET subject matter requirements.
Support	The appropriateness and quality of the supporting evidence in relation to relevant CSET subject matter requirements.
Depth and Breadth of Understanding	The degree to which the response demonstrates understanding of the relevant CSET subject matter requirements.

Scoring Scale for CSET: English Subtest III

Scores will be assigned to each response to the constructed-response questions on CSET: English Subtest III according to the following scoring scale.

Score Point	Score Point Description
4	The "4" response reflects a thorough command of the relevant knowledge and skills as defined in the subject matter requirements for CSET: English. • The purpose of the assignment is fully achieved. • There is a substantial and accurate application of relevant subject matter knowledge. • The supporting evidence is sound; there are high-quality, relevant examples. • The response reflects a comprehensive understanding of the assignment.
3	The "3" response reflects a general command of the relevant knowledge and skills as defined in the subject matter requirements for CSET: English. • The purpose of the assignment is largely achieved. • There is a largely accurate application of relevant subject matter knowledge. • The supporting evidence is adequate; there are some acceptable, relevant examples. • The response reflects an adequate understanding of the assignment.
2	The "2" response reflects a limited command of the relevant knowledge and skills as defined in the subject matter requirements for CSET: English. • The purpose of the assignment is partially achieved. • There is limited accurate application of relevant subject matter knowledge. • The supporting evidence is limited; there are few relevant examples. • The response reflects a limited understanding of the assignment.
1	The "1" response reflects little or no command of the relevant knowledge and skills as defined in the subject matter requirements for CSET: English. • The purpose of the assignment is not achieved. • There is little or no accurate application of relevant subject matter knowledge. • The supporting evidence is weak; there are no or few relevant examples. • The response reflects little or no understanding of the assignment.
U	The "U" (Unscorable) is assigned to a response that is unrelated to the assignment, illegible, primarily in a language other than English, or does not contain a sufficient amount of original work to score.
B	The "B" (Blank) is assigned to a response that is blank.

Subtest IV: Speech, Media, and Creative Performance

Content Domains for Subject Matter Understanding and Skill in English

Here is a list of the areas on which you will be tested. This information is also available at the CSET Website. It is reproduced here for your convenience.

Communications: Speech, Media, and Creative Performance (SMR Domain 4)

Candidates demonstrate knowledge of the foundations and contexts of the speech, media, and creative performance contained in the *English-Language Arts Content Standards for California Public Schools* (1997) as outlined in the *Reading/Language Arts Framework for California Public Schools: Kindergarten Through Grade Twelve* (1999) at a post secondary level of rigor. Candidates have both broad and deep conceptual knowledge of the subject matter. The Reading/Language Arts Framework for California Public Schools (1999) puts consistent emphasis on analysis and evaluation of oral and media communication as well as on effective public speaking and performance. The candidate must possess the breadth of knowledge needed to integrate journalism, technological media, speech, dramatic performance, and creative writing into the language arts curriculum, including sensitivity to cultural approaches to communication. The subject matter preparation program should include opportunities for candidates to obtain knowledge and experience in these areas. The candidate skillfully applies the artistic and aesthetic tools and sensitivities required for creative expression. Candidates will be able to:

0001 Oral Communication Processes (SMR 4.1)

a. Identify features of, and deliver oral performance in, a variety of forms (e.g., impromptu, extemporaneous, persuasive, expository, interpretive, debate).

b. Demonstrate and evaluate individual performance skills (e.g., diction, enunciation, vocal rate, range, pitch, volume, body language, eye contact, response to audience).

c. Articulate principles of speaker/audience interrelationship (e.g., interpersonal communication, group dynamics, public address).

d. Identify and demonstrate collaborative communication skills in a variety of roles (e.g., listening supportively, facilitating, synthesizing, stimulating higher level critical thinking through inquiry).

(*English-Language Arts Content: Standards for California Public Schools,* Grade 6, Reading: 1.1, Listening and Speaking: 1.1–8, 2.0; Grade 7, Listening and Speaking: 1.1–7, 2.0; Grade 8, Listening and Speaking: 1.1–8, 2.0; Grades 9–10, Listening and Speaking: 1.1, 1.3–6, 1.8–13, 2.0; Grades 11–12, Reading: 2.6, Listening and Speaking: 1.4–6, 1.8–13, 2.0)

0002 Media Analysis and Journalistic Applications (SMR 4.2)

a. Analyze the impact on society of a variety of media forms (e.g., television, advertising, radio, Internet, film).

b. Recognize and evaluate strategies used by the media to inform, persuade, entertain, and transmit culture.

c. Identify aesthetic effects of a media presentation.

d. Demonstrate effective and creative application of these strategies and techniques to prepare presentations using a variety of media forms and visual aids.

(*English-Language Arts Content Standards for California Public Schools,* Grade 6, Reading: 2.1–2, 2.6, Listening and Speaking: 1.9; Grade 7, Reading: 2.1, Listening and Speaking: 1.8–9; Grade 8, Reading: 2.1, 2.3, Listening and Speaking: 1.8–9; Grades 9–10, Reading: 2.1, Listening and Speaking: 1.1–2, 1.7, 1.9, 1.14; Grades 11–12, Reading: 2.1, Writing: 2.6, Listening and Speaking: 1.1–4, 1.9, 1.14, 2.4; *Visual and Performing Arts Content Standards for California Public Schools,* Theatre, Grades 6–12, 5.0: Connections, Relationships, Applications)

0003 Dramatic Performance (SMR 4.3)

a. Describe and use a range of rehearsal strategies to effectively mount a production (e.g., teambuilding, scheduling, organizing resources, setting priorities, memorization techniques, improvisation, physical and vocal exercises).

b. Employ basic elements of character analysis and approaches to acting, including physical and vocal techniques, that reveal character and relationships.

c. Demonstrate basic knowledge of the language of visual composition and principles of theatrical design (e.g., set, costume, lighting, sound, props).

d. Apply fundamentals of stage directing, including conceptualization, blocking (movement patterns), tempo, and dramatic arc (rising and falling action).

e. Demonstrate facility in a variety of oral performance traditions (e.g., storytelling, epic poetry, recitation).

(*English-Language Arts Content Standards for California Public Schools,* Grade 6, Listening and Speaking: 2.1, 2.3; Grade 7, Listening and Speaking: 2.1; Grade 8, Listening and Speaking: 1.1, 2.1–2, 2.5; Grades 9–10, Listening and Speaking: 2.1, 2.4; Grades 11–12, Listening and Speaking: 1.7, 1.9–10, 2.5; *Visual and Performing Arts Content Standards for California Public Schools,* Theatre, Grades 6–12, 1.0: Artistic Perception, 2.0: Creative Expression, 3.0: Historical and Cultural Context, 4.0: Aesthetic Valuing)

0004 Creative Writing (SMR 4.4)

a. Demonstrate facility in creative composition in a variety of genres (e.g., poetry, stories, plays, film).

b. Understand and apply processes and techniques that enhance the impact of the creative writing product (e.g., workshopping; readings; recasting of genre, voice, perspective).

c. Demonstrate skill in composing creative and aesthetically compelling responses to literature.

(*English-Language Arts Content Standards for California Pubic Schools,* Grades 6-12, Writing: 2.1)

Subtest IV: Communications: Speech, Media, and Creative Performance

Directions: Below is a set of constructed-response questions that are similar to the questions you will see on Subtest IV of CSET: English. You are encouraged to respond to the questions without looking at the responses provided in the next section and to compare your answers with the provided responses.

1. Complete the exercise that follows.

   Many factors contribute to a successful speech or oral presentation. Among these factors are appearance, posture, the approach to the lectern or stage, gestures, facial expressions, eye contact, voice, involving the audience, audio-visual aids, the speech or presentation itself, and the question-and-answer period. Choose one of these factors and write a response in which you describe how this element can be used to best effect. Write your response on the lined pages of Assignment 1 Response Sheet, provided after these questions.

2. Complete the exercise that follows.

   Briefly discuss the ways in which technology has improved the appearance, effectiveness, and impact of television news broadcasts since the 1950s. Write your response on the lined pages of Assignment 2 Response Sheet, provided after these questions.

3. Complete the exercise that follows.

   You have been asked to participate in an oral storytelling session for a group of children. Describe how you would prepare for the experience and explain the techniques you would use to make the experience enjoyable for the audience. Write your response on the lined pages of Assignment 3 Response Sheet, provided after these questions.

4. Read the paragraph below from *Snow Falling on Cedars* by David Guterson; then complete the exercise that follows.

   Hatsue grew up digging clams at South Beach, picking blackberries, collecting mushrooms, and weeding strawberry plants. She was mother, too, to four sisters. When she was ten a neighborhood boy taught her how to swim and offered her the use of his glass-bottomed box so that she could look beneath the surface of the waves. The two of them clung to it, their backs warmed by the Pacific sun, and together watched starfish and rock crabs. The water evaporated against Hatsue's skin, leaving a residue of salt behind. Finally, one day, the boy kissed her. He asked if he might, and she said nothing either way, and then he leaned across the box and put his lips on hers for no more than a second. She smelled the warm, salty interior of his mouth before this boy pulled away and blinked at her. Then they went on looking through the glass at anemones, sea cucumbers, and tube worms. Hatsue would remember on the day of her wedding that her first kiss had been from this boy, Ishmael Chambers, while they clung to a glass box and floated in the ocean. But when her husband asked if she had kissed anyone before, Hatsue had answered *never.*

   Using your knowledge of literary criticism, evaluate this paragraph in terms of its aesthetic value. Write your response on the lined pages of Assignment 4 Response Sheet, provided after these questions.

Sample Written Response Document for CSET: English Subtest IV

For Questions 1–4, you will record your written response to each question on a one-page response sheet located in your answer document. The length of your response to each question is limited to the lined space available on the response sheet. Response sheets similar to what you will be given at the testing center are provided here.

Assignment 1 Response Sheet

_____

_____

_____

_____

_____

_____

_____

_____

_____

_____

_____

_____

_____

_____

_____

_____

_____

_____

_____

_____

_____

_____

_____

Assignment 2 Response Sheet

_____

_____

_____

_____

_____

_____

_____

_____

_____

_____

_____

_____

_____

_____

_____

_____

_____

_____

_____

_____

_____

_____

_____

Assignment 3 Response Sheet

_____

_____

_____

_____

_____

_____

_____

_____

_____

_____

_____

_____

_____

_____

_____

_____

_____

_____

_____

Assignment 4 Response Sheet

Examples of Responses to Sample Constructed-Response Questions for CSET: English Subtest IV

Communication: Speech, Media, and Creative Performance

Question #1 (Score Point 3 Response)

Eye contact is essential in establishing rapport with an audience. The benefits of maintaining eye contact are as follows:

- *It gives the impression that the speaker is interested in the audience.*
- *It conveys a sense that the speaker has confidence, power, and authority. It also indicates openness and honesty.*
- *Eye contact involves members of the audience and keeps them interested.*

The speaker should pick out a friendly face and address remarks to that person, maintaining eye contact for three to five seconds. Any less than that, and the speaker appears shifty and nervous. Any longer than that, and the audience member feels as if he or she is being stared at. The speaker should then change to someone else, preferably in another section of the audience. Addressing one section of the audience for too long makes the rest of the audience feel left out.

Question #1 (Score Point 2 Response)

One of the worst things you can do as a speaker is to hold your arms stiffly at your sides. You need to move your arms in appropriate gestures to emphasize your points. Your gestures should appear spontaneous, not rehearsed. This doesn't mean that you shouldn't rehearse them. The point is to make them seem to be spontaneous, fitting the text. Don't use just your hands or the lower part of your arms. You need to move the whole body in a way that looks natural with the gesture.

In addition, you should be aware of your body language as you use gestures. Your facial expression should mirror the emotion you might be demonstrating. For example, if you are talking about something frightening and are holding up your arm as if to protect yourself, your face should have a fearful expression.

Question #1 (Score Point 1 Response)

Voice is important when you are giving a speech. In a small room, you don't have to talk very loudly. In a big room, you'll have to raise your voice so everyone can hear you. One thing you can do to make sure you are being heard is to stop and ask, "Can everyone hear me?"

Question #2 (Score Point 3 Response)

In the 1950s, news reports were very dull affairs compared to news reports of today. For one thing, the anchor sat at a desk and read from sheets of paper held in his hand. To try to maintain eye contact with the viewers, he would bob his head up and down as he read the news. Today's teleprompter, a lighted electronic scroll located next to the camera lens, has freed the news anchor from hand-held notes, giving the illusion that the anchor is looking straight at the viewer, speaking spontaneously.

We also have on-the-spot coverage today. Reporters deliver the news from locations outside the studio, perhaps from a battle zone, at the site of a natural disaster, or standing in front of the White House. This is made possible by our more sophisticated means of transmittal, including communications satellites.

Question #2 (Score Point 2 Response)

In the 1950s, news reporting did not have the variety it has today. The entire broadcast took place in the studio. Backgrounds never changed, so all the viewer had to look at was the anchor as he (it was always a "he") read notes from papers on a desk. Today, we have fancier sets that even include locations outside the studio. Because of satellites, we are able to transmit news from where it is happening, which adds to the excitement and interest of the report.

Question #2 (Score Point 1 Response)

News reports are quite different today from what they were like in the 1950s. For one thing, we have more ethnic and gender diversity in the anchors and other reporters. In the 1950s, there was no diversity at all!

We also have more interesting theme music to accompany the news. National news usually has a more dramatic type of theme music than local news.

Question #3 (Score Point 3 Response)

To prepare for a storytelling session for children, I would first spend some time picking out a suitable story. I would look for a story with an age-appropriate theme and a well-developed plot. The story should also include vivid word pictures and pleasing sounds and rhythm. Characterization should be strong, and the story should have some dramatic appeal.

Once I have chosen a story, I would read it several times in order to know it well. I would consider the images I want my listeners to see and the mood I want to create. I would research the background and cultural meanings of the story, learning everything that I could about it. Once I am able to visualize each scene in the story—imagining the sights, sounds, scents, tastes—I would start practicing the story orally, developing different voices for different characters.

Before the session, I would make sure the setting is free of distractions. If possible, I would use props, a costume, or a backdrop to create atmosphere.

While telling the story, I would use appropriate gestures and facial expressions to go along with the plot. I would vary the pace to fit the demands of the plot, slowing down for dialogue and speeding up while narrating action.

Question #3 (Score Point 2 Response)

If I were asked to tell a story to a group of children, I would take great care in choosing the story. It has to be appropriate for the age group, and it has to be interesting and entertaining. I would learn the story inside out and practice telling it many times before the session itself.

At the session itself, I would use my voice, gestures, and facial expressions to create the atmosphere called for by the story. When a character in the story had a line of dialogue, I would give him or her a unique voice so the children could visualize the character better. I might even use different body language for each character.

Question #3 (Score Point 1 Response)

To prepare for an oral storytelling session for children, I would pick out a book with an interesting plot and colorful pictures. The day of the reading, I would sit on a chair while the children sat on a rug in front of me. I would read each page and then hold the book up so they could see the pictures. I would not allow them to talk during the reading, but at the end I would ask them what they thought of the story.

Question #4 (Score Point 3 Response)

This passage from <u>Snow Falling on Cedars</u> is an excellent example of David Guterson's ability to describe character and setting. Without saying "Hatsue worked hard" or "Ishmael was respectful," Guterson lets the reader know what the characters are like. He lets us know by telling us what the characters did. We have to admire a young girl who digs clams, picks blackberries, collects mushroom, weeds strawberry plants, and acts as a mother to her four sisters. And we would like to know a young boy who teaches a girl how to swim, shares a glass-bottomed box, and asks permission before offering her a kiss.

Guterson uses concrete language that makes it easy for the reader to visualize the scenes. When we read about Hatsue and Ishmael looking at sea life below the surface, we can almost taste and smell the salty air and feel the warm sun. Mention of the residue of salt on Hatsue's skin and the salty smell of Ishmael's mouth emphasizes the imagery. We learn about their personalities when Ishmael asks permission to kiss her, and ten-year-old Matsue says nothing either way. The kiss is short and sweet, yet important enough to Hatsue that she remembers it on her wedding night.

Question #4 (Score Point 2 Response)

This passage is beautifully written. David Guterson has described two children in an interesting, seaside setting. The boy has taught the girl how to swim, and he has shared the glass-bottomed box that he uses for viewing underwater life. As Guterson presents the picture of the two children floating near the shore, peering through the glass-bottomed box, and viewing starfish, rock crabs, anemones, sea cucumbers, and tube worms, the reader can almost feel the sun on their backs. This is a lovely scene, skillfully described.

Question #4 (Score Point 1 Response)

There are several confusing aspects to this passage. Let's first consider this sentence: "She was mother, too, to four sisters." Does this mean that when she grew up she had four children, all girls? Or does it mean she acted as a mother to her own sisters? In the next sentence, the author refers to the time Hatsue was ten, so the time frame seems a bit mixed up.

Another confusing aspect is why Hatsue lied to her husband about the kiss she had when she was ten. It was no big deal. What was she hiding? She could have just told him, shared with him that sweet memory from her childhood.

Scoring Information for CSET: English Subtest IV

The following information is available at the CSET Website. It is reproduced here for your convenience.

There are four constructed-response questions in Subtest IV of CSET: English. Each of these constructed-response questions is designed so that a response can be completed within a short amount of time—approximately 10–15 minutes. Responses to the constructed-response questions are scored by qualified California educators using focused holistic scoring. Scorers will judge the overall effectiveness of your responses while focusing on the performance characteristics that have been identified as important for this subtest (see below). Each response will be assigned a score based on an approved scoring scale (see page 139).

Your performance on the subtest will be evaluated against a standard determined by the California Commission on Teacher Credentialing based on professional judgments and recommendations of California educators.

Performance Characteristics for CSET: English Subtest IV

The following performance characteristics will guide the scoring of responses to the constructed-response questions on CSET: English Subtest IV.

Purpose	The extent to which the response addresses the constructed-response assignment's charge in relation to relevant CSET subject matter requirements.
Subject Matter Knowledge	The application of accurate subject matter knowledge as described in the relevant CSET subject matter requirements.
Support	The appropriateness and quality of the supporting evidence in relation to relevant CSET subject matter requirements.

Scoring Scale for CSET: English Subtest IV

Scores will be assigned to each response to the constructed-response questions on CSET: English Subtest III according to the following scoring scale.

Score Point	Score Point Description
3	The "3" response reflects a command of the relevant knowledge and skills as defined in the subject matter requirements for CSET: English. • The purpose of the assignment is fully achieved. • There is an accurate application of relevant subject matter knowledge. • There is appropriate and specific relevant supporting evidence.
2	The "2" response reflects a general command of the relevant knowledge and skills as defined in the subject matter requirements for CSET: English. • The purpose of the assignment is largely achieved. • There is a largely accurate application of relevant subject matter knowledge. • There is acceptable relevant supporting evidence.
1	The "1" response reflects a limited command of the relevant knowledge and skills as defined in the subject matter requirements for CSET: English. • The purpose of the assignment is only partially or not achieved. • There is limited or no application of relevant subject matter knowledge. • There is little or no relevant supporting evidence.
U	The "U" (Unscorable) is assigned to a response that is unrelated to the assignment, illegible, primarily in a language other than English, or does not contain a sufficient amount of original work to score.
B	The "B" (Blank) is assigned to a response that is blank.

(Remove this sheet and use it to mark your answers to the multiple-choice questions.)

Answer Sheet

1 Ⓐ Ⓑ Ⓒ Ⓓ		26 Ⓐ Ⓑ Ⓒ Ⓓ
2 Ⓐ Ⓑ Ⓒ Ⓓ		27 Ⓐ Ⓑ Ⓒ Ⓓ
3 Ⓐ Ⓑ Ⓒ Ⓓ		28 Ⓐ Ⓑ Ⓒ Ⓓ
4 Ⓐ Ⓑ Ⓒ Ⓓ		29 Ⓐ Ⓑ Ⓒ Ⓓ
5 Ⓐ Ⓑ Ⓒ Ⓓ		30 Ⓐ Ⓑ Ⓒ Ⓓ
6 Ⓐ Ⓑ Ⓒ Ⓓ		31 Ⓐ Ⓑ Ⓒ Ⓓ
7 Ⓐ Ⓑ Ⓒ Ⓓ		32 Ⓐ Ⓑ Ⓒ Ⓓ
8 Ⓐ Ⓑ Ⓒ Ⓓ		33 Ⓐ Ⓑ Ⓒ Ⓓ
9 Ⓐ Ⓑ Ⓒ Ⓓ		34 Ⓐ Ⓑ Ⓒ Ⓓ
10 Ⓐ Ⓑ Ⓒ Ⓓ		35 Ⓐ Ⓑ Ⓒ Ⓓ
11 Ⓐ Ⓑ Ⓒ Ⓓ		36 Ⓐ Ⓑ Ⓒ Ⓓ
12 Ⓐ Ⓑ Ⓒ Ⓓ		37 Ⓐ Ⓑ Ⓒ Ⓓ
13 Ⓐ Ⓑ Ⓒ Ⓓ		38 Ⓐ Ⓑ Ⓒ Ⓓ
14 Ⓐ Ⓑ Ⓒ Ⓓ		39 Ⓐ Ⓑ Ⓒ Ⓓ
15 Ⓐ Ⓑ Ⓒ Ⓓ		40 Ⓐ Ⓑ Ⓒ Ⓓ
16 Ⓐ Ⓑ Ⓒ Ⓓ		41 Ⓐ Ⓑ Ⓒ Ⓓ
17 Ⓐ Ⓑ Ⓒ Ⓓ		42 Ⓐ Ⓑ Ⓒ Ⓓ
18 Ⓐ Ⓑ Ⓒ Ⓓ		43 Ⓐ Ⓑ Ⓒ Ⓓ
19 Ⓐ Ⓑ Ⓒ Ⓓ		44 Ⓐ Ⓑ Ⓒ Ⓓ
20 Ⓐ Ⓑ Ⓒ Ⓓ		45 Ⓐ Ⓑ Ⓒ Ⓓ
21 Ⓐ Ⓑ Ⓒ Ⓓ		46 Ⓐ Ⓑ Ⓒ Ⓓ
22 Ⓐ Ⓑ Ⓒ Ⓓ		47 Ⓐ Ⓑ Ⓒ Ⓓ
23 Ⓐ Ⓑ Ⓒ Ⓓ		48 Ⓐ Ⓑ Ⓒ Ⓓ
24 Ⓐ Ⓑ Ⓒ Ⓓ		49 Ⓐ Ⓑ Ⓒ Ⓓ
25 Ⓐ Ⓑ Ⓒ Ⓓ		50 Ⓐ Ⓑ Ⓒ Ⓓ

CUT HERE

Practice Test 2

Subtest I: Literature and Textual Analysis; Composition and Rhetoric

Part 1: Content Domains for Subject Matter Understanding and Skill in English

Following is a list of the areas on which you will be tested. This information is also available at the CSET Website. It is reproduced here for your convenience.

Literature and Textual Analysis (SMR Domain 1)

Candidates demonstrate knowledge of the foundations and contexts of the literature and textual analysis contained in the *English-Language Arts Content Standards for California Public Schools Kindergarten Through Grade Twelve* (1999) at a post secondary level of rigor. Candidates have both broad and deep conceptual knowledge of the subject matter. The candidate's preparation should include breadth of knowledge in literature, literary analysis and criticism, as well as nonliterary test analysis. Literary analysis presumes in-depth exploration of the relationship between form and content. The curriculum should embrace representative selections from different literary traditions and major works from diverse cultures. Advanced study of multicultural writers is also fundamental preparation for teaching these works. Shakespeare remains integral to the secondary school curriculum; advanced study of his work is, therefore, essential to future secondary teachers. Candidates must be enthusiastic readers and writers, who know and apply effective reading strategies and compose thoughtful well-crafted responses to literary and nonliterary tests. Candidates will be able to:

0001 Literary Analysis (SMR 1.1)

a. Recognize, compare, and evaluate different literary traditions to include:

- American (inclusive of cultural pluralism)
- British (inclusive of cultural pluralism)
- World literature and literature in translation (inclusive of cross-cultural literature)
- Mythology and oral tradition

b. Trace development of major literary movements in historical periods (e.g., Homeric Greece, medieval, neoclassic, romantic, modern).

c. Describe the salient features of adolescent/young adult literature.

d. Analyze and interpret major works by representative writers in historical, aesthetic, political, and philosophical contexts.

(*English-Language Arts Content Standards for California Public Schools*, Grade 6, Reading: 2.4; Grades 11–12, Reading: 2.2, 3.5–7)

0002 Literary Elements (SMR 1.2)

a. Distinguish salient features of genres (e.g., short stories, non-fiction, drama, poetry, novel).

b. Define and analyze basic elements of literature (e.g., plot, setting, character, point of view, theme, narrative structure, figurative language, tone, diction, style).

c. Articulate the relationship between the expressed purposes and the characteristics of different forms of dramatic literature (e.g., comedy, tragedy, drama, dramatic monologue).

d. Develop critical thinking and analytic skill through close reading of texts.

(*English-Language Arts Content Standards for California Public Schools,* Grade 6, Reading: 1.1–2, 2.1, 2.4, 2.6, 2.8, 3.0; Grade 7, Reading: 1.1, 2.4, 3.1–5; Grade 8, Reading: 1.1, 2.7, 3.0; Grades 9–10, Reading: 1.1, 2.8, 3.1–4, 3.7–10; Grades 11–12, Reading: 2.2, 3.1–4)

0003 Literary Criticism (SMR 1.3)

a. Research and apply criticism of major texts and authors using print and/or electronic resources.

b. Research and apply various approaches to interpreting literature (e.g., aesthetic, historical, political, philosophical).

(*English-Language Arts Content Standards for California Public Schools,* Grade 6, Reading: 2.1–2, 2.6–8, 3.6; Grade 7, Reading: 2.1, 2.4, 2.6, 3.0; Grade 8, Reading: 2.2, 2.6, 3.0; Grades 9–10, Reading: 2.2, 2.4, 2.8, 3.5–7, 3.11–12; Writing: 1.6–7; Grades 11–12, Reading: 2.2, 2.4, 3.8–9, Writing: 1.6–7)

0004 Analysis of Non-Literary Texts (SMR 1.4)

a. Compare various features of print and visual media (e.g., film, television, Internet).

b. Evaluate structure and content of a variety of consumer, workplace, and public documents.

c. Interpret individual works in their cultural, social, and political contexts.

(*English-Language Arts Content Standards for California Public Schools,* Grade 6, Reading: 2.0, 3.0; Grade 7, Reading: 2.1–5, 3.0; Grade 8, Reading: 2.1–7, 3.0; Grades 9–10, Reading: 2.1, 2.2, 2.4–7, 3.0; Grades 11–12, Reading: 2.1–3, 2.6, 3.0)

Composition and Rhetoric (SMR Domain 3)

Candidates demonstrate knowledge of the foundations and contexts of the composition and rhetoric contained in the *English-Language Arts Content Standards for California Public Schools* (1997) as outlined in the *Reading/Language Arts Framework for California Public Schools: Kindergarten Through Grade Twelve* (1999) at a post-secondary level of rigor. Candidates have both broad and deep conceptual knowledge of the subject matter. Candidates face dynamic challenges in the domains of oral and written communication. They must make appropriate use of current text-production technologies and develop sensitivity to patterns of communication used by different social and cultural groups. Candidates are competent writers and speakers who are able to communicate appropriately in various rhetorical contexts, using effective text structures, word choice, sentence options, standard usage conventions, and advanced research methods as needed. The subject matter preparation program provides opportunities for candidates to develop skills and confidence in public speaking. Candidates will be able to:

0005 Written Composing Processes (Individual and Collaborative) (SMR 3.1)

a. Reflect on and describe their own writing processes.

b. Investigate and apply alternative methods of prewriting, drafting, responding, revising, editing, and evaluating.

c. Employ such strategies as graphic organizers, outlines, notes, charts, summaries, or précis to clarify and record meaning.

d. Integrate a variety of software applications (e.g., databases, graphics, spreadsheets) to produce print documents and multi-media presentations.

(*English-Language Arts Content Standards for California Public Schools,* Grade 6, Reading: 2.1–2, 2.4, Writing: 1.4–6; Grade 7, Reading: 2.3–4, Writing: 1.3–4, 1.6–7; Grade 8, Reading: 2.4, Writing: 1.1, 1.4–6, Listening and Speaking: 1.4; Grades 9–10, Reading: 2.4, Writing: 1.8–9; Grades 11–12, Writing: 1.4, 1.7–9, Listening and Speaking: 2.4)

0006 Rhetorical Features of Literary and Non-Literary, Oral and Written Texts (SMR 3.2)

a. Recognize and use a variety of writing applications (e.g., short story, biographical, autobiographical, expository, persuasive, business and technical documents, historical investigation).

b. Demonstrate awareness of audience, purpose, and context.

c. Recognize and use various text structures (e.g., narrative and non-narrative organizational patterns).

d. Apply a variety of methods to develop ideas within an essay (e.g., analogy, cause and effect, compare and contrast, definition, illustration, description, hypothesis).

e. Apply critical thinking strategies to evaluate methods of persuasion, including but not limited to:

- Types of appeal (e.g., appeal to reason, emotion, morality)
- Types of persuasive speech (e.g., propositions of fact, value, problem, policy)
- Logical fallacies (e.g., bandwagon, red herring, glittering generalities, ad hominem)
- Advertising techniques (e.g., Maslow's hierarchy of needs)
- Logical argument (e.g., inductive/deductive reasoning, syllogisms, analogies)
- Classical argument (e.g., claim, qualifiers, rules of evidence, warrant)

(*English-Language Arts Content Standards for California Public Schools,* Grade 6, Reading: 2.1–2, 2.4, 2.6, 2.8, Writing: 1.1–3, 1.6, 2.1–5, Listening and Speaking: 1.8–9; Grade 7, Reading: 1.3, 2.2–3, Writing: 1.1–3, 1.7, 2.1–5, Listening and Speaking: 1.1, 1.3; Grade 8, Reading: 1.3, 2.2, Writing: 1.1–3, 1.5, 2.1–6, Listening and Speaking: 1.8; Grades 9–10, Writing: 1.1–2, 1.4, 1.9, 2.1–6, Listening and Speaking: 1.5, 1.10, 1.13; Grades 11–12, Reading: 1.3, 2.2, 2.4–6, Writing: 1.1–5, 1.9, 2.1–6, Listening and Speaking: 1.4, 1.12–13)

0007 Rhetorical Effects of Grammatical Elements (SMR 3.3)

a. Employ precise and extensive vocabulary and effective diction to control voice, style, and tone.

b. Use clause joining techniques (e.g., coordinators, subordinators, punctuation) to express logical connections between ideas.

c. Identify and use clausal and phrasal modifiers to control flow, pace, and emphasis (e.g., adjective clauses, appositives, participle and verbal phrases, absolutes).

d. Identify and use devices to control focus in sentence and paragraph (e.g., active and passive voice, expletives, concrete subjects, transitional phrases).

e. Maintain coherence through use of cohesive devices.

(*English-Language Arts Content Standards for California Public Schools,* Grade 6, Reading: 1.1, Writing: 1.2, 1.6, Written and Oral English Language Conventions: 1.1–5; Grade 7, Writing: 1.1, 1.7, Written and Oral English Language Conventions: 1.1–7; Grade 8, Writing: 1.2, 1.6, Written and Oral English Language Conventions: 1.1–6, Listening and Speaking: 1.5–6; Grades 9–10, Writing: 1.1–2, 1.6, 1.9, Written and Oral English Language Conventions: 1.1–5; Grades 11–12, Reading: 2.1–2, Writing: 1.2–5, 1.9, Written and Oral English Language Conventions: 1.1–3, Listening and Speaking: 1.5)

0008 Conventions of Oral and Written Language (SMR 3.4)

a. Apply knowledge of linguistic structure to identify and use the conventions of Standard Edited English.

b. Recognize, understand, and use a range of conventions in both spoken and written English, including:

- Conventions of effective sentence structure (e.g., clear pronoun reference, parallel structure, appropriate verb tense)
- Preferred usage (e.g., verb/subject agreement, pronoun agreement, idioms)
- Conventions of pronunciation and intonation
- Conventional forms of spelling
- Capitalization and punctuation

(*English-Language Arts Content Standards for California Public Schools,* Grade 6, Reading: 1.1, Written and Oral English Language Conventions: 1.1–5; Grade 7, Written and Oral English Language Conventions: 1.1–7; Grade 8, Writing: 1.2, Written and Oral English Language Conventions: 1.1–6, Listening and Speaking: 1.6; Grades 9–10, Writing: 1.9, Written and Oral English Language Conventions: 1.9; Grades 11–12, Writing: 1.4, Written and Oral English Language Conventions: 1.1–3, Listening and Speaking: 1.8)

0009 Research Strategies (SMR 3.5)

a. Develop and apply research questions.

b. Demonstrate methods of inquiry and investigation.

c. Identify and use multiple resources (e.g., oral, print, electronic; primary and secondary), and critically evaluate the quality of the sources.

d. Interpret and apply findings.

e. Use professional conventions and ethical standards of citation and attribution.

f. Demonstrate effective presentation methods, including multi-media formats.

(*English-Language Arts Content Standards for California Public Schools,* Grade 6, Reading: 1.1, 2.1, 2.3, 2.6–8, Writing: 1.4–5, Listening and Speaking: 1.1–2, 1.6–7, 2.1, 2.3; Grade 7, Reading: 2.2, 2.6, Writing: 1.4–5, Listening and Speaking: 1.2, 1.6–7, 2.1, 2.3; Grade 8, Reading: 2.2, 2.7, Writing: 1.3–6, Listening and Speaking: 1.2–3, 1.6–8, 2.3; Grades 9–10, Reading: 2.2–5, 2.8, Writing: 1.3–8, Listening and Speaking: 1.7, 2.2; Grades 11–12, Writing: 1.4, 1.6–8, Listening and Speaking: 2.4)

Subtest I: Literature and Textual Analysis; Composition and Rhetoric

Directions: Each of the questions or statements below is followed by four suggested answers or completions. Select the one that is best in each case.

1. The first medieval dramas were performed for the purpose of:

   A. distracting the public from their squalid conditions.

   B. entertaining the monarch.

   C. bringing culture to the masses.

   D. making religious instruction and rites vivid.

Questions 2–4 are based on the following excerpt from Charles Dickens's *Hard Times*.

     It was a town of red brick, or of brick that would have been red if the smoke and ashes had allowed it; but as matters stood, it was a town of unnatural red and black, like the painted face of a savage. It was a town of machinery and tall chimneys, out of which interminable serpents of smoke trailed themselves for ever and ever, and never got uncoiled. It had a black canal in it, and a river that ran purple with ill-smelling dye, and vast piles of building full of windows where there was a rattling and a trembling all day long, and where the piston of the steam-engine worked monotonously up and down, like the head of an elephant in a state of melancholy madness. It contained several large streets all very like one another, and many small streets still more like one another, inhabited by people equally like one another, who all went in and out at the same hours, with the same sound upon the same pavements, to do the same work, and to whom every day was the same as yesterday and tomorrow, and every year the counterpart of the last and the next.

2. This passage most clearly reflects the Victorian world view that:

   A. people are all alike.

   B. the new industrial conditions have led to serious social problems.

   C. elephants and savages don't belong in big cities.

   D. the industrial revolution has improved the lives of the people.

3. The clause "where the piston of the steam-engine worked monotonously up and down, like the head of an elephant in a state of melancholy madness" contains examples of:

   I.   simile.

   II.   alliteration.

   III.   hyperbole.

   IV.   onomatopoeia.

   A. I and II

   B. I and III

   C. I and IV

   D. II and IV

4. The tone of this passage might be described as:

   A. informal.

   B. playful.

   C. serious.

   D. condescending.

GO ON TO THE NEXT PAGE

Questions 5 and 6 are based on this poem by Walt Whitman.

A Noiseless Patient Spider

A noiseless patient spider,

I mark'd where on a little promontory it stood isolated,

Mark'd how to explore the vacant vast surrounding,

It launch'd forth filament, filament, filament, out of itself,

Ever unreeling them, ever tirelessly speeding them.

And you, O my soul, where you stand,

Surrounded, detached, in measureless oceans of space,

Ceaselessly musing, venturing, throwing, seeking the spheres to connect them,

Till the bridge you will need be form'd, till the ductile anchor hold,

Till the gossamer thread you fling catch somewhere, O my soul.

5. This poem is an example of:
   A. a sonnet.
   B. free verse.
   C. blank verse.
   D. a ballad.

6. This poem most clearly illustrates which of the following poetic devices?
   A. the use of metaphor to suggest that the human spirit has much in common with the world of nature
   B. the use of personification to stress how human beings are superior to animals
   C. the use of irony to emphasize the futility of trying to make sense of the universe
   D. the use of apostrophe to emphasize the soul's disconnection from the body

7. In which of the following periods in American literature were these literary works written?

   Henry David Thoreau's *Walden*

   Ralph Waldo Emerson's "Self-Reliance"

   Nathaniel Hawthorne's *The Scarlet Letter*

   Herman Melville's *Moby-Dick*

   A. the Colonial Period
   B. the Federalist Age
   C. the Romantic Period
   D. the Realistic Period

8. As a reaction to the Renaissance, the Neo-Classic Period displayed:
   I. great appreciation for the emotional side of human nature.
   II. a reverence for order and a delight in reason and rules.
   III. a view that human beings are imperfect and limited.
   IV. a fascination with the occult, the mysterious, and the exotic.

   A. I and IV
   B. I and III
   C. II and III
   D. III and IV

9. Zora Neale Hurston is best known for:

    I. collecting black folklore.
    II. the use of dialect.
    III. her lyric poetry.
    IV. her contributions to the Harlem Renaissance.

    A. I and II
    B. II and III
    C. II, III, and IV
    D. I, II, and IV

Questions 10 and 11 are based on this excerpt from *The Epic of Gilgamesh.*

A stupor of despair went up to heaven when the god of the storm turned daylight to darkness, when he smashed the land like a cup. One whole day the tempest raged, gathering fury as it went, it poured over the people like the tides of battle; a man could not see his brother nor the people be seen from heaven. Even the gods were terrified at the flood, they fled to the highest heaven, the firmament of Anu; they crouched against the walls, cowering like curs. . . .

For six days and six nights the winds blew; torrent and tempest and flood overwhelmed the world; tempest and flood raged together like warring hosts.

10. Which of the following best describes the mood of the passage?

    A. awe
    B. terror
    C. excitement
    D. confusion

11. This passage reveals that its audience was:

    A. polytheistic.
    B. monotheistic.
    C. atheistic.
    D. naturalistic.

Questions 12–14 are about the following excerpt from an Edgar Allan Poe poem.

Once upon a midnight dreary, while I pondered, weak and weary,

Over many a quaint and curious volume of forgotten lore—

While I nodded, nearly napping, suddenly there came a tapping,

As of some one gently rapping, rapping at my chamber door—

"'Tis some visitor," I muttered, "tapping at my chamber door—

    Only this and nothing more."

12. Which of the following is the correct title of the poem from which this excerpt is taken?

    A. "The Black Raven"
    B. "Once Upon a Midnight Dreary"
    C. "The Raven"
    D. "Nevermore"

13. Which of the following describes the meter of most of the lines above?

    A. iambic hexameter
    B. trochaic octameter
    C. anapestic octameter
    D. dactylic tetrameter

14. Which of the following poetic devices does Poe <u>not</u> use in this excerpt?

    A. internal rhyme
    B. alliteration
    C. repetition
    D. personification

GO ON TO THE NEXT PAGE

Questions 15–17 are based on this excerpt from *House of Sand and Fog* by Andre Dubus III.

Last spring, after our thirty-day fast of Ramadan, I from an Arab purchased a shirt in his shop near the overpass bridge. He was an Iraqi, an enemy of my people, and the Americans had recently killed thousands of them in the desert. He was a short man, but he had large arms and legs beneath his clothes. Of course he began speaking to me right away in his mother tongue, in Arabic, and when I to him apologized and said I did not speak his language, he knew I was Persian, and he offered to me tea from his samovar, and we sat on two low wooden stools near his display window and talked of America and how long it had been since we'd last been home. He poured for me more tea, and we played backgammon and did not speak at all.

15. The tone of this passage can best be described as:

    A. sarcastic.
    B. sorrowful.
    C. ironic.
    D. amused.

16. Which sentence has the least to do with the main point in this paragraph?

    A. Last spring, after our thirty-day fast of Ramadan, I from an Arab purchased a shirt in his shop near the overpass bridge.
    B. He was an Iraqi, an enemy of my people, and the Americans had recently killed thousands of them in the desert.
    C. He was a short man, but he had large arms and legs beneath his clothes.
    D. He poured for me more tea, and we played backgammon and did not speak at all.

17. The ideas in this passage most clearly reflect the political context of our time by:

    I.   commenting on the tensions in the Middle East.
    II.   suggesting that America should stay out of the Middle East.
    III.   suggesting that America should stay involved in the Middle East.
    IV.   inferring that many cultures can peacefully coexist in America.

    A. I and II
    B. II and IV
    C. I and III
    D. I and IV

Questions 18 and 19 are based on this poem by Lillian Morrison.

The Sidewalk Racer

or On the Skateboard

<u>Skimming</u>

an asphalt sea

I swerve, I curve, I

sway; I speed to whirring

sound an inch above the

ground; I'm the sailor

and the sail, I'm the

driver and the wheel

I'm the one and only

single engine

human auto

mobile.

18. This poem is an example of:

   A. a ballad.
   B. a limerick.
   C. a haiku.
   D. a concrete poem.

19. The characteristic feature of this type of poem is that:

   A. its shape suggests its subject.
   B. it tells a story.
   C. it has short lines.
   D. it suggests a mood.

20. The drunken porter scene in *Macbeth* is an example of:

   A. realistic comedy.
   B. dramatic monologue.
   C. comic relief.
   D. a soliloquy.

Questions 21–23 are based on this excerpt from a short story by Rosario Castellanos called "The Luck of Teodoro Méndez Acúbal."

Selection from "The Luck of Teodoro Méndez Acúbal" from Another Way to Be: Selected Works of Rosario Castellanos, *by Rosario Castellanos, Foreword by Edward D. Terry. Copyright (c) 1990 by The University of Georgia Press.*

Wallking along the streets of Jobel (with his eyes cast downward as custom dictates for those of his humble station), Teodoro Méndez Acúbal spotted a coin. All but lost in the dust, caked with mud, worn from years of use, it had been ignored by the white *caxlanes*. For the *caxlanes* walk with their heads held high. Moved by pride, they contemplate from afar the important matters that absorb them.

Teodoro stopped, more out of disbelief than greed. Kneeling as if to fasten one of his sandals, he waited until

no one was looking to pick up what he had found. He hid it quickly in the folds of his sash.

He stood again, swaying, overcome by a kind of dizziness. Weak-kneed and dry-mouthed, his eyes blurred as he felt his heart pounding, pulsing between his eyebrows.

Staggering from side to side as if in a drunken stupor, Teodoro began to make his way down the street. From time to time the passersby had to push him aside to avoid bumping into him. But Teodoro's spirit was too troubled to be bothered by what was going on around him. The coin, hidden in his sash, had transformed him into another man—a stronger man than before, it is true. But also more fearful.

21. Which of the following best describes the use of a literary device in this passage?

   A. Use of the third-person point of view emphasizes the narrator's disdain of Teodoro.
   B. Descriptive details highlight Teodoro's position in the lowest socioeconomic class in this society.
   C. Sensory language helps convey a feeling about the time and place.
   D. Dramatic irony stresses the distance between what Teodoro thinks is true and what is really true.

22. Which of the following does the reader know about Teodoro at this point?

   I.   He is poor.
   II. He has a strong religious faith.
   III. He is afraid of those in higher social positions.
   IV. He has a drinking problem.

   A. I and II
   B. II and II
   C. III and IV
   D. I and III

GO ON TO THE NEXT PAGE

23. Which is the best prediction about what will happen by the end of the story?

    A. Teodoro's life will be changed for the better because of the coin.

    B. The finding of the coin will have a negative effect on Teodoro's life.

    C. Teodoro will buy basic necessities with the coin.

    D. Teodoro's wife will become angry when he doesn't give her the coin.

24. In Elizabethan drama, the function of the chorus can best be described as:

    A. to provide prologue and epilogue and interact comment.

    B. to add a musical element to the performance.

    C. to serve as a foil to the protagonist.

    D. to entertain the audience during scene changes.

25. Which is the best description of a dramatic monologue?

    A. one person's ranting on stage, along with dramatic hand gestures

    B. a conversation about a dramatic incident between two characters in a novel

    C. a lyric poem in which one character in a dramatic situation speaks to a silent listener

    D. a one-act play in which a dramatic incident is recreated

26. Which of the following could be applied to the work of both Gabriel García Márquez and Isabel Allende?

    A. Like William Faulkner, the author has created a fictional setting that serves as the backdrop for nearly every novel.

    B. Rather than develop many characters in a single novel, the author focuses on one or two.

    C. The author seeks to portray the political vicissitudes of the country in a realistic manner.

    D. This author's style is marked by surrealism and exuberance, sensory language, and magical realism.

Questions 27–29 are based on this excerpt from a February 3, 1995, speech by Barbra Streisand. She was speaking at the John F. Kennedy School of Government of Harvard University, defending the role of the arts in American society and politics.

Art was a way out for me. I represent a generation of kids who happened to benefit from government support of the arts in public schools. I was a member of the choral club at Erasmus Hall High School in Brooklyn. Sadly, this current generation of young people does not have the same opportunities.

How can we accept a situation in which there are no longer orchestras, choruses, libraries, or art classes to nourish our children? We need *more* support for the arts, not less—particularly to make this rich world available to young people whose vision is choked by a stark reality. How many children, who have no other outlet in their lives for their grief, have found solace in an instrument to play or a canvas to paint on? When you take into consideration the development of the human heart, soul, and imagination, don't the arts take on just as much importance as math or science?

27. Which of the following is the main claim being advanced in the excerpt?

    A. Art is a good way to deal with grief.

    B. Barbra Streisand got her start in the choral club of her high school.

    C. It is important that students have access to education in the arts.

    D. Many children enjoy playing instruments and painting.

28. We can assume that at the time Barbra Streisand gave this speech:

   A. funding for the arts in education was at an all-time high.

   B. public funding for art education was in jeopardy.

   C. most Americans didn't care one way or the other about this issue.

   D. art education in the schools had been completely phased out.

29. The strongest feature to support Streisand's argument in this excerpt is:

   A. the reference to the grief that children might have in their lives.

   B. the comparison and contrast between Streisand's educational opportunities and those of the current generation.

   C. the use of items in a series, such as "human heart, soul, and imagination."

   D. the use of rhetorical questions to call attention to the obvious answers.

Questions 30–31 are based on this excerpt from Willa Cather's *My Ántonia*.

Winter comes down savagely over a little town on the prairie. The wind that sweeps in from the open country strips away all the leafy screens that hide one yard from another in summer, and the houses seem to draw closer together. The roofs, that looked so far away across the green tree-tops, now stare you in the face, and they are so much uglier than when their angles were softened by vines and shrubs.

30. Which remark by a critic could best be applied to this excerpt?

   A. "*My Ántonia* is notable particularly for its lucid and moving depiction of the prairie and the people who live close to it—the farmers whose lives are controlled by storm and drought and the spring rains." (*Benet's Reader's Encyclopedia of American Literature*)

   B. "[Willa Cather's] greatest achievement remained her portrayals, with fine simplicity and what she called 'the gift of sympathy,' of simple men and women who struggled to find meaningful lives in the midst of adversity and who stood for the noble ideals of an age that had passed." (*Anthology of American Literature*, Geroge McMichael, General Editor)

   C. "Willa Cather, like the greatest of her predecessors among women in English fiction, Jane Austen, was extraordinarily consistent in her art from beginning to end." (*Literary History of the United States*, Robert E. Spiller, et al.)

   D. "*My Ántonia*, another story of Nebraska, celebrated the land and the immigrant pioneers, and linked the enduring figure of Ántonia to the life-force itself." (www.kirjasto.sci.fi/weather.htm)

31. Which of the following literary devices is used in the last sentence of the excerpt?

   A. simile

   B. metaphor

   C. personification

   D. onomatopoeia

GO ON TO THE NEXT PAGE

32. Which of the following best expresses the goal of formalist criticism?

    A. to consider such elements as style, structure, tone, and imagery that are found within the text and determine how they work together to shape the text's effects upon readers

    B. to investigate the social, cultural, and intellectual context of a work and determine its effect upon its original readers

    C. to examine the work in the cultural, political, and economic context in which it is written, and to determine the interaction between the artist and society

    D. to examine the recurring universal patterns underlying the work and determine the relationship between the work and the mythologies and archetypes common to all literature

33. Read this quotation from Alfred Kazin's *On Native Grounds,* and answer the question that follows:

    Though the book [*The Grapes of Wrath*] was as urgent and as obvious a social tract for its time as *Uncle Tom's Cabin* had been for another, it was also the first novel of its kind to dramatize the inflictions of the crisis without mechanical violence and hatred. The bitterness was there, as it should have been, the sense of unspeakable human waste and privation and pain. But in the light of Steinbeck's strong sense of fellowship, his simple indignation at so much suffering, the Joads, while essentially symbolic marionettes, did illuminate something more than the desperation of the time: they became a living and challenging part of the forgotten American procession.

    Which of the following choices best describes this approach to literary criticism?

    A. reader-response criticism

    B. biographical criticism

    C. psychological criticism

    D. historical criticism

34. The novel *My Side of the Mountain* by Jean Craighead George is categorized as adolescent/young adult literature because:

    A. the chapters are short.

    B. the themes in it appeal to young people.

    C. the protagonist is an adolescent boy.

    D. the sentences are not too complicated.

35. Which of the following activities are parts of the prewriting process?

    I.   brainstorming for ideas

    II. checking grammar, mechanics, and spelling

    III. gathering information through interviews and research

    IV. making an outline

    A. I and II

    B. II and III

    C. III and IV

    D. I, III, and IV

36. Although peer review can be used at any stage of the writing process, its best use is in the:

    A. prewriting stage.

    B. drafting stage.

    C. revising stage.

    D. proofreading stage.

37. Writing has been called a recursive process. What does this mean?

    A. You start with prewriting and move sequentially through a series of steps until you are finished.

    B. You might have to return to previous stages in the process as you develop your ideas.

    C. You must always follow the same steps in the same order.

    D. You do your best work if you are by yourself in a quiet room.

38. Which of the following is an *ad hominem* argument?

   A. You should try Brite White toothpaste. Nine out of ten dentists recommend it.

   B. Amanda claims that tax breaks for corporations are good for the economy. She just says that because she's the CEO of a corporation.

   C. You wouldn't want your sweet little baby to fall behind, would you? Our product, Baby Genius, will give your little angel a head start before he even gets to preschool.

   D. These light bulbs are good for the environment. Do the right thing, and replace all your light bulbs now.

39. Daniel is giving a speech to first-graders, welcoming them to their field trip at the tide pools. Which of the following sentences would be most appropriately included in that speech?

   A. Starfish are marine invertebrates belonging to the phylum Echinodermata, class Asteroidea.

   B. A typical starfish has five or more "arms" radiating out from an indistinct disk.

   C. Starfish use a hydraulic water vascular system as an aid in locomotion.

   D. Did you know that if a starfish loses an arm, it can grow another one?

40. Read the following excerpt from "Self-Reliance" by Ralph Waldo Emerson, and answer the question that follows.

A foolish consistency is the hobgoblin of little minds, adored by little statesmen and philosophers and divines. With consistency a great soul has simply nothing to do. He may as well concern himself with his shadow on the wall. Speak what you think now in hard words, and tomorrow speak what tomorrow thinks in hard words again, though it contradict everything you said today.—"Ah, so you shall be sure to be misunderstood."—Is it so bad, then, to be misunderstood? Pythagoras was misunderstood, and Socrates, and Jesus, and Luther, and Copernicus, and Galileo, and Newton, and every pure and wise spirit that ever took flesh. To be great is to be misunderstood.

In this passage, Emerson refers to great and respected thinkers in order to:

   A. elicit respect in his readers over the fact that he is so well read.

   B. inspire his readers to study the teachings of those men.

   C. support his point that being misunderstood is not necessarily a bad thing.

   D. suggest that those thinkers were inconsistent in what they said and taught.

41. A speaker wants to convey a serious tone. Which of these sentences best contributes to that tone?

   A. Who would ever have guessed that Jim and Caroline would get together?

   B. Caroline, always full of surprises, has chosen Jim to be her husband.

   C. Marriage is a solemn commitment, and Jim and Caroline have chosen to make that commitment.

   D. Much to our surprise, Jim and Caroline have shown up at the altar today.

42. Read these two sentences, and answer the question that follows.

Joanne was exhausted. She went to the party.

Which of the following sentences show logical connections between the ideas?

   I.   Even though Joanne was exhausted, she went to the party.

   II.   Joanne was exhausted, so she went to the party.

   III.   Joanne was exhausted after she went to the party.

   IV.   Because Joanne was exhausted, she went to the party.

   A. I and II

   B. I and III

   C. II and IV

   D. III and IV

GO ON TO THE NEXT PAGE

43. Which sentence has an adjective clause?

    A. Elizabeth Blackwell, who graduated from medical school in 1849, was the first woman doctor in the modern era.

    B. Graduating first in her class in 1849, Elizabeth Blackwell was the first woman doctor in the modern era.

    C. Elizabeth Blackwell, the first woman doctor in the modern era, graduated first in her class in 1849.

    D. Elizabeth Blackwell wanted to be a doctor, so she went to medical school, graduating in 1849.

44. What do we call the underlined part of this sentence?

The rapids ahead being rough, we decided to cut short our kayaking excursion.

    A. a subordinate clause

    B. an independent clause

    C. an absolute phrase

    D. an appositive

45. Which of the following sentences has a pronoun antecedent that is not clear?

    A. Bryan told Ian, "You are mistaken."

    B. Bryan told Ian that he was mistaken.

    C. Bryan told Ian, "I am mistaken."

    D. Ian told Bryan, "You are mistaken."

46. Which statements are true about this sentence?

Senators are elected for six-year terms.

    I.   It is a simple sentence.

    II. It is a compound sentence.

    III. It is in the passive voice.

    IV. It is in the active voice.

    A. I and III

    B. I and IV

    C. II and III

    D. II and IV

47. Which sentence has an appositive?

    A. The American industrialist J. Paul Getty once said, "If you can actually count your money, then you are not really a rich man."

    B. Was it J. Paul Getty who once said, "If you can actually count your money, then you are not really a rich man"?

    C. J. Paul Getty, who was an American industrialist, once said, "If you can actually count your money, then you are not really a rich man."

    D. J. Paul Getty was an American industrialist who once said, "If you can actually count your money, then you are not really a rich man."

48. Read the following passage and answer the question that follows.

Macbeth leaves Lady Macbeth and makes his way to King Duncan's room. There he took a dagger from a sleeping guard and murdered the king.

Which of the following are valid revisions?

    I.   Macbeth leaves Lady Macbeth and made his way to King Duncan's room. There he took a dagger from a sleeping guard and murdered the king.

    II. Macbeth leaves Lady Macbeth and makes his way to King Duncan's room. There he takes a dagger from a sleeping guard and murders the king.

    III. Macbeth left Lady Macbeth and made his way to King Duncan's room. There he took a dagger from a sleeping guard and murdered the king.

    IV. Macbeth leaves Lady Macbeth and makes his way to King Duncan's room. There he takes a dagger from a sleeping guard and murdered the king.

    A. I and II

    B. II and III

    C. III and IV

    D. I and IV

49. Which of the following online sources would be considered the *least* reliable?

A. those with a domain name that includes a tilde (~)

B. those with a domain name ending in .org

C. those with a domain name ending in .edu

D. those with a domain name ending in .gov

50. A researcher wants to find out who wrote the musical score for the film *Dances with Wolves*. What is the best way for the researcher to find this information?

A. Rent the movie and pay close attention to the credits.

B. Look it up on the Internet.

C. Consult an encyclopedia.

D. Look in an almanac.

Annotated Responses for CSET: English Subtest I

Literature and Textual Analysis

The parenthetical information about SMR codes in the following answers refers to the standards being tested. For further clarification of these codes, see the information reprinted from the CSET Website at the beginning of this practice test.

1. **D.** (SMR Code: 1.1) The first medieval dramas, the morality plays, developed out of the rites that commemorated the birth and the resurrection of Christ. Although these dramas might have distracted the public from their squalid conditions, entertained the monarch, and brought culture to the masses, these were not their original purposes.

2. **B.** (SMR Code:1.2) The passage highlights the negative effects of industrialization on the fictional city of Coketown, a cotton manufacturing town, in northern England. Although it is true that the people mentioned in the passage have lives of similar monotony, that is not the focus of the passage; elephants and savages are mentioned only in similes that compare aspects of the town to them; and there is no evidence in this passage that the people's lives have been improved.

3. **A.** (SMR Code: 1.2) The clause is an example of a simile because it compares two things, using the word *like;* it is also an example of alliteration because it repeats the initial consonant sound *m* in "melancholy madness." Hyperbole is the use of exaggeration, and onomatopoeia is the use of a word that sounds like what it names (for example, *plop, boom,* and *crackle*).

4. **C.** (SMR Code: 1.2) Word choice and imagery in this passage contribute to the serious tone. For example, "interminable serpents of smoke," "ill-smelling dye," "rattling and trembling all day long," are far from playful or informal. No evidence demonstrates that Dickens has a condescending attitude toward the town; rather, we get the impression that he sympathizes with the people. Hence, "serious" best describes the tone of this passage.

5. **B.** (SMR Code: 1.2) Free verse is poetry with an irregular metrical pattern, using a variety of rhythmical effects instead. It is clearly not a sonnet (a lyric poem of 14 lines), or a ballad (a poem that tells a story), nor does it use blank verse (unrhymed iambic pentameter).

6. **A.** (SMR Code: 1.2) The poem most clearly illustrates the use of a metaphor, comparing the spider's activity to that of the human soul seeking something to connect to. It does not use personification because the spider does not take on human characteristics, nor is any irony implied. The poem does use apostrophe, addressing the soul, but not in a way to emphasize the soul's disconnection from the body.

7. **C.** (SMR Code: 1.1) The listed works were written during the Romantic Period, sometimes called the American Renaissance. This period extended from about 1830 to 1865. *Walden* came out in 1854, "Self-Reliance" in 1841, *The Scarlet Letter* in 1850, and *Moby-Dick* in 1851.The Colonial Period and the Federalist Age were earlier, and the Realistic Period was later.

8. **C.** (SMR Code: 1.1) During the Neo-Classic Period, writers reacted against the excesses of the Romantic Period, returning to a reverence for order and a delight in reason and rules. They also expressed the view that human beings are imperfect and limited. Choices I and IV apply to the Romantic Period.

9. **D.** (SMR Code: 1.1) Zora Neale Hurston wrote novels and short stories, not lyric poetry. She was one of the writers of the Harlem Renaissance, and she worked closely with Franz Boaz, a professor of anthropology at Barnard. With Boaz's help, she won a six-month grant to collect African-American folklore. It is generally acknowledged that she had a wonderful ear for the dialect spoken by African Americans and was able to duplicate its sounds in her novels.

10. **B.** (SMR Code: 1.2) Words and phrases such as "stupor of despair," gathering fury," "terrified," and "cowering like curs" contribute to the mood of terror. Although it is true that awe, excitement, and confusion might have been experienced by those who witnessed the storm, the dominant mood is terror.

11. **A.** (SMR Code: 1.2) The reference to the "gods" reveals that the audience was polytheistic.

12. **C.** (SMR Code: 1.1) The passage is the opening lines of Poe's "The Raven."

13. B. (SMR Code: 1.2) Most of the lines are in trochaic (one stressed syllable followed by an unstressed syllable) octameter (eight measures, or feet). Iambic hexameter would be six feet of iambs (one unstressed syllable followed by a stressed one); anapestic octameter would be eight feet of anapests (two unstressed syllables followed by a stressed one); and dactylic tetrameter would be three feet of dactyls (one stressed syllable followed by two unstressed ones).

14. D. (SMR Code: 1.2) Poe uses internal rhyme (for example, *dreary* and *weary* in the first line); alliteration (the repetition of initial identical consonant sounds or any vowel sounds in closely associated words or syllables) in the words *weak, weary* and *nodded, nearly napping;* and *repetition* (of the word *rapping)*. He does not use personification (a figure of speech endowing animals, ideas, abstractions, and inanimate objects with human characteristics) in this excerpt, although it is true that he personifies the raven later on in the poem.

15. C. (SMR Code: 1/2) The tone is clearly ironic. Even though the narrator and the Iraqi would have been enemies if they lived back home, here in America they can sit down and enjoy some tea and a game of backgammon. The narrator is not being sarcastic, nor is he sorrowful or amused.

16. C. (SMR Code: 1.2) If this sentence were deleted from the passage, the reader would still get the main point: that the narrator and the Iraqi can coexist peacefully in their new environment. All the other answer choices support the main point.

17. D. (SMR Code: 1.1) The passage makes no suggestions for or against American involvement in the Middle East. It acknowledges that there are tensions and demonstrates that many cultures can peacefully exist in America.

18. D. (SMR Code: 1.2) The poem is not a ballad (which tells a story), a limerick (a five-line poem of anapests, in which the first, second and fifth have three feet and rhyme, and the third and fourth have two feet and rhyme), or a haiku (a seventeen-syllable poem divided into three lines of five, seven, and five syllables).

19. A. (SMR Code: 1.2) The definition of a concrete poem is that its shape suggests its subject.

20. C. (SMR Code: 1.2) The drunken porter scene in Macbeth is one of the most famous examples of comic relief in literature. Comic relief is a humorous scene, incident, or speech appearing in a serious fiction or drama. The term *realistic comedy* describes a particular type of comedy and does not refer to a single scene. A dramatic monologue is a lyric poem in which one character in a dramatic situation speaks to a silent listener. A soliloquy is a speech delivered by a character in a play while the speaker is alone; it is designed to reveal the character's thoughts or to give information about other characters in the drama.

21. B. (SMR Code: 1.2) Descriptive details, such as the downcast eyes, the fear that anyone else might see him picking up the coin, and his being jostled by other pedestrians, highlight Teodoro's low social position. There is no evidence that the narrator feels disdain for Teodoro. The sensory language does convey a feeling about the time and place, but this is not the main thrust of the passage, which stresses the character more than the setting. At this point, the reader has no indication that there is a gap between what Teodoro thinks is true and what is really true.

22. D. (SMR Code: 1.2) We know that Teodoro is poor because the coin means so much to him. We also know that he fears those in higher social positions because he takes such pains to conceal his action from them. There is no mention of a strong religious faith, nor is there evidence of a drinking problem. Don't be fooled by the phrase "drunken stupor"—just because he is walking "as if in a drunken stupor" doesn't mean that he is in one.

23. B. (SMR Code: 1.2) It is a safe prediction that the coin will affect Teodoro's life negatively—otherwise, why is he so fearful about having found it? There is no evidence that his life will be changed for the better, nor that he will buy basic necessities, nor that he even has a wife.

24. A. (SMR Code: 1.2) The function of the chorus in Elizabethan drama is to provide prologue and epilogue and inter-act comment. Even though the chorus may add music to the performance, this is not the best description of its function. As for choice C, the chorus does not interact at all with the protagonist. And as for choice D, while the chorus might have entertained the audience during scene changes, this was not its main function.

25. C. (SMR Code: 1.2) This is the definition of a dramatic monologue.

26. **D.** (SMR Code: 1.3) Gabriel García Márquez and Isabel Allende are known for their use of "magical realism," which employs surrealism, exuberance, and sensory language. Choice A doesn't work because the backdrops of the novels of García Márquez and Allende change from book to book. Choice B is clearly wrong, as both writers are known for the multiplicity of characters in their novels. Choice C doesn't work, either—most of the writings of these authors are anything but realistic.

27. **C.** (SMR Code: 1.4) Although choices A, B, and D are true, they are not the main claim being advanced in the excerpt.

28. **B.** (SMR Code: 1.4) Choice B is the most logical choice. If Choice A were true, there would have been no need for her impassioned plea. We have no grounds to assume that most Americans didn't care one way or another, and we know that art education was never completely phased out.

29. **D.** (SMR Code: 1.4) Although all the choices support Streisand's argument, you're looking for the strongest feature here, which is choice D, the use of rhetorical questions to call attention to the obvious answers.

30. **A.** (SMR Code: 1.3) Choice A most clearly applies to the excerpt given. Choice B refers exclusively to portrayals of simple men and women, who are not mentioned in the excerpt. There is no evidence in the excerpt alone to support such a sweeping statement as choice C. And choice D, which mentions Ántonia herself, does not apply to the excerpt.

31. **C.** (SMR Code: 1.2) The last sentence uses personification when it says that the roofs "now stare you in the face."

32. **A.** (SMR Code: 1.3) Formalist criticism holds that the work contains within itself all the elements necessary for understanding it. Choice B describes historical criticism; choice C describes sociological criticism, and choice D describes mythological criticism.

33. **D.** (SMR Code: 1.3) The Kazin excerpt is an example of historical criticism, using the facts of the Depression as a way to understand *The Grapes of Wrath*.

34. **B.** (SMR Code: 1.1) It is a characteristic of adolescent/young adult literature that its themes appeal to young people. The other choices, although they might be true about the book in question, are not necessarily characteristics of the genre.

Composition and Rhetoric

35. **D.** (SMR Code: 3.1) Choices I, III, and IV are part of the prewriting process. The actions mentioned in choice II, checking grammar, mechanics, and spelling, are part of the editing process and should be among the last steps taken by the writer.

36. **C.** (SMR Code: 3.1) During the revising stage, the advice of a peer reviewer can be most helpful, for it is during this stage that the writer gives the most careful consideration to organization, ideas, style, focus, diction, and audience.

37. **B.** (SMR Code: 3.1) *Recursive* is a cognate of the word *recur,* which suggests doing something over and over. Hence, choice B makes the most sense.

38. **B.** (SMR Code: 3.2) *Ad hominem* means "against the man." Therefore, an *ad hominem* argument attacks the person who makes the statement rather than attacking the statement itself on logical grounds. Choice A is an example of an appeal to authority; choice C is an appeal to emotion; and choice D is an appeal to morality.

39. **D.** (SMR Code: 3.2) Choice D is clearly the best sentence to address to a first-grader. The vocabulary in choices A, B, and C is a bit too scientific for that age group.

40. **C.** (SMR Code: 3.2) There is no evidence in the excerpt to support choices A, B, and D.

41. **C.** (SMR Code: 3.3) Choices A, B, and D have a more humorous, light-hearted tone. The only sentence with a serious tone is choice C.

42. **B.** (SMR Code: 3.3) Choices II and IV don't make sense. Only choices I and III show the logical connection between Joanne being exhausted and going to the party.

43. A. (SMR Code: 3.3) A clause has to have a verb, and choice A is the only one with an adjective clause. Choices B and D have participial phrases acting as adjectives, and choice C has an appositive.

44. C. (SMR Code: 3.3) An absolute phrase consists of a noun followed by a participle or a participial phrase. It is called "absolute" because it modifies no single word in the sentence, but it does have a thought relationship to the entire sentence or part of it. Choices A and B are incorrect because a clause requires a verb. Choice D is incorrect because an appositive is a noun or pronoun (word or phrase) that identifies in different words a preceding noun or pronoun.

45. B. (SMR Code: 3.4) In choice B, the pronoun "he" could refer to either Bryan or Ian.

46. A. (SMR Code: 3.4) It is a simple sentence because it is an independent clause without any other subordinate clauses. It is in the passive voice because the subject is the receiver rather than the doer of the action.

47. A. (SMR Code: 3.3) The name "J. Paul Getty" is in apposition to "industrialist"; that is, the name identifies in different words the preceding noun.

48. B. (SMR Code: 3.4) Choices I and IV are not consistent in verb tense, switching from present tense to past tense. Choice II is valid because all verbs are in the present tense; choice III is valid because all verbs are in the past tense.

49. A. (SMR Code: 3.5) Domain names that include a tilde are usually personal home pages.

50. B. (SMR Code: 3.5) Choice A is far too complicated, although it is one way to find the information. The information is not the type of information that can be found in an encyclopedia or almanac. Choice B is the easiest and fastest way to find the information.

(Remove this sheet and use it to mark your answers to the multiple-choice questions.)

Answer Sheet

1 Ⓐ Ⓑ Ⓒ Ⓓ	26 Ⓐ Ⓑ Ⓒ Ⓓ	
2 Ⓐ Ⓑ Ⓒ Ⓓ	27 Ⓐ Ⓑ Ⓒ Ⓓ	
3 Ⓐ Ⓑ Ⓒ Ⓓ	28 Ⓐ Ⓑ Ⓒ Ⓓ	
4 Ⓐ Ⓑ Ⓒ Ⓓ	29 Ⓐ Ⓑ Ⓒ Ⓓ	
5 Ⓐ Ⓑ Ⓒ Ⓓ	30 Ⓐ Ⓑ Ⓒ Ⓓ	
6 Ⓐ Ⓑ Ⓒ Ⓓ	31 Ⓐ Ⓑ Ⓒ Ⓓ	
7 Ⓐ Ⓑ Ⓒ Ⓓ	32 Ⓐ Ⓑ Ⓒ Ⓓ	
8 Ⓐ Ⓑ Ⓒ Ⓓ	33 Ⓐ Ⓑ Ⓒ Ⓓ	
9 Ⓐ Ⓑ Ⓒ Ⓓ	34 Ⓐ Ⓑ Ⓒ Ⓓ	
10 Ⓐ Ⓑ Ⓒ Ⓓ	35 Ⓐ Ⓑ Ⓒ Ⓓ	
11 Ⓐ Ⓑ Ⓒ Ⓓ	36 Ⓐ Ⓑ Ⓒ Ⓓ	
12 Ⓐ Ⓑ Ⓒ Ⓓ	37 Ⓐ Ⓑ Ⓒ Ⓓ	
13 Ⓐ Ⓑ Ⓒ Ⓓ	38 Ⓐ Ⓑ Ⓒ Ⓓ	
14 Ⓐ Ⓑ Ⓒ Ⓓ	39 Ⓐ Ⓑ Ⓒ Ⓓ	
15 Ⓐ Ⓑ Ⓒ Ⓓ	40 Ⓐ Ⓑ Ⓒ Ⓓ	
16 Ⓐ Ⓑ Ⓒ Ⓓ	41 Ⓐ Ⓑ Ⓒ Ⓓ	
17 Ⓐ Ⓑ Ⓒ Ⓓ	42 Ⓐ Ⓑ Ⓒ Ⓓ	
18 Ⓐ Ⓑ Ⓒ Ⓓ	43 Ⓐ Ⓑ Ⓒ Ⓓ	
19 Ⓐ Ⓑ Ⓒ Ⓓ	44 Ⓐ Ⓑ Ⓒ Ⓓ	
20 Ⓐ Ⓑ Ⓒ Ⓓ	45 Ⓐ Ⓑ Ⓒ Ⓓ	
21 Ⓐ Ⓑ Ⓒ Ⓓ	46 Ⓐ Ⓑ Ⓒ Ⓓ	
22 Ⓐ Ⓑ Ⓒ Ⓓ	47 Ⓐ Ⓑ Ⓒ Ⓓ	
23 Ⓐ Ⓑ Ⓒ Ⓓ	48 Ⓐ Ⓑ Ⓒ Ⓓ	
24 Ⓐ Ⓑ Ⓒ Ⓓ	49 Ⓐ Ⓑ Ⓒ Ⓓ	
25 Ⓐ Ⓑ Ⓒ Ⓓ	50 Ⓐ Ⓑ Ⓒ Ⓓ	

Subtest II: Language, Linguistics, and Literacy

Content Domains for Subject Matter Understanding and Skill in English

Here is a list of the areas on which you will be tested. This information is also available at the CSET Website. It is reproduced here for your convenience.

Language, Linguistics, and Literacy (SMR Domain 2)

Candidates demonstrate knowledge of the foundations and contexts of the language, linguistics, and literacy contained in the *English-Language Arts Content Standards for California Public Schools Kindergarten Through Grade Twelve* (1999) at a post secondary level of rigor. Candidates have both broad and deep conceptual knowledge of the subject matter. Many California students, coming from a variety of linguistic and sociocultural backgrounds, face specific challenges in mastering the English language. The diversity of this population requires the candidate to understand the principles of language acquisition and development. Candidates must become knowledgeable about the nature of human language, language variation, and historical and cultural perspectives on the development of English. In addition, candidates must acquire a complex understanding of the development of English literacy among both native and non-native speakers. Candidates will be able to:

0001 Human Language Structures (SMR 2.1)

a. Recognize the nature of human language, differences among languages, the universality of linguistic structures, and changes across time, locale, and communities.

b. Demonstrate knowledge of word analysis, including sound patterns (phonology) and inflection, derivation, compounding, roots and affixes (morphology).

c. Demonstrate knowledge of sentence structures (syntax), word and sentence meanings (semantics), and language function in communicative context (pragmatics).

d. Use appropriate print and electronic sources to research etymologies; recognize conventions of English orthography and changes in word meaning and pronunciation.

(*English-Language Arts Content: Standards for California Public Schools,* Grade 6, Reading: 1.1–5; Grades 7–8, Reading: 1.2; Grades 9–10, Reading: 1.1–3)

0002 Acquisition and Development of Language and Literacy (SMR 2.2)

a. Explain the influences of cognitive, affective, and sociocultural factors on language acquisition and development.

b. Explain the influence of a first language on second language development

c. Describe methods and techniques for developing academic literacy (e.g., tapping prior knowledge through semantic mapping, word analogies, cohesion analysis)

(*English-Language Arts Content Standards for California Public Schools,* Grades 6–12, Reading: 1.0)

0003 Literacy Studies (SMR 2.3)

a. Recognize the written and oral conventions of Standard English, and analyze the social implications of mastering them.

b. Describe and explain cognitive elements of reading and writing processes (e.g., decoding and encoding, construction of meaning, recognizing and using text conventions of different genres).

c. Explain metacognitive strategies for making sense of text (e.g., pre-reading activities, predicting, questioning, word analysis, concept formation).

(*English-Language Arts Content Standards for California Public Schools,* Grades 6–12, Reading: 1.0)

0004 Grammatical Structures of English (SMR 2.4)

a. Identify methods of sentence construction (e.g., sentence combining with coordinators and subordinators; sentence embedding and expanding with clausal and phrasal modifiers).

b. Analyze parts of speech and their distinctive structures and functions (e.g. noun phrases including count and non-count nouns and the determiner system; prepositions, adjectives, and adverbs; word transformations).

c. Describe the forms and functions of the English verb system (e.g. modals, verb complements, verbal phrases).

(*English-Language Arts Content Standards for California Pubic Schools,* Grade 8, Reading: 1.2)

Subtest II: Language, Linguistics, and Literacy

Directions: Each of the questions or statements below is followed by four suggested answers or completions. Select the one that is best in each case.

1. Which fact is the best support for Chomsky's idea of an innate universal grammar?

   A. An English child surrounded by people speaking Chinese will learn to speak Chinese.
   B. Most plurals in English and in Spanish end with an *s*.
   C. Many languages grew out of Latin.
   D. Even though Latin is a dead language, people can still learn to speak it.

2. Read the passage below; then answer the question that follows.

   This pattern of speech is characterized by a higher pitch, often as much as an octave higher than normal speech. It also has a slower tempo and wider fluctuations in intonation. It is thought to be an effective way of encouraging the use of language to communicate.

   Which of the following linguistic phenomena is described in the above passage?

   A. creolization
   B. hypercorrection
   C. motherese
   D. deep structure

3. Read the passage below; then answer the question that follows.

   People from three different countries begin to interact, mostly for the sake of trade. No one understands the others' languages. They begin to develop a language that has some features from each of the base languages. This language has its own grammar, but both the vocabulary and grammar are much simpler than they are in any of the base languages.

   What is this simplified contact language called?

   A. mother tongue
   B. Esperanto
   C. slang
   D. pidgin

4. Why are some languages called Romance languages?

   A. It's easier to make rhyming poems in them because so many of their words have similar endings.
   B. They have more words for love than any other language.
   C. They grew out of Latin, the language spoken by Romans during the Holy Roman Empire.
   D. They were used for commerce in ancient Roman cities and towns.

5. Which of the following do American English and British English have in common?

   I. grammar
   II. pronunciation
   III. intonation
   IV. syntax

   A. I and II
   B. II and III
   C. III and IV
   D. I and IV

6. The fact that the Latin word *tabula* became *tabla* in Spanish is an example of:

   A. phonetics.
   B. syncope.
   C. creolization.
   D. euphony.

GO ON TO THE NEXT PAGE

7. In British English, the word *laboratory* is pronounced with an emphasis on the second vowel. In American English, the second vowel is not even pronounced. This is an example of:

   A. elision.

   B. pragmatism.

   C. laziness.

   D. practicality.

8. Which of the following words come from Greek roots?

   I.   significant

   II. cyclone

   III. photograph

   IV. manufacture

   A. I and II

   B. II and III

   C. III and IV

   D. I, II, and III

9. Which of the following best describes how a compound word gets into the language?

   A. It starts out as a solid compound, then changes to a hyphenated compound, and finally becomes two words.

   B. It begins as a hyphenated compound, then becomes two words, and finally develops into a single word.

   C. It starts out as two words, then develops into a hyphenated compound, and finally becomes a single word.

   D. Its original spelling as two words slowly changes into a single word and finally to a hyphenated compound.

10. Which of the following suffixes change a root word into a noun?

   I.   -ize

   II. -ish

   III. -ism

   IV. -ation

   A. I and II

   B. I and III

   C. II and IV

   D. III and IV

11. Use the diagram below to answer the question that follows.

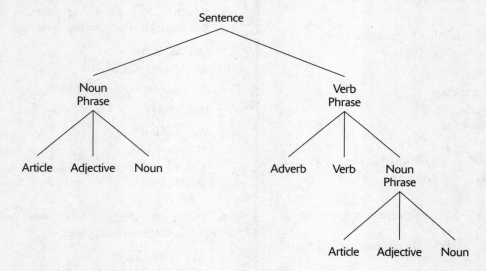

The diagram represents the structure of which of the following sentences?

   A. The boy in the wetsuit enjoys daily surfing.

   B. The best defense is a good offense.

   C. A spectacular dress often causes an audible gasp.

   D. This mortgage loan requires no down payment.

12. Which of the following pronunciations suggests that Stella doesn't want to go to the park, but she might like to go to the museum instead?

A. *Stella* doesn't want to go to the park.
B. Stella *doesn't* want to go to the park.
C. Stella doesn't *want* to go to the park.
D. Stella doesn't want to go to the *park*.

13. Which of the following best defines the word *etymology?*

A. the internal structure of words
B. the arrangement and relationship of words in phrases and sentences
C. the study of the similarities and differences among different languages
D. the study of word origins, development, and meaning

14. A student recognizes that in the following sentence, the underlined section is a subordinate clause used as an adverb.

Katie told us that she had a weakness for dark chocolate, <u>which I had always suspected</u>.

This recognition by the student is an example of:

A. pragmatic competence.
B. syntactical knowledge.
C. a grammatical error.
D. code-switching.

15. Identify the compound-complex sentence or sentences.

I. The fox chased the rabbit, but the rabbit, which was extremely fast, managed to escape.

II. The ship sails at noon, so you should get there by eleven.

III. Blueberries, which taste great on corn flakes, provide important antioxidants, and they're on sale this week.

IV. Dan and Peter plan to play golf on Saturday if it doesn't rain.

A. I
B. II
C. II, III, and IV
D. I and III

16. Identify the simple sentence or sentences.

I. I think; therefore, I am.

II. I'm thinking about a long-lost love.

III. Are you thinking, or are you day-dreaming?

IV. George and Marie talked for hours about miscellaneous subjects.

A. I and II
B. II
C. II and IV
D. III and IV

17. The best way to research the etymology of a word is to:

A. ask a native speaker of the language about it.
B. type the word into the subject line of your search engine.
C. consult the *Oxford English Dictionary.*
D. write to a college professor of English.

18. Read the passage below; then answer the question that follows.

The original meaning of the word *silly,* in Old English times, was "blessed." Perhaps because those who are blessed are often seen as innocent and guileless, the word's meaning gradually evolved into "innocent." And what makes a person innocent? Is it that he or she lacks the brains to be anything else? And if not that, then it is perhaps true that the innocent are so unsuspecting that they are often targets for those who want to take advantage of them. So, as time passed, the word gradually came to mean "foolish," the meaning of *silly* today.

This change in the meaning of the word *silly* is an example of:

A. pejoration.
B. amelioration.
C. extension.
D. narrowing.

GO ON TO THE NEXT PAGE

19. Read the passage; then answer the question that follows.

Suppose you were a farmer a hundred years ago. When you got ready to cast seeds out, you might have said you were going to *broadcast* them. With the advent of radio and television, the word's meaning was extended to apply to the transmission of audio and video signals. Today, the word is rarely used in its original meaning.

This most recent change in the meaning of the word *broadcast* demonstrates:

A. euphemism.
B. narrowing.
C. political correctness.
D. metonymy.

20. When discussing funeral arrangements with a client, a funeral director refers to "the loved one." This is an example of:

A. semantic shift.
B. semantic drift.
C. figurative language.
D. euphemism.

21. Which of the following activities would best help a kinesthetic learner in the acquisition of language skills?

A. listening to a lecture
B. watching a slide show
C. reading aloud
D. acting out scenes from a play

22. Students who are new to speaking English may prefer to remain silent for some time, just listening in class. If this happens, the teacher's best response is to:

A. call on the student frequently to force him or her to participate.
B. respect this preference and not put any pressure on the student.
C. get the student involved in discussion groups with other students.
D. have frequent one-on-one conversations with the student, slowly drawing the student out.

23. Read the passage below; then answer the question that follows.

An ESL teacher knows that her young student understands the sentence "Get your pencil." She then tells the student, "Get my pencils." She knows that by slightly altering the phrase, she can provide an appropriate cognitive and linguistic challenge, offering new information that builds on the student's prior knowledge.

Which principle of second-language acquisition is illustrated by this example?

A. S. P. Corder's "error analysis" method
B. Merrill Swain's "comprehensible output" hypothesis
C. Stephen Krashen's "comprehensible input" hypothesis
D. Rod Ellis's theories about the sequence of acquisition

24. Which of the following best explains the Critical Period Hypothesis as it relates to second-language acquisition?

  A. A language learner must put in at least two hours of study a week in order to acquire a second language.

  B. Studying a second language in the few hours before going to sleep is the most effective way to learn.

  C. The human brain is malleable, in terms of language, for a limited time—usually from birth to puberty.

  D. If a language learner is criticized too much by the teacher, he or she will never learn the language.

25. It has been observed that nouns, verbs, and adjectives all exist in languages that have never interacted. This fact lends support to:

  A. Noam Chomsky's idea of a universal grammar.

  B. the idea that grammar should be taught in the primary grades.

  C. the idea that it should be easy to learn a second language.

  D. the fact that all modern languages can be traced back to a single original language.

26. A teacher who is aware of Stephen Krashen's Affective Filter Hypothesis would facilitate her students' experience with second-language acquisition by:

  A. using various kinds of computer software to enable the students to listen to and speak the second language.

  B. providing a nonthreatening environment in which the students would not feel anxiety, embarrassment, or anger.

  C. insisting that each student speak the second language for at least 15 minutes a day.

  D. correcting her students' mistakes consistently so they can avoid forming bad habits.

27. An effective second-language teacher develops appropriate teaching strategies to guide students along a continuum of language development, beginning with:

  I. cognitively undemanding communication, such as storytelling activities that include visual props.

  II. context-reduced communication, such as a paragraph written on the chalkboard.

  III. cognitively demanding communication, such as a social studies lecture.

  IV. context-embedded communication, such as a one-to-one conversation with physical gestures.

  A. I and III

  B. I and IV

  C. II and III

  D. II and IV

28. Which of the following types of reading would a student do in order to get a general idea of what is written?

  A. scanning

  B. skimming

  C. reading intensively

  D. rereading

29. Which of the following techniques would most likely help a student understand how a season of the year can compare to a phase in a person's life?

  A. tapping prior knowledge about the vicissitudes of old age

  B. making a list of all the educational goals that might interest a nine-year-old

  C. making a semantic map listing all the words one might associate with winter

  D. making an analogy between youth and springtime

GO ON TO THE NEXT PAGE

30. To help her students expand their vocabulary, a teacher has them complete a diagram like this:

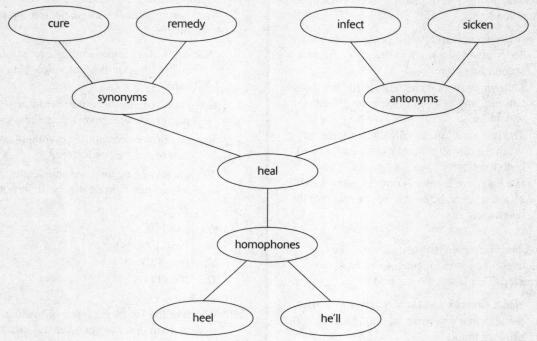

The teacher is using the technique of:

 A. cohesion analysis.
 B. word analogies.
 C. semantic mapping.
 D. free-writing.

31. Which of the following is an appropriate closing to a business letter?

 I. Yours truly,
 II. Your friend,
 III. Love,
 IV. Sincerely,

 A. I and II
 B. II and III
 C. I and IV
 D. IV

32. It is appropriate to include the recipient's address on the first page of a letter when you are writing:

 A. a friendly letter.
 B. a business letter.
 C. an e-mail.
 D. an invitation to a party.

33. If a job applicant misspells a few words in a résumé or a cover letter, what is likely to happen?

 A. The job applicant will not be asked in for an interview.
 B. The potential employer will overlook the errors if the applicant has experience.
 C. The potential employer will point out the errors during the interview.
 D. It is unlikely anyone would even notice.

34. If a teacher wanted students to evaluate the effectiveness of an author's technique, she might say:

 A. How well do you think the author develops the main character in this story?
 B. What is the theme of this story?
 C. Have you ever had an experience similar to the one described in this story?
 D. How does the setting in Chapter 1 compare to the setting in Chapter 2?

35. Which of the following are elements of a fable?

    I.   animal characters with anthropomorphic qualities

   II.   red herrings

  III.   suspense leading to the solving of a mysterious puzzle

  IV.   a moral, which may be expressed explicitly at the end

    A.   I and II

    B.   I, II, and IV

    C.   I and III

    D.   I and IV

36. Which of the following features or characteristics are common to myths?

    I.   stanza divisions

   II.   narrative fiction

  III.   a plot involving gods and heroes

  IV.   a theme expressing a culture's ideology

    A.   I, III, and IV

    B.   II and IV

    C.   II, III, and IV

    D.   III and IV

37. Which of the following might help a student decode an unfamiliar word?

    I.   considering context clues

   II.   choral reading

  III.   knowledge of prefixes, suffixes, and root words

  IV.   constructing a semantic map

    A.   I and III

    B.   II and IV

    C.   II and III

    D.   III and IV

38. Which of the following best defines the technique of modeling in order to aid in comprehension?

    A.   Student peers get together and do a choral reading of a text.

    B.   The teacher asks students about their prior knowledge of a particular subject.

    C.   Students make predictions about what will happen next in a story.

    D.   The teacher thinks or talks aloud to share his or her thought process while reading.

39. What study strategy is described below?

On a page in his or her notebook, a student draws a vertical line down the middle. On the left side, he or she takes notes while reading a text or listening to a lecture. Later, the student rereads the notes and records his or her reactions, thoughts, and observations in the right-hand column.

    A.   double-entry page

    B.   SQ3R

    C.   K-W-L chart

    D.   outlining

40. The best use of a Venn diagram is to:

    A.   show cause and effect.

    B.   indicate solutions to problems.

    C.   compare and contrast.

    D.   show the sequence of events.

41. Identify the compound sentence or sentences.

    I.   Lorraine Hansberry's play *A Raisin in the Sun* debuted on Broadway in 1959; it was the first play by an African American woman ever produced on Broadway.

   II.   The original cast included Sidney Poitier and Ruby Dee.

  III.   Lorraine Hansberry's play was very successful, but her career was cut short by cancer.

  IV.   She died at the tragically young age of thirty-four.

    A.   I and III

    B.   II

    C.   III and IV

    D.   III

GO ON TO THE NEXT PAGE

Questions 42 and 43 are based on these two sentences.

Herman Melville wrote *Moby-Dick.*

Herman Melville was a contemporary of Ralph Waldo Emerson.

42. Which sentence or sentences use a subordinate clause to combine the two sentences?

   I. Herman Melville, who wrote *Moby-Dick,* was a contemporary of Ralph Waldo Emerson.

   II. Herman Melville, the author of *Moby-Dick,* was a contemporary of Ralph Waldo Emerson.

   III. Herman Melville wrote *Moby-Dick;* he was a contemporary of Ralph Waldo Emerson.

   IV. Herman Melville, who was a contemporary of Ralph Waldo Emerson, wrote *Moby-Dick.*

   A. I and II
   B. I and IV
   C. II and III
   D. I

43. Which of the following combines the sentences and then expands them with an appositional phrase?

   A. Herman Melville, the author of *Moby-Dick* and a contemporary of Ralph Waldo Emerson, lived in the nineteenth century.
   B. Herman Melville, a contemporary of Ralph Waldo Emerson, wrote *Moby-Dick, Omoo,* and *Typee.*
   C. Herman Melville, the author of *Moby-Dick,* was a contemporary of Ralph Waldo Emerson, who wrote "Self-Reliance."
   D. Herman Melville, the author of *Moby-Dick,* was a contemporary of Ralph Waldo Emerson, the author of "Self-Reliance."

44. Which of the following questions does an adverb answer?

   I. Which one?
   II. Where?
   III. How?
   IV. What kind?

   A. I and II
   B. II and III
   C. III and IV
   D. I and IV

45. Which sentence contains a prepositional phrase that functions as an adjective?

   A. That singer has the voice of an angel.
   B. She sings with such emotion!
   C. Every time I hear that song, I get chills.
   D. I'll play it for you if you'd like.

46. Which of the following is the definition of a noncount noun?

   A. a noun whose plural form is made by adding *-s* or *-es*
   B. a noun whose plural form is made in an irregular manner
   C. a noun that has both a singular and a plural form
   D. a noun that has only a singular form

47. Which of the following sentences has a participial phrase that acts as an adjective?

   A. To relieve her nervousness about the verdict, Melanie tapped her fingers on the desk.
   B. Tapping her fingers nervously on the desk did little to ease Melanie's mind about the verdict.
   C. Tapping her fingers nervously on the desk, Melanie wondered what the verdict would be.
   D. Melanie wondered what the verdict would be as she tapped her fingers nervously on the desk.

48. In which of the following sentences is the word *while* used as a conjunction?

    A. While you chop the vegetables, I'll get the sauce ready.

    B. Maya likes to while away her afternoons by the pool.

    C. Let's rest here, in the shade of this tree, for a while.

    D. It will be a while before the order can be shipped.

49. Which sentence has an indirect object?

    A. Stan wondered what to get for Margie's birthday.

    B. Margie had hinted that she'd like a diamond ring.

    C. Stan didn't pick up on the hint.

    D. Stan bought Margie a gaudy hat.

50. What is the function of the underlined verbal phrase in this sentence?

Victoria maintains her resolve by <u>visualizing herself thinner.</u>

    A. direct object

    B. object of a preposition

    C. adverb

    D. adjective

Annotated Responses for CSET: English Subtest II

Language, Linguistics, and Literacy

Human Language Structures

1. **A.** (SMR Code: 2.1) By the same token, a Chinese child who grows up in the United States will learn to speak English. These facts indicate that people are not genetically programmed for a specific language, but, rather, that we are all born with a basic template that can serve for any language. Chomsky calls this "universal grammar."

2. **C.** (SMR Code: 2.1) *Motherese* refers to the way adults and older siblings (not just mothers) talk to infants. It is sometimes called "baby talk."

3. **D.** (SMR Code: 2.1) Pidgin is a language that has no native speakers; rather, it is a language that is a hybrid of three or more different languages, put together by its speakers for practical reasons. A pidgin language has features of all the base languages and blends them in matters of grammar and function. The vocabulary and grammar of the pidgin language are less complicated when compared with each base language. A later stage of this language occurs when it becomes the mother-tongue for many people, especially children. As the language develops, its structure changes, and it becomes richer than the pidgin language; at this stage it is called a creole language.

4. **C.** (SMR Code: 2.1) As the Holy Roman Empire expanded throughout Europe, the Vulgar Latin (also known as Popular Latin) spoken by the soldiers, settlers, and merchants of the conquerors became the dominant language in the Empire. As the Empire declined in the fifth century, the languages gradually developed into the Romance languages we know today (for example, French, Spanish, Italian, Portuguese, and Rumanian).

5. **D.** (SMR Code: 2.1) Intonation and pronunciation are obviously different, but the grammar and syntax of American English and British English are alike. This explains why written English is often easier to understand than spoken English, given the many accents that exist.

6. **B.** (SMR Code: 2.1) The word *syncope* comes from a Greek word (*koptein*), meaning "to strike or cut off." The word refers to the loss of one or more sounds or letters in the interior of a word. Other examples include *fo'c'sle* for *forecastle*, and the pronunciation of the word *parliament*, in which the *i* is no longer pronounced.

7. **A.** (SMR Code: 2.1) *Elision* and *syncope* are synonyms. Elision is often used as a technique in poetry to maintain meter.

8. **B.** (SMR Code: 2.1) *Cyclone* comes from the Greek root *cycl*, meaning "circle" or "ring." *Photograph* comes from two Greek words: *photo*, meaning "light" and *graph*, meaning "to write." The other two words, *significant* and *manufacture*, come from Latin roots.

9. **C.** (SMR Code: 2.1) The usual progression of a compound word is from two separate words, to a hyphenated compound, to a closed compound. In most cases, the spelling of each word does not change, as in *doghouse, basketball*, and *uptown*. Sometimes, however, the spelling of one word changes, as in *almighty* and *wherever*.

10. **D.** (SMR Code: 2.1) The noun-forming suffixes on this list are *-ism*, which means "doctrine of," and *-ation*, which means "state or quality of." The suffix *-ize* is a verb-forming suffix that means "to make," and the suffix *-ish* is an adjective-forming suffix that means "relating to."

11. **C.** (SMR Code: 2.1) The sentences in which the first noun phrase includes an adjective are choices B, C, and D, so you can eliminate choice A immediately. The only verb phrase that includes an adverb is choice C, with the adverb *often*. Further proof that choice C is the correct answer is the noun phrase that acts as a direct object of the verb *causes*. That noun phrase, *an audible gasp*, is made up of an article, an adjective, and a noun, thus fitting the diagram.

12. **D.** (SMR Code: 2.1) The emphasis on the word *park* suggests that a clause beginning with *but* might be added, such as "but she might like to go somewhere else." Choice A suggests that someone else besides Stella might like to go to the park, and choices B and C simply emphasize how strongly Stella feels about her position.

13. D. (SMR Code: 2.1) Choice A refers to morphology; choice B refers to syntax; and choice C refers to comparative linguistics. The only choice remaining is the correct one: etymology is the study of word origins, development, and meaning.

14. B. (SMR Code: 2.1) Since syntax is the arrangement and relationship of words in phrases and sentences, Katie's analysis of the sentence indicates that she has syntactical knowledge. Pragmatic competence refers to the ability to adjust one's language to the social situation, so you can eliminate choice A. Katie has not committed a grammatical error, so you can eliminate choice C. And code-switching—using words and expressions from one language or dialect when speaking or writing another—does not apply.

15. D. (SMR Code: 2.1) A compound sentence has two independent clauses, joined by a comma and a coordinating conjunction or by a semicolon. A complex sentence has an independent clause and one or more subordinate clauses. A compound-complex sentence is a combination of the two. Sentences I and III are the only ones that fit the definition, so answer choice D is correct. Both sentences have two independent clauses ("The fox chased the rabbit" and "the rabbit managed to escape;" and "Blueberries provide important antioxidants" and "they're on sale this week." Each one also has a subordinate clause, "which was extremely fast" and "which taste great on corn flakes." Sentence II is a compound sentence, and sentence IV is a complex sentence.

16. C. (SMR Code: 2.1) A simple sentence has one independent clause. Sentences II and IV fit the description. Sentences I and III are compound sentences.

17. C. (SMR Code: 2.1) Although you might be able to find answers about word etymologies by asking a native speaker, researching it online, or asking a college professor, the *best* way to do so is to consult the *Oxford English Dictionary,* which includes word etymologies with their definitions.

18. A. (SMR Code: 2.1) Pejoration occurs as a word loses positive connotations and/or develops negative connotations over the years. Another example is the word *slick,* in its colloquial sense. Its original slang meaning was "excellent, fine, enjoyable, or attractive." Today, the word's colloquial meaning is "clever in deception or trickery."

19. B. (SMR Code: 2.1) This is an example of a word that once enjoyed extension of meaning, changing from "casting of seeds" to "transmitting audio and video signals," and later underwent narrowing of meaning, losing the first meaning almost entirely.

20. D. (SMR Code: 2.1) A euphemism is the substitution of a less offensive, less upsetting, or less distasteful word for its more direct synonym. Euphemisms are common in the funeral industry, as well as in any references to sex or bathroom matters. For example, rather than "died," one might say "passed away."

Acquisition and Development of Language and Literacy

21. D. (SMR Code: 2.2) Kinesthetic learners process information through movement and action. Hence, activities such as acting out scenes, putting on plays, and counting out measures with foot tapping are all effective teaching methods for them. Listening to a lecture and reading aloud are good methods for auditory learners, and watching a slide show works well for visual learners.

22. B. (SMR Code: 2.2) The silent period, when a second-language learner is listening to the new language, is very common. In fact, most learners go through this period. It may last only for a few hours, or it may last for weeks or even months. Research has shown that many silent learners are actually engaging in "self-talk" during this time, in which they are silently rehearsing the new language patterns they are hearing. It's best not to put the student on the spot during this stage.

23. C. (SMR Code: 2.2) Stephen Krashen believes that students who hear language slightly beyond what they already understand, but based on what they do understand, will improve. When supplying "comprehensible input" to a student, the teacher might also use concrete objects, gestures, and graphic organizers to make the meaning clearer.

24. C. (SMR Code: 2.2) The Critical Period Hypothesis refers to that time that the human brain is most open to the acquisition of language, which appears to be up to the age of puberty. After that, even though a person may learn a new language, he or she will likely never become completely fluent in the sense that a native speaker would be.

25. **A.** (SMR Code: 2.2) This is one of many points that Chomsky uses to support his idea of a universal grammar. As for choice D, the phrase "the fact that" gives this away as an incorrect answer. Although linguists have been trying to trace all languages back to a single original language, they have not been successful.

26. **B.** (SMR Code: 2.2) Krashen's Affective Filter Hypothesis contends that anxiety, lack of motivation, and low self-esteem interfere with a learner's ability to learn a second language. Therefore, the teacher who provides a nonthreatening environment has taken the first step toward helping students learn.

27. **B.** (SMR Code: 2.2) The key phrase in the question stem is *beginning with.* Students must begin with easier tasks before they can move on to more difficult ones. Hence, cognitively undemanding communication comes before cognitively demanding communication. And context-embedded communication is easier to understand than context-reduced communication.

28. **B.** (SMR Code: 2.2) Skimming is looking quickly through a book, chapter, or section to get a general sense of its contents. It is a prereading activity that tells the student what to expect from a closer reading. Scanning is closely related to skimming in that it involves quickly looking over a text, but scanning involves looking for specific information, such as the definition of a key word or an explanation of a difficult term.

29. **D.** (SMR Code: 2.2) The key word in the question is *compare,* which is the essence of an analogy. An analogy compares two unlike things, pointing out an area of similarity. The other choices relate to only one idea (old age, educational goals of a nine-year-old, or winter words) and do not make any comparisons between those ideas and others.

30. **C.** (SMR Code: 2.2) Semantic mapping is making a graphic organizer to show the relationships between various bits of information or knowledge. It is a good way to expand vocabulary, as in this example. It can also be used to show relationships between ideas.

Literacy Studies

31. **C.** (SMR Code: 2.3) Choices I and IV are the only two from this list that are appropriate for a business letter. The other choices are more appropriate for a friendly letter. Additional choices for a business letter include Best regards, Warm regards, Kind regards, Cordially, Sincerely yours, Very truly yours, and Yours sincerely, among others.

32. **B.** (SMR Code: 2.3) The recipient's address on the first page of a letter, also known as the "inside address," is appropriate in a business letter. It is not necessary for any of the other forms of communication listed.

33. **A.** (SMR Code: 2.3) It is most likely that the job applicant will not be asked in for an interview. Even if spelling is not an important part of the job, misspellings on such important forms of communication indicate carelessness and lack of attention to detail.

34. **A.** (SMR Code: 2.3) When you evaluate something, you judge its merits. Therefore, choice A is the only one that fits.

35. **D.** (SMR Code: 2.3) A fable is defined as a brief story that usually features animal characters and that teaches a moral or a lesson. The other choices both apply to mysteries, not fables.

36. **C.** (SMR Code: 2.4) Items II, III, and IV apply to myths, so choice C is the correct answer. Since myths are narrative fiction, you can eliminate item I, stanza divisions, which would be found only in poetry.

37. **A.** (SMR Code: 2.4) Context clues and a knowledge of word parts are useful in decoding unfamiliar words. Choral reading, or reading aloud with a group, would shed no light on the meaning of an unfamiliar word, and constructing a semantic map would be impossible if one didn't know what the word meant in the first place.

38. **D.** (SMR Code: 2.4) Modeling involves a think-aloud, in which the teacher or an able student recollects aloud how he or she deciphered a passage.

39. **A.** (SMR Code: 2.4) The strategy described is a double-entry page. SQ3R means Survey, Question, Read, Recite, Review, the steps a student takes while reading a text. A K-W-L chart is a three-column chart in which the student fills in "What I *Know,*" "What I *Want* to Know," and, later, "What I *Learned.*" Outlining is a method of recording the important points and showing their order of importance.

40. C. (SMR Code: 2.4) A Venn diagram is two intersecting circles, with the area of intersection being used to show what is alike about two things. The independent sections outside the intersection are used to show what is unique about two things.

Grammatical Structures of English

41. A. (SMR Code: 2.4) Compound sentences have two or more independent clauses joined by a comma and a coordinating conjunction, or by a semicolon. Items I and III match this definition, so choice A is the correct answer. Item II is a simple sentence with a compound object; item IV is a simple sentence.

42. B. (SMR Code: 2.4) A clause is a group of related words that contains a subject and a predicate; a subordinate clause is one that cannot stand alone. In item I, the subordinate clause is "who wrote *Moby-Dick.*" Item 2 combines the sentences using a phrase. Item III combines the sentences by making them into two independent clauses joined by a semicolon. In item IV, the subordinate clause is "who was a contemporary of Ralph Waldo Emerson."

43. D. (SMR Code: 2.4) The appositional phrase is "the author of 'Self-Reliance.'"

44. B. (SMR Code: 2.4) Adverbs also answer the questions *when* and *to what extent.* The other choices, I and IV, are answered by adjectives.

45. A. (SMR Code: 2.4) The prepositional phrase "of an angel" functions as an adjective modifying *voice.* Choice B has a prepositional phrase, "with such emotion," that functions as an adverb modifying the verb *sings.* Choices C and D include adverbial clauses.

46. D. (SMR Code: 2.4) Noncount nouns have only singular forms, such as homework, enjoyment, advice, patience, knowledge, sleeping, tennis, and so on.

47. C. (SMR Code: 2.4) "Tapping her fingers nervously on the desk" is a participial phrase modifying the noun *Melanie.* Choice A has an infinitive phrase acting as an adverb. Choice B has a participial phrase acting as a noun, the subject of the sentence. Choice D has a subordinate clause acting as an adverb.

48. A. (SMR Code: 2.4) In choice A, *while* is used as a subordinating conjunction. In choice B, *while* is part of an infinitive used as the direct object. Choices C and D use *while* as a noun.

49. D. (SMR Code: 2.4) An indirect object has an imaginary *to* or *for* in front of the word, telling to whom or for whom something was done. In choice D, the word *for* could be inserted before *Margie* without changing the meaning.

50. B. (SMR Code: 2.4) The underlined verbal phrase is the object of the preposition *by.*

Subtest III: Composition and Rhetoric; Literature and Textual Analysis

Content Domains for Subject Matter Understanding and Skill in English

Here is a list of the areas on which you will be tested. This information is also available at the CSET Website. It is reproduced here for your convenience.

Composition and Rhetoric (SMR Domain 3)

Candidates demonstrate knowledge of the foundations and contexts of the composition and rhetoric contained in the *English-Language Arts Content Standards for California Public Schools* (1997) as outlined in the *Reading/Language Arts Framework for California Public Schools: Kindergarten Through Grade Twelve* (1999) at a post secondary level of rigor. Candidates have both broad and deep conceptual knowledge of the subject matter. Candidates face dynamic challenges in the domains of oral and written communication. They must make appropriate use of current text-production technologies and develop sensitivity to patterns of communication used by different social and cultural groups. Candidates are competent writers and speakers who can communicate appropriately in various rhetorical contexts, using effective text structures, word choice, sentence options, standard usage conventions, and advanced research methods as needed. The subject matter preparation program provides opportunities for candidates to develop skills and confidence in public speaking. Candidates will be able to:

0001 Written Composing Processes (Individual and Collaborative) (SMR 3.1)

a. Reflect on and describe their own writing processes.

b. Investigate and apply alternative methods of prewriting, drafting, responding, revising, editing, and evaluating.

c. Employ such strategies as graphic organizers, outlines, notes, charts, summaries, or précis to clarify and record meaning.

d. Integrate a variety of software applications (e.g., databases, graphics, spreadsheets) to produce print documents and multi-media presentations.

(*English-Language Arts Content: Standards for California Public Schools,* Grade 6, Reading: 2.1–2, 2.4, Writing: 1.4–6; Grade 7, Reading: 2.3–4, Writing: 1.3–4, 1.6–7; Grade 8, Reading: 2.4, Writing: 1.1, 1.4–6, Listening and Speaking: 1.4; Grades 9–10, Reading: 2.4, Writing: 1.8–9; Grades 11–12, Writing: 1.4, 1.7–9, Listening and Speaking: 2.4)

0002 Rhetorical Features of Literary and Non-Literary, Oral and Written Texts (SMR 3.2)

a. Recognize and use a variety of writing applications (e.g., short story, biographical, autobiographical, expository, persuasive, business and technical documents, historical investigation).

b. Demonstrate awareness of audience, purpose, and context.

c. Recognize and use various text structures (e.g., narrative and non-narrative organizational patterns).

d. Apply a variety of methods to develop ideas within an essay (e.g., analogy, cause and effect, compare and contrast, definition, illustration, description, hypothesis).

e. Apply critical thinking strategies to evaluate methods of persuasion, including but not limited to:

- Types of appeal (e.g., appeal to reason, emotion, morality)
- Types of persuasive speech (e.g., propositions of fact, value, problem, policy)
- Logical fallacies (e.g., bandwagon, red herring, glittering generalities, ad hominem)
- Advertising techniques (e.g., Maslow's hierarchy of needs)

- Logical argument (e.g., inductive/deductive reasoning, syllogisms, analogies)
- Classical argument (e.g., claim, qualifiers, rules of evidence, warrant)

(*English-Language Arts Content Standards for California Public Schools,* Grades 6, Reading: 2.1–2, 2.4, 2.6. 2.8, Writing: 1.1–3, 1.6, 2.1–5, Listening and Speaking: 1.8–9; Grade 7, Reading: 1.3, 2.2–3, Writing: 1.1–3, 1.7, 2.1–5, Listening and Speaking: 1.1, 1.3; Grade 8, Reading: 1.3, 2.2, Writing: 1.1–3, 1.5, 2.1–6, Listening and Speaking: 1.8; Grades 9–10, Writing: 1.1–2, 1.4, 1.9, 2.1–6, Listening and Speaking: 1.5, 1.10, 1.13; Grades 11–12, Reading: 1.3, 2.2, 2.4–6, Writing: 1.1–5, 1.9, 2.1–6, Listening and Speaking: 1.4, 1.12–13)

0003 Rhetorical Effects of Grammatical Elements (SMR 3.3)

a. Employ precise and extensive vocabulary and effective diction to control voice, style, and tone.

b. Use clause joining techniques (e.g., coordinators, subordinators, punctuation) to express logical connections between ideas.

c. Identify and use clausal and phrasal modifiers to control flow, pace, and emphasis (e.g., adjective clauses, appositives, participles and verbal phrases, absolutes).

d. Identify and use devices to control focus in sentence and paragraph (e.g., active and passive voice, expletives, concrete subjects, transitional phrases).

e. Maintain coherence through use of cohesive devices.

(*English-Language Arts Content Standards for California Public Schools,* Grade 6, Reading: 1.1, Writing: 1.2, 1.6, Written and Oral English Language Conventions: 1.1–5; Grade 7, Writing: 1.1, 1.7, Written and Oral English Language Conventions: 1.1–7; Grade 8, Writing: 1.2, 1.6, Written and Oral English Language Conventions: 1.1–6, Listening and Speaking: 1.5–6; Grades 9–10, Writing: 1.1–2, 1.6, 1.9, Written and Oral English Language Conventions: 1.1–5; Grades 11–12, Reading: 2.1–2, Writing: 1.2–5, 1.9, Written and Oral English Language Conventions: 1.1–3, Listening and Speaking: 1.5)

0004 Conventions of Oral and Written Language (SMR 3.4)

a. Apply knowledge of linguistic structure to identify and use the conventions of Standard Edited English.

b. Recognize, understand, and use a range of conventions in both spoken and written English, including:

- Conventions of effective sentence structure (e.g., clear pronoun reference, parallel structure, appropriate verb tense)
- Preferred usage (e.g., verb/subject agreement, pronoun agreement, idioms)
- Conventions of pronunciation and intonation
- Conventional forms of spelling
- Capitalization and punctuation

(*English-Language Arts Content Standards for California Pubic Schools,* Grade 6, Reading: 1.1, Written and Oral English Language Conventions: 1.1–5; Grade 7, Written and Oral English Language Conventions: 1.1–7; Grade 8, Writing: 1.2, Written and Oral English Language Conventions: 1.1–6, Listening and Speaking: 1.6; Grades 9–10, Writing: 1.9, Written and Oral English Language Conventions: 1.9; Grades 11–12, Writing: 1.4, Written and Oral English Language Conventions: 1.1–3, Listening and Speaking: 1.8)

0005 Research Strategies (SMR 3.5)

a. Develop and apply research questions.

b. Demonstrate methods of inquiry and investigation.

c. Identify and use multiple resources (e.g., oral, print, electronic; primary and secondary) and critically evaluate the quality of the sources.

d. Interpret and apply findings.

e. Use professional conventions and ethical standards of citation and attribution.

f. Demonstrate effective presentation methods, including multi-media formats.

(*English-Language Arts Content Standards for California Pubic Schools,* Grade 6, Reading: 1.1, 2.1, 2.3, 2.6–8, Writing: 1.4–5, Listening and Speaking: 1.1–2, 1.6–7, 2.1, 2.3; Grade 7, Reading: 2.2, 2.6, Writing: 1.4–5, Listening and Speaking: 1.2, 1.6–7, 2.1, 2.3; Grade 8, Reading: 2.2, 2.7, Writing: 1.3–6, Listening and Speaking: 1.2–3, 1.6–8, 2.3; Grades 9–10, Reading: 2.2–5, 2.8, Writing: 1.3–8, Listening and Speaking: 1.7, 2.2; Grades 11–12, Writing: 1.4, 1.6–8, Listening and Speaking: 2.4)

Literature and Textual Analysis (SMR Domain 1)

Candidates demonstrate knowledge of the foundations and contexts of the literature and textual analysis contained in the *English-Language Arts Content Standards for California Public Schools* (1997) as outlined in the *Reading/Language Arts Framework for California Public Schools: Kindergarten Through Grade Twelve* (1999) at a post secondary level of rigor. Candidates have both broad and deep conceptual knowledge of the subject matter. The candidate's preparation should include breadth of knowledge in literature, literary analysis and criticism, as well as non-literary text analysis. Literary analysis presumes in-depth exploration of the relationship between form and content. The curriculum should embrace representative selections form different literary traditions and major works from diverse cultures. Advanced study of multicultural writers is also fundamental preparation for teaching these works. Shakespeare remains integral to the secondary school curriculum; advanced study of his work is, therefore, essential to future secondary teachers. Candidates must be enthusiastic readers and writers, who know and apply effective reading strategies and compose thoughtful, well-crafted responses to literary and non-literary texts. Candidates will be able to:

0006 Literary Analysis (SMR 1.1)

a. Recognize, compare, and evaluate different literary traditions to include:

- American (inclusive of cultural pluralism)
- British (inclusive of cultural pluralism)
- World literature and literature in translation (inclusive of cross-cultural literature)
- Mythology and oral tradition

b. Trace development of major literary movements in historical periods (e.g., Homeric Greece, medieval, neoclassic, romantic, modern).

c. Describe the salient features of adolescent/young adult literature.

d. Analyze and interpret major works by representative writers in historical, aesthetic, political, and philosophical contexts.

(*English-Language Arts Content Standards for California Public Schools,* Grade 6, Reading: 2.4: Grades 11–12, Reading: 2.2, 3.5–7)

0007 Literary Elements (SMR 1.2)

a. Distinguish salient features of genres (e.g., short stories, non-fiction, drama, poetry, novel).

b. Define and analyze basic elements of literature (e.g., plot, setting, character, point of view, theme, narrative structure, figurative language, tone, diction, style).

c. Articulate the relationship between the expressed purposes and the characteristics of different forms of dramatic literature (e.g., comedy, tragedy, drama, dramatic monologue).

d. Develop critical thinking and analytic skill through close reading of texts.

(*English-Language Arts Content Standards for California Public Schools,* Grade 6, Reading: 1.1–2, 2.1, 2.4, 2.6, 2.8, 3.0; Grade 7, Reading: 1.1, 2.4, 3.1–5; Grade 8, Reading: 1.1, 2.7, 3.0; Grades 9–10, Reading: 1.1, 2.8, 3.1–4, 3.7–10; Grades 11–12, Reading: 2.2, 3.1–4)

0008 Literary Criticism (SMR 1.3)

a. Research and apply criticism of major texts and authors using print and/or electronic resources.

b. Research and apply various approaches to interpreting literature (e.g., aesthetic, historical, political, philosophical).

(*English-Language Arts Content Standards for California Public Schools,* Grade 6, Reading: 2.1–2, 2.6–8, 3.6; Grade 7, Reading: 2.1, 2.4, 2.6, 3.0; Grade 8, Reading: 2.2, 2.6, 3.0; Grades 9–10, Reading: 2.2, 2.4, 2.8, 3.5–7, 3.11–12, Writing: 1.6–7; Grades 11–12, Reading: 2.2, 2.4, 3.8–9, Writing: 1.6–7)

0009 Analysis of Non-Literary Texts (SMR 1.4)

a. Compare various features of print and visual media (e.g., film, television, Internet).

b. Evaluate structure and content of a variety of consumer, workplace, and public documents.

c. Interpret individual works in their cultural, social, and political contexts.

(*English-Language Arts Content Standards for California Public Schools,* Grade 6, Reading: 2.0, 3.0; Grade 7, Reading: 2.1–5, 3.0; Grade 8, Reading: 2.1–7, 3.0; Grades 9–10, Reading: 2.1, 2.2, 2.4–7, 3.0; Grades 11–12, Reading: 2.1–3, 2.6, 3.0)

Subtest III: Composition and Rhetoric; Literature and Textual Analysis

Directions: Below is a set of constructed-response questions that are similar to the questions you will see on Subtest III of CSET: English. You are encouraged to respond to the questions without looking at the responses provided in the next section. Record your responses on the test booklets that follow the questions and compare them with the provided responses.

1. Complete the exercise that follows.

Read the following excerpt, the opening chapter of *The Waves* by Virginia Woolf. In your own words, identify the author's main idea in the excerpt and analyze the method of development she uses. Explain how this method of development clarifies and supports the author's main idea. Comment on her use of various literary and style elements (sentence structure, word choice, figurative language). As you respond, assume that you are writing for an educated audience familiar with literary criticism and make sure to support your points with evidence from the text. Write your response on the lined pages of Response Booklet A.

The sun had not yet risen. The sea was indistinguishable from the sky, except that the sea was slightly creased as if a cloth had wrinkles in it. Gradually as the sky whitened a dark line lay on the horizon dividing the sea from the sky and the grey cloth became barred with thick strokes moving, one after another, beneath the surface, following each other, pursuing each other, perpetually.

As they neared the shore each bar rose, heaped itself, broke and swept a thin veil of white water across the sand. The wave paused, and then drew out again, sighing like a sleeper whose breath comes and goes unconsciously. Gradually the dark bar on the horizon became clear as if the sediment in an old wine-bottle had sunk and left the glass green. Behind it, too, the sky cleared as if the white sediment there had sunk, or as if the arm of a woman crouched beneath the horizon had raised a lamp and flat bars of white, green and yellow, spread across the sky like the blades of a fan. Then she raised her lamp higher and the air seemed to become fibrous and to tear away from the green surface flickering and flaming in red and yellow fibres like the smoky fire that roars from a bonfire. Gradually the fibres of the burning bonfire were fused into one haze, one incandescence which lifted the weight of the woollen grey sky on top of it and turned it to a million atoms of soft blue. The surface of the sea slowly became transparent and lay rippling and sparkling until the dark stripes were almost rubbed out. Slowly the arm that held the lamp raised it higher and then higher until a broad flame became invisible; an arc of fire burnt on the rim of the horizon, and all round it the sea blazed gold.

The light struck upon the trees in the garden, making one leaf transparent and then another. One bird chirped high up; there was a pause; another chirped lower down. The sun sharpened the walls of the house, and rested like the tip of a fan upon a white blind and made a blue fingerprint of shadow under the leaf by the bedroom window. The blind stirred slightly, but all within was dim and unsubstantial. The birds sang their blank melody outside.

2. Complete the exercise that follows.

Read the following poem, "Cargoes" by John Mansfield, carefully. Comment on the meaning of the poem. Then discuss the elements of poetry that Mansfield uses to express that meaning. Cite at least three specific examples from the poem to argue your points about Mansfield's technique and style in this poem. Assume that you are writing for an educated audience and support your points with evidence from the poem. Write your response on the lined pages of Response Booklet B.

Quinquireme of Nineveh from distant Ophir,

Rowing home to haven in sunny Palestine,

With a cargo of ivory,

And apes and peacocks,

Sandalwood, cedarwood, and sweet white wine.

Stately Spanish galleon coming from the Isthmus,

Dipping through the Tropics by the palm-green shores,

With a cargo of diamonds,

Emeralds, amethysts,

Topazes, and cinnamon, and gold moidores.

Dirty British coaster with salt-caked smoke stack,

Butting through the Channel in the mad March days,

With a cargo of Tyne coal,

Road-rail, pig-lead,

Firewood, iron-ware, and cheap tin trays.

Written Response Document for CSET: English Subtest III

For both questions 1 and 2, you will record your written response to each question on a four-page response document. The length of your response to each question is limited to the lined space available in the response document. Samples of the response documents are provided on the following pages.

Written Response Booklet A

Written Response Booklet A continued

Written Response Booklet A continued

Written Response Booklet A continued

Written Response Booklet B

Written Response Booklet B continued

_____

_____

_____

_____

_____

_____

_____

_____

_____

_____

_____

_____

_____

_____

_____

_____

_____

_____

Written Response Booklet B continued

Written Response Booklet B continued

_____

_____

_____

_____

_____

_____

_____

_____

_____

_____

_____

_____

_____

_____

_____

_____

_____

_____

_____

_____

Examples of Responses to Sample Constructed-Response Questions for CSET: English Subtest III

Composition and Rhetoric; Literature and Textual Analysis

Question #1 (Score Point 4 Response)

In this excerpt, the opening chapter of <u>The Waves</u>, Virginia Woolf describes the beauty of dawn as seen from the shoreline. She opens with a simple sentence describing the moment just before the rising of the sun, when the horizon is not even visible. She develops her description with a series of compound, complex, and compound-complex sentences, as if to mirror the growing complexity of the scene as the sun rises.

In this masterful description, Woolf uses similes, metaphors, alliteration, and imagery to great effect. She compares the sea to a slightly <u>c</u>reased <u>c</u>loth with wrinkles on it, using alliteration and simile at the same time. Those wrinkles, of course, are the waves that race toward shore, "<u>p</u>ursuing each other, <u>p</u>erpetually." She uses alliteration and simile again when she describes a wave that has reached the shore drawing out again, "<u>s</u>ighing like a <u>s</u>leeper."

She compares the appearance of the horizon to an old wine bottle in which the sediment has sunk. She compares the rising sun to a lamp raised by the arm of a "woman crouched beneath the horizon," the light spreading "like the blades of a fan." When she describes the "green surface flickering and flaming in red and yellow fibres like the smoky fire that roars from a bonfire," the reader has no trouble picturing the scene. In language that appeals to every sense, Woolf has given us a memorable description of the dramatic sight of dawn at sea, until the moment when the "sea blazed gold."

She follows both chronological and spatial order, describing the changes in the appearance of the sea and the sky as the sun gradually rises, lightening the sky in the distance and moving closer to the shore.

As light fills the sky, it eventually strikes the trees in the garden, revealing the transparency of the leaves and awakening the birds, who begin to chirp. Finally, the sunlight falls on the walls of a house, resting on the blinds of a bedroom window. Woolf closes, as she had begun, with a simple sentence. The reader is left in suspense, wondering what would be revealed inside the bedroom if the blinds were open.

Question #1 (Score Point 3 Response)

This excerpt from <u>The Waves</u> by Virginia Woolf is a description of morning, as the sun rises over the sea. As the passage opens, the perspective is from the shore, looking out toward the horizon. From that perspective, the unnamed viewer cannot tell, at first, where the sea ends and the sky begins. Only gradually, as the sky grows lighter, can the viewer see the difference between the sky and the sea.

The main idea is that the sun gradually fills the sky, revealing more details about the sea. Waves continue to move toward the shore, breaking on the beach and then slowly being drawn back out to sea. In the end, the sunlight reaches the backyard of a house, revealing the leaves in the trees and dancing off the blinds of a bedroom window.

To develop this description, Woolf follows chronological order, beginning with the moment just before the sun lightens the sky and gradually moving forward until the sky is ablaze with color. She also follows spatial order, moving from the horizon to the backyard of the house. These two methods of development are perfect for her purpose, for they follow the way anyone would appreciate the sunrise, watching the light.

The sentence structure, like the scenery, is varied. She opens with a simple sentence ("The sun had not yet risen."), which reflects the simplicity of the scene at that point. She moves on to a mixture of compound, complex, and compound-complex sentences, reflecting the growing complexity of the scene as more details become visible.

Woolf uses similes and metaphors to enhance her descriptions. She says the sea "was slightly creased as if a cloth had wrinkles in it," an apt description of the waves that ruffle the surface of the sea. When she describes breaking waves sweeping "a thin veil of white water across the sand," continuing the comparison to cloth, the reader is surprised to realize how like a veil that foamy water is. Other similes and metaphors include the image of a woman holding up a lamp that lights up the sky, as the light spreads out "like the blades of a fan." The color in the sky is likened to a flickering, flaming bonfire.

Woolf's use of alliteration adds to the pleasing effect of her description. Waves rush toward the shore, "<u>p</u>ursuing each other, <u>p</u>erpetually." Waves draw back toward the sea, "<u>s</u>ighing like a <u>s</u>leeper." Later, the "<u>s</u>urface of the <u>s</u>ea <u>s</u>lowly became transparent."

Question #1 (Score Point 2 Response)

This excerpt from Virginia Woolf's <u>The Waves</u> is a description of the process of sunrise. It starts out when it is still dark, when the narrator can't tell the difference between the sky and the sea. Gradually, as the sun rises higher in the sky, details in the scenery can be distinguished. Waves can be seen beneath the surface of the sea as they move toward shore. Then they break on the beach and are drawn back out. As light fills the sky, it finally shines on the trees in a garden and on the blinds of a house. Birds begin to chirp, so we know morning has broken.

Some of the comparisons Woolf uses don't make much sense. She says the sea is like a wrinkled cloth. Well, cloth and the sea don't have anything in common. They don't look alike, they don't feel alike, and they don't act alike.

I did like the comparison of receding waves, "sighing like a sleeper whose breath comes and goes unconsciously." Waves sound just like that, when you think about it.

But I thought she was stretching it a bit to compare the light of the sun to a lamp being raised by the arm of a woman. Then she keeps jumping from the image of a lamp to the image of a bonfire. She should stick to one or the other.

All in all, I thought she spent too much time describing the dawn. I wanted her to get into the real story. What's going to happen? Will the house have anything to do with it? What's behind that bedroom window?

Question #1 (Score Point 1 Response)

This is a very confusing description of dawn. A narrator is standing in a place where the ocean, the beach, and a house are visible, but we never find out who the narrator is. Where exactly is he or she standing? Does he or she have something to do with the people who live in the house? Is he or she going to be one of the characters in the book?

In any case, the narrator goes on and on, describing dawn and how its light changes the appearance of everything. Well, of course it does! At first, everything's dark, and then it gets light enough to see things. No surprise there.

The narrator mixes up metaphors from paragraph to paragraph. First, the sea is compared to a wrinkled cloth. Then, the foam of breaking waves is compared to a veil. Then the receding waves are compared to a sighing sleeper. As if that weren't enough comparisons, the narrator goes on to compare the rising light to a lamp being held by a woman. I don't know of any woman strong enough to hold a lamp that size! But is it a lamp or a fire— a "burning bonfire"? Maybe in those days, lamps were actually fires—in fact, I guess electricity hadn't been invented yet. But even so, it's a very confusing description.

I was glad when the narrator finally started describing the garden next to the house. With the birds chirping and the blind on the bedroom window stirring slightly, I felt as if something was about to happen.

Question #2 (Score Point 4 Response)

On a literal level, "Cargoes" by John Masefield is a simple lyric poem about ships and their cargoes, but its connotations make it a bit more complex than that.

The poem is made up of three five-line stanzas, each dealing with a different type of ship and its unique cargo. The first two lines of each stanza name the type of ship and describe how it moves. The last three lines of each stanza describe the cargo carried by the ship. In each stanza, lines one, two, and five are relatively long, and lines three and four are relatively short. Only lines two and five of each stanza rhyme.

The ship named in the first stanza is a quinquireme, a large vessel used for trade in the Mediterranean area in ancient times. The word evokes images of the long-distant past, when ships were propelled by rows of oarsmen. The quinquireme travels from "distant Ophir" to "sunny Palestine," with an exotic cargo of ivory, apes, peacocks, fragrant woods, and wine, all luxury items. The reader can picture the final destination of these items: some luxurious palace where the rich are waited on by servants or slaves, and peacocks roam free around the palace grounds.

The second stanza brings us ahead to the sixteenth or seventeenth century, when the Spanish conquest of South America was in full progress. The ship is a "Stately Spanish galleon," another large ship, this one propelled by sails. Notice that its cargo is the plunder taken from the New World, being brought back to the Old World for profit. This plunder consists of precious and semi-precious stones, cinnamon, and gold coins—not quite as exotic as the cargo of the quinquireme but appealing nonetheless.

The third stanza moves forward in time to the Industrial Revolution. The "Dirty British coaster" uses neither oars nor sails, but a steam engine instead. It does not move gracefully but, rather, like an animal "butting through the channel." Its cargo is things to burn (coal and firewood) and manufactured metal products (road-rail, iron-ware, tin trays). The visual image is one of far less color and sparkle than in the previous two stanzas.

It is interesting to note the change in sound from one stanza to another. The first stanza has long words that flow easily in a melodic manner. Quinquireme, Ninevah, Palestine, sandalwood, cedarwood: these anapests are fun to say aloud. In the second stanza, Masefield again uses anapests, but not as many of them: emeralds, amethysts, topazes, cinnamon. By the time the British coaster is chugging along in the Channel, Masefield has dropped the anapests and is now using spondees, the better to match the motion of the ship: road-rail, pig-lead, firewood.

Question #2 (Score Point 3 Response)

In his poem "Cargoes," John Masefield uses three short stanzas to describe three different ships from three different historical periods. Each stanza is devoted to one ship. He moves from the very distant past to the relatively recent past, and as he does so, the images become less romantic and exotic and more utilitarian and industrial.

He starts out by describing a quinquireme, an ancient ship propelled by rows of oarsmen. This ancient ship carries an exotic, colorful, and luxurious cargo: ivory, apes, peacocks, sandalwood, cedarwood, and sweet white wine. This cargo appeals to the reader on a sensual level: we can imagine the colors, tastes, sounds, and aromas associated with the items.

The second stanza describes a Spanish galleon on its way back from the New World. It is laden with treasures either stolen from or obtained by trade with the natives: diamonds, emeralds, amethysts, topazes, cinnamon, and gold moidores. These treasures appeal to the reader mostly on a visual level; we can imagine the sparkles of the gems and the gold coins. The cinnamon is the only cargo item that appeals to other senses.

The third stanza is about a "Dirty British coaster." The word coaster just doesn't have the same appeal as quinquireme or galleon. Like the sound of its name, this boat chugs along in a jerky fashion, "butting through the Channel in the mad March days." The coaster is carrying a very boring, though utilitarian, cargo: coal, firewood, and manufactured metal goods. There are no bright colors and no sparkles here.

At first glance, Masefield seems to be saying that the modern world is inferior to the ancient world. After all, who would prefer "cheap tin trays" to the exotic cargo of the first two ships? But perhaps Masefield actually admires the British coaster. It does get along on its own power, not relying on the labor of oarsmen or the whims of the wind. And its cargo includes useful things that will make life easier for the common person: coal and wood to heat homes, rails to build train tracks, and cheap tin trays for home use.

I think the most interesting thing about this poem is the way the tempo and words match the subject matter. More exotic words go with the more exotic cargo; more utilitarian words go with the more utilitarian cargo.

Question #2 (Score Point 2 Response)

John Masefield's poem "Cargoes" is interesting if a bit difficult to understand. Three different ships from three different historical periods carry different cargoes. Do the cargoes tell us something about each period? Do the ships tell us something about each period? Masefield makes no comment about what it all means—he just sets these images in front of the reader, and the reader has to make sense of it.

In stanza one, the ship is called a quinquireme. At least, I'm assuming that a quinquireme is a ship. I never heard the word before, but since it has a "cargo," and it's "rowing home," it must be a ship. This ship is "of Nineveh from distant Ophir." That must mean the ship belongs to someone in Nineveh and has traveled to Ophir to pick up its cargo. But it's going home to "sunny Palestine." Maybe the owner in Nineveh has moved to Palestine. In any case, it doesn't really matter. What matters is that it has an interesting and varied cargo that includes ivory, apes, peacocks, sandalwood, cedarwood, and sweet white wine.

In stanza two, the ship is a Spanish galleon. It is laden with treasures, mostly valuable gems. The cargo also includes cinnamon and "gold moidores." That could be money or maybe some kind of jewelry. It doesn't matter—we get the impression that the cargo is valuable, colorful, and sparkly.

Stanza three describes a "Dirty British coaster" with an uninspiring cargo. Of all the three ships, this is the one I'd least like to be on. The ship moves in a herky-jerky way ("Butting through the Channel in the mad March days"), unlike the graceful motion of the Spanish galleon ("Dipping through the Tropics") and the quinquireme ("Rowing home to haven").

Question #2 (Score Point 1 Response)

John Masefield's poem "Cargoes" is made up of three stanzas. Each stanza has five lines, but some lines are long and some are short. It would probably look better if Masefield had combined lines three and four of each stanza—then the lines would be roughly the same length, and the poem would look more balanced.

Each stanza describes a different kind of ship and its cargo. The poem goes from beautiful, exotic images from the ancient past to ugly, pedestrian images from the more recent past. I think Masefield is saying that our world has gotten uglier as time has passed.

I think this poem would be greatly improved if it had footnotes explaining some of the unfamiliar words. That way, the reader wouldn't be stopped cold by the first word: "Quinquireme." It's fun to say, but what does it mean? You have to read on, to find out it's "rowing home" and it has a "cargo" before you realize it's a type of ship. It would also be helpful to know where Nineveh and Ophir are (or were) and what a moidore is exactly.

Scoring Information for CSET: English Subtest III

The following information is available at the CSET Website. It is reproduced here for your convenience.

There are two constructed-response questions in Subtest III of CSET: English. Each of these constructed-response questions is designed so that a response can be completed within approximately 45–60 minutes. Responses to the constructed-response questions are scored by qualified California educators using focused holistic scoring. Scorers will judge the overall effectiveness of your responses while focusing on the performance characteristics that have been identified as important for this subtest (see below). Each response will be assigned a score based on an approved scoring scale (see page 204).

Your performance on the subtest will be evaluated against a standard determined by the California Commission on Teacher Credentialing based on professional judgments and recommendations of California educators.

Performance Characteristics for CSET: English Subtest III

The following performance characteristics will guide the scoring of responses to the constructed-response questions on CSET: English Subtest III.

Purpose	The extent to which the response addresses the constructed-response assignment's charge in relation to relevant CSET subject matter requirements.
Subject Matter Knowledge	The application of accurate subject matter knowledge as described in the relevant CSET subject matter requirements.
Support	The appropriateness and quality of the supporting evidence in relation to relevant CSET subject matter requirements.
Depth and Breadth of Understanding	The degree to which the response demonstrates understanding of the relevant CSET subject matter requirements.

Scoring Scale for CSET: English Subtest III

Scores will be assigned to each response to the constructed-response questions on CSET: English Subtest III according to the following scoring scale.

Score Point	Score Point Description
4	The "4" response reflects a thorough command of the relevant knowledge and skills as defined in the subject matter requirements for CSET: English. • The purpose of the assignment is fully achieved. • There is a substantial and accurate application of relevant subject matter knowledge. • The supporting evidence is sound; there are high-quality, relevant examples. • The response reflects a comprehensive understanding of the assignment.
3	The "3" response reflects a general command of the relevant knowledge and skills as defined in the subject matter requirements for CSET: English. • The purpose of the assignment is largely achieved. • There is a largely accurate application of relevant subject matter knowledge. • The supporting evidence is adequate; there are some acceptable, relevant examples. • The response reflects an adequate understanding of the assignment.
2	The "2" response reflects a limited command of the relevant knowledge and skills as defined in the subject matter requirements for CSET: English. • The purpose of the assignment is partially achieved. • There is limited accurate application of relevant subject matter knowledge. • The supporting evidence is limited; there are few relevant examples. • The response reflects a limited understanding of the assignment.
1	The "1" response reflects little or no command of the relevant knowledge and skills as defined in the subject matter requirements for CSET: English. • The purpose of the assignment is not achieved. • There is little or no accurate application of relevant subject matter knowledge. • The supporting evidence is weak; there are no or few relevant examples. • The response reflects little or no understanding of the assignment.
U	The "U" (Unscorable) is assigned to a response that is unrelated to the assignment, illegible, primarily in a language other than English, or does not contain a sufficient amount of original work to score.
B	The "B" (Blank) is assigned to a response that is blank.

Subtest IV: Speech, Media, and Creative Performance

Content Domains for Subject Matter Understanding and Skill in English

Here is a list of the areas on which you will be tested. This information is also available at the CSET Website. It is reproduced here for your convenience.

Communications: Speech, Media, and Creative Performance (SMR Domain 4)

Candidates demonstrate knowledge of the foundations and contexts of the speech, media, and creative performance contained in the *English-Language Arts Content Standards for California Public Schools* (1997) as outlined in the *Reading/Language Arts Framework for California Public Schools: Kindergarten Through Grade Twelve* (1999) at a post secondary level of rigor. Candidates have both broad and deep conceptual knowledge of the subject matter. The Reading/Language Arts Framework for California Public Schools (1999) puts consistent emphasis on analysis and evaluation of oral and media communication as well as on effective public speaking and performance. The candidate must possess the breadth of knowledge needed to integrate journalism, technological media, speech, dramatic performance, and creative writing into the language arts curriculum, including sensitivity to cultural approaches to communication. The subject matter preparation program should include opportunities for candidates to obtain knowledge and experience in these areas. The candidate skillfully applies the artistic and aesthetic tools and sensitivities required for creative expression. Candidates will be able to:

0001 Oral Communication Processes (SMR 4.1)

a. Identify features of, and deliver oral performance in, a variety of forms (e.g., impromptu, extemporaneous, persuasive, expository, interpretive, debate).

b. Demonstrate and evaluate individual performance skills (e.g., diction, enunciation, vocal rate, range, pitch, volume, body language, eye contact, response to audience).

c. Articulate principles of speaker/audience interrelationship (e.g., interpersonal communication, group dynamics, public address).

d. Identify and demonstrate collaborative communication skills in a variety of roles (e.g., listening supportively, facilitating, synthesizing, stimulating higher level critical thinking through inquiry).

(*English-Language Arts Content: Standards for California Public Schools,* Grade 6, Reading: 1.1, Listening and Speaking: 1.1–8, 2.0; Grade 7, Listening and Speaking: 1.1–7, 2.0; Grade 8, Listening and Speaking: 1.1–8, 2.0; Grades 9–10, Listening and Speaking: 1.1, 1.3–6, 1.8–13, 2.0; Grades 11–12, Reading: 2.6, Listening and Speaking: 1.4–6, 1.8–13, 2.0)

0002 Media Analysis and Journalistic Applications (SMR 4.2)

a. Analyze the impact on society of a variety of media forms (e.g., television, advertising, radio, Internet, film).

b. Recognize and evaluate strategies used by the media to inform, persuade, entertain, and transmit culture.

c. Identify aesthetic effects of a media presentation.

d. Demonstrate effective and creative application of these strategies and techniques to prepare presentations using a variety of media forms and visual aids.

(*English-Language Arts Content Standards for California Public Schools,* Grade 6, Reading: 2.1–2, 2.6, Listening and Speaking: 1.9; Grade 7, Reading: 2.1, Listening and Speaking: 1.8–9; Grade 8, Reading: 2.1, 2.3, Listening and Speaking: 1.8–9; Grades 9–10, Reading: 2.1, Listening and Speaking: 1.1–2, 1.7, 1.9, 1.14; Grades 11–12, Reading: 2.1, Writing: 2.6, Listening and Speaking: 1.1–4, 1.9, 1.14, 2.4; *Visual and Performing Arts Content Standards for California Public Schools,* Theatre, Grades 6–12, 5.0: Connections, Relationships, Applications)

0003 Dramatic Performance (SMR 4.3)

a. Describe and use a range of rehearsal strategies to effectively mount a production (e.g., teambuilding, scheduling, organizing resources, setting priorities, memorization techniques, improvisation, physical and vocal exercises).

b. Employ basic elements of character analysis and approaches to acting, including physical and vocal techniques, that reveal character and relationships.

c. Demonstrate basic knowledge of the language of visual composition and principles of theatrical design (e.g., set, costume, lighting, sound, props).

d. Apply fundamentals of stage directing, including conceptualization, blocking (movement patterns), tempo, and dramatic arc (rising and falling action).

e. Demonstrate facility in a variety of oral performance traditions (e.g., storytelling, epic poetry, recitation).

(*English-Language Arts Content Standards for California Public Schools,* Grade 6, Listening and Speaking: 2.1, 2.3; Grade 7, Listening and Speaking: 2.1; Grade 8, Listening and Speaking: 1.1, 2.1–2, 2.5; Grades 9–10, Listening and Speaking: 2.1, 2.4; Grades 11–12, Listening and Speaking: 1.7, 1.9–10, 2.5; *Visual and Performing Arts Content Standards for California Public Schools,* Theatre, Grades 6–12, 1.0: Artistic Perception, 2.0: Creative Expression, 3.0: Historical and Cultural Context, 4.0: Aesthetic Valuing)

0004 Creative Writing (SMR 4.4)

a. Demonstrate facility in creative composition in a variety of genres (e.g., poetry, stories, plays, film).

b. Understand and apply processes and techniques that enhance the impact of the creative writing product (e.g., workshopping; readings; recasting of genre, voice, perspective).

c. Demonstrate skill in composing creative and aesthetically compelling responses to literature.

(*English-Language Arts Content Standards for California Pubic Schools,* Grades 6–12, Writing: 2.1)

Subtest IV: Communications: Speech, Media, and Creative Performance

Directions: Below is a set of constructed-response questions that are similar to the questions you will see on Subtest IV of CSET: English. You are encouraged to respond to the questions without looking at the responses provided in the next section and to compare your answers with the provided responses.

1. Complete the exercise that follows.

   Identify the features of Lincoln-Douglas debates and parliamentary debates. What is alike about them? What is different? Write your response on the lined pages of Assignment 1 Response Sheet, provided after these questions.

2. Complete the exercise that follows.

   Name, describe, and give an example of five commonly used advertising techniques. Write your response on the lined pages of Assignment 2 Response Sheet, provided after these questions.

3. Complete the exercise that follows.

   A director is staging a realistic play. At one point, it is crucial that the audience's attention be focused on one particular actor. Because the play is realistic, the director does not want to use a single tight spot of light on that actor. How might the director solve this problem? Give two suggestions, and explain why each one would work. Write your response on the lined pages of Assignment 3 Response Sheet, provided after these questions.

4. Read the paragraph below, taken from *Lord Jim* by Joseph Conrad.

   It was the dusk of a winter's day. The gale had freshened since noon, stopping the traffic on the river and now blew with the strength of a hurricane in fitful bursts that boomed like salvoes of great guns firing over the ocean. The rain slanted in sheets that flicked and subsided, and between whiles Jim had threatening glimpses of the tumbling tide, the small craft jumbled and tossing along the shore, the motionless buildings in the driving mist, the broad ferry-boats pitching ponderously at anchor, the vast landing-stages heaving up and down and smothered in sprays. The next gust seemed to blow all this away. The air was full of flying water. There was a fierce purpose in the gale, a furious earnestness in the screech of the wind, in the brutal tumult of earth and sky, that seemed directed at him, and made him hold his breath in awe. He stood still. It seemed to him he was whirled around.

   Using your knowledge of literary genres, write a haiku that captures the same feeling. Write your response on the lined pages of Assignment 4 Response Sheet, provided after these questions.

GO ON TO THE NEXT PAGE

Sample Written Response Document for CSET: English Subtest IV

For Questions 1–4, you will record your written response to each question on a one-page response sheet located in your answer document. The length of your response to each question is limited to the lined space available on the response sheet. Response sheets similar to what you will be given at the testing center are provided here.

Assignment 1 Response Sheet

Assignment 2 Response Sheet

Assignment 3 Response Sheet

Assignment 4 Response Sheet

Examples of Responses to Sample Constructed-Response Questions for CSET: English Subtest IV

Communications: Speech, Media, and Creative Performance

Question #1 (Score Point 3 Response)

Lincoln-Douglas debates and parliamentary debates have these features in common:

- *They are structured, controlled, and judged contests between two sides that take opposite positions on the same topic.*
- *They begin with the affirmative side speaking for a predetermined number of minutes, followed by the negative side speaking. These periods are followed by a rebuttal period by each side, during which no new evidence can be introduced.*
- *Final rebuttal is made by the affirmative side.*

The main differences between Lincoln-Douglas debates and parliamentary debates are as follows:

- *Lincoln-Douglas debates are between two individuals, and parliamentary debates are between two two-person teams.*
- *For a Lincoln-Douglas debate, the individuals have days, weeks, or even months to prepare their arguments, whereas for a parliamentary debate, team members usually have about 30 minutes to prepare.*
- *In a Lincoln-Douglas debate, each side cross-examines the other briefly, immediately after the other side speaks and before the rebuttals. This is not true in parliamentary debate.*

Question #1 (Score Point 2 Response)

Lincoln-Douglas debates are based on the historical debates between Abraham Lincoln and Stephen Douglas in 1858. Following their example, these debates are between two individuals, each one arguing a different side of a question. They take turns speaking, the affirmative side going first. They then have a three-part rebuttal period, in this order: affirmative, negative, affirmative.

Parliamentary debates, on the other hand, are between two two-person teams. They pretty much follow the same format, with affirmative speaking first and also getting the last rebuttal.

Preparation time varies as well. For Lincoln-Douglas debates, the preparation time might be as long as several months. For parliamentary debates, the topic is usually announced about 30 minutes ahead.

Question #1 (Score Point 1 Response)

Debates are arguments between people or teams. The Lincoln-Douglas debates took place in the mid 1800s between Abraham Lincoln and Stephen Douglas as they were campaigning to be a senator from Illinois. Douglas must have won the debates, for he went on to become a senator.

Parliamentary debates take place mainly in England. The affirmative side is argued by the prime minister and a member of government. The opposition side is argued by the leader of the opposition and a member of the opposition.

Question #2 (Score Point 3 Response)

Five commonly used advertising techniques are as follows:

1.   Avante Garde: This is the suggestion that by buying a product, the user will be ahead of the times; for example, a car company shows a new car being driven in a futuristic setting.

2.   Patriotism: This is the suggestion that by buying a certain product, the user can demonstrate love of country; for example, a company stresses the fact that its product is made in America by American workers.

3. Peer approval: This is the suggestion that use of this product will help the user get the approval of friends; for example, a company shows its product being enjoyed by a happy group of friends at a party.

4.   Facts and figures: This type of advertising provides specific numbers or scientific proofs that a product works; for example, a toothpaste company claims that its users had an 85% reduction in the number of cavities.

5.   Snob appeal: This suggests that use of the product will ensure the user's inclusion in an elite group; for example, a mustard manufacturer shows well-dressed people in very expensive cars asking for its brand.

Question #2 (Score Point 2 Response)

The bandwagon technique encourages people to join the crowd and buy a product, saying things like "Don't be left out!"

Weasel words are used to suggest a positive attribute without really guaranteeing anything, such as "Use of this product may diminish wrinkles."

Bribery is used to make people think they are getting an extra desirable something; an example is when a restaurant offers free chips and salsa with the purchase of two drinks.

A testimonial is a statement by a famous personality who endorses the product.

Question #2 (Score Point 1 Response)

Some commonly used advertising techniques are billboards, radio, television, sides of buses, flyers, magazine ads, outdoor furniture such as benches at bus stops, community bulletin boards, backs of receipts or movie stubs, and so on. I think the five best ones are billboards, radio, television, magazine ads, and Internet pop-up ads.

Question #3 (Score Point 3 Response)

The director could have the character perform some movement on stage. This is a good way to draw attention to the character because the human eye is naturally attracted by motion. Suppose one character has just delivered a line that will cause a strong reaction in another character—a reaction that the director wants the audience to observe. Even if the second character does not have a line to speak, he or she can suddenly stand up, or take a step, or sit down. The audience will immediately watch that character, especially if the other characters on stage are remaining fairly still.

Sound is another way of attracting attention. The audience's attention is naturally attracted to the character who is speaking (or making some other kind of sound) rather than to characters who are silent. If the director wants the audience to look at one particular character to the exclusion of the others, he or she can have all the other characters remain silent while the important one speaks.

Question #3 (Score Point 2 Response)

Height is one factor that helps draw attention to a character. The audience will naturally look at the character who is taller or in a higher position on the stage. An actor who is standing draws more attention than one who is sitting. So, to direct the audience's attention to a particular actor, he or she might have the actor stand up while the others on stage remain seated.

Another way to draw attention to an actor is to have him or her face the audience directly. The director could have the other actors on the stage turn a profile toward the audience, or be three-quarters turned away. The audience is more likely to look at the character who is facing them.

Question #3 (Score Point 1 Response)

The best way to draw attention to an actor on stage is to direct a light on him or her. But if the director does not want to do that, his or her choices are limited. I would suggest having all the other actors on stage look at the other actor. This will hint to the audience that they should look in that same direction.

Question #4 (Score Point 3 Response)

Standing on the deck
In a driving winter storm—
Holding breath in awe!

Question #4 (Score Point 2 Response)

So scary on deck!
A gale like a hurricane
Whirls him around.

Question #4 (Score Point 1 Response)

At dusk on a winter's day,
He stood and watched the windy fray.
Sheet-like rain and tumbling tide—
The man would rather be inside.

Scoring Information for CSET: English Subtest IV

The following information is available at the CSET Website. It is reproduced here for your convenience.

There are four constructed-response questions in Subtest IV of CSET: English. Each of these constructed-response questions is designed so that a response can be completed within a short amount of time—approximately 10–15 minutes. Responses to the constructed-response questions are scored by qualified California educators using focused holistic scoring. Scorers will judge the overall effectiveness of your responses while focusing on the performance characteristics that have been identified as important for this subtest (see below). Each response will be assigned a score based on an approved scoring scale (see page 226).

Your performance on the subtest will be evaluated against a standard determined by the California Commission on Teacher Credentialing based on professional judgments and recommendations of California educators.

Performance Characteristics for CSET: English Subtest IV

The following performance characteristics will guide the scoring of responses to the constructed-response questions on CSET: English Subtest IV.

Purpose	The extent to which the response addresses the constructed-response assignment's charge in relation to relevant CSET subject matter requirements.
Subject Matter Knowledge	The application of accurate subject matter knowledge as described in the relevant CSET subject matter requirements.
Support	The appropriateness and quality of the supporting evidence in relation to relevant CSET subject matter requirements.

Scoring Scale for CSET: English Subtest IV

Scores will be assigned to each response to the constructed-response questions on CSET: English Subtest III according to the following scoring scale.

Score Point	Score Point Description
3	The "3" response reflects a command of the relevant knowledge and skills as defined in the subject matter requirements for CSET: English. • The purpose of the assignment is fully achieved. • There is an accurate application of relevant subject matter knowledge. • There is appropriate and specific relevant supporting evidence.
2	The "2" response reflects a general command of the relevant knowledge and skills as defined in the subject matter requirements for CSET: English. • The purpose of the assignment is largely achieved. • There is a largely accurate application of relevant subject matter knowledge. • There is acceptable relevant supporting evidence.
1	The "1" response reflects a limited command of the relevant knowledge and skills as defined in the subject matter requirements for CSET: English. • The purpose of the assignment is only partially or not achieved. • There is limited or no application of relevant subject matter knowledge. • There is little or no relevant supporting evidence.
U	The "U" (Unscorable) is assigned to a response that is unrelated to the assignment, illegible, primarily in a language other than English, or does not contain a sufficient amount of original work to score.
B	The "B" (Blank) is assigned to a response that is blank.

PART IV

CLOSING THOUGHTS

This section includes two study timelines, a long one (three months or more) and a short one (one month). Use the one that works for your schedule. This section also includes a few last study tips and a list of resources that should help you study effectively for your CSET: English test.

These tips and resources should help you pass the CSET: English test.

Registration

Remember that the CSET: English test contains four subtests. You might consider taking only one or two tests during one session and going back another time or times to take the rest of the tests. Taking the CSET: English test is an exhausting and intense experience. Even though it is possible to take all four subtests in the five-hour span that is allowed, think about how tired you might be in that last hour. Would you do better on the last test if you were fresh and well-rested? Only you can answer the question of whether you want to take all four subtests at once.

The easiest and most efficient way to complete registration is to do it online. Go to the CSET Website:

> http://www.cset.nesinc.com

There, you can find all the information you need for registration.

If you're eligible for alternative testing arrangements due to physical or learning disabilities or for religious reasons (unable to take a test on Saturday), complete the required documentation prior to registering for the test. Mail in any necessary forms early. Make sure that the alternative arrangements are available at the testing location you request. The testing service keeps your documentation on file for one year, so if you are planning to complete all four subtests within the year, you do not have to resubmit the documentation. You do, however, have to submit new registration forms for each test date that you select.

Studying

Make a study plan and stick to it. It takes discipline to study for a big test like this, so don't let yourself be distracted from your plan.

Think about your own strengths and weaknesses as a test-taker and student based on your past performance. Are you generally a strong test-taker? If so, review this book's content and take the practice tests. Are you generally an anxious or not-so-strong test-taker? If so, use this book to become familiar with the format and content of the CSET: English test and plan to use additional resources, such as English and education course textbooks, to prepare yourself for the test. If test anxiety is a problem for you, you might want to seek the support of your university's or college's counseling services. You can also find a free guide about test anxiety at the following Website:

> http://www.ets.org/Media/Tests/PRAXIS/pdf/01361anxiety.pdf

This book has helped prepare you for the format of the test and to determine the content you need to review. If multiple-choice questions are not your strong suit, for example, then study more of those questions. If you're having a problem with reading comprehension, writing, or the fundamental English or language arts content, focus your attention on those sections to better prepare for the CSET: English.

Remember, all eight of the practice tests in this book can help you prepare for the content of the CSET: English test. Some people have found that reading the answers and explanations for each practice test is especially useful in reviewing content.

Exam Day

Follow these tips to be at your best and well prepared for the test:

- Be sure to get a good night's sleep the night before your test.
- Eat a healthful, adequate lunch before the test. The CSET: English test is administered only in the afternoon session (at the time of the publication of this book), with a reporting time of 1:30, which allows time for distribution of materials and communication of directions before the starting time of approximately 2:00. The afternoon session ends at approximately 7:00 P.M.; if you have skipped lunch, you will no doubt run out of energy.
- Remember your admission ticket, a government-issued form of identification with your photograph and signature on it, and several sharpened #2 pencils with erasers (no pens). Pencils are not distributed at the test site, so be sure you have enough.

Study Planning Guide

If You Have Three Months (or more)	
When	**What to Do**
3 months (or more) before the CSET: English	Register for the subtests you plan to take. Complete the paperwork for alternative testing arrangements, if applicable. Read the Introduction and Part I of this book. Review your old English textbooks or borrow some from the library. Use your favorite Web browser to access the CSET Website (www.cset.nesinc.com) and browse the site for information about the English test. Also browse the Internet for information about content areas that you need to review. Bookmark these Websites for future use.
2 months (or more) before the CSET: English	Make sure that you have registered. Also, be sure to set aside proof of registration in a safe place. Read Parts I and II of this book to help you understand the format and content of the subtests. Use your favorite Websites—the ones you bookmarked last month—to help you prepare for the test.
1 month (or more) before the CSET: English	On a Saturday, at about lunchtime, take a test drive to the building where you'll be taking your test. Time how long it takes and note the traffic conditions. Take the full-length practice tests in Part III of this book to simulate test-taking conditions and determine which areas you still need to study. Use your Websites and English textbooks to fill in any missing pieces of content.
1 week before the CSET: English	Set aside your proof of registration, a few #2 pencils with erasers, and a valid form of photo identification with your signature. Retake any or all of the full-length practice tests in this book. Review Part II of this book to refresh your memory on the test content.
The night before the CSET: English	Talk only to people who make you feel good and confident. Pack a water bottle (a clear bottle without a label and with a secure lid). You'll be allowed to bring this into the test site, and you'll need it if you're there for the full five hours of testing time. Get enough rest. Do not cram all night.
The day of the CSET: English	Think positive thoughts. Relax. Eat well. Remember to bring your water bottle, proof of registration, ID, and pencils. Arrive at the test center no later than 1:30 P.M.

If You Have One Month

When	What to Do
1 month before the CSET: English	Register for the subtests you plan to take. You must register at least 29 days before the test in order to avoid late fees. If you register less than 29 days and up to 11 days ahead of time (late registration), you have to pay late fees, and if you register less than 11 days ahead of time and up to 4 days ahead of time (emergency registration), you have to pay even more fees. Complete the paperwork for alternative testing arrangements, if applicable. Read the Introduction and Part I of this book.
3 weeks before the CSET: English	Read Parts I and II of this book to help you understand the format and content of the subtests. On a Saturday, at about lunchtime, take a test drive to the building where you'll be taking your test. Time how long it takes and note the traffic conditions.
2 weeks before the CSET: English	Take the full-length practice tests in Part III of this book to simulate test-taking conditions and determine which areas you still need to study. Review the content outlines in Part II of this book to fill in information in areas whose content you are still learning.
1 week before the CSET: English	Set aside your proof of registration, a few #2 pencils with erasers, and a valid form of photo identification with your signature. Retake any or all of the full-length practice tests in this book. Review Part II of this book to refresh your memory on the test content.
The night before the CSET: English	Talk only to people who make you feel good and confident. Pack a water bottle (a clear bottle without a label and with a secure lid). You'll be allowed to bring this into the test site, and you'll need it if you're there for the full five hours of testing time. Get enough rest. Do not cram all night.
The day of the CSET: English	Think positive thoughts. Relax. Eat well. Remember to bring your water bottle, proof of registration, ID, and pencils. Arrive at the test center no later than 1:30 P.M.

This section provides a list of resources that you might find helpful as you prepare for the content of the CSET: English test.

Suggested References

The suggested references in this section might help prepare you for the CSET: English and might prove useful in your English classroom in the future. This list also appears on the CSET: English Website and is reproduced here for your convenience.

Literature and Textual Analysis

Buss, Kathleen; Karnowski, Lee; and Granum, O. Alfred. (2002) *Reading and Writing Nonfiction Genres*. Newark, DE: International Reading Association.

California Department of Education. (1990) *Recommended Literature, Grades Nine Through Twelve*. Sacramento, CA: California Department of Education.

Donelson, K. L., and Nilsen, A. P. (2000). *Literature for Today's Young Adults* (6th edition). New York, NY: Longman.

Hall, Donald E. (2001). *Literary and Cultural Theory: From Basic Principles to Advanced Applications*. Boston, MA: Houghton Mifflin.

Olson, Carol Booth. (2003) *The Reading/Writing Connection: Strategies for Teaching and Learning in the Secondary Classroom*. New York, NY: Allyn & Bacon/Longman.

Composition and Rhetoric

Buss, Kathleen; Karnowski, Lee; and Granum, O. Alfred. (2002) *Reading and Writing Nonfiction Genres*. Newark, DE: International Reading Association.

Fowler, H. Ramsey; Aaron, Jane E.; and Anderson, Daniel. (2000). *The Little, Brown Handbook* (8th edition). New York, NY: Longman.

Graves, R. (1990). *Rhetoric and Composition: A Sourcebook for Teachers and Writers*. Portsmouth, NH: Heinemann.

Harris, Joseph. (1996). *A Teaching Subject: Composition Since 1966*. New York, NY: Prentice Hall.

Moore, David; Moore, Sharon; Cunningham, Patricia; and Cunningham, James. (2003). *Developing Readers and Writers in the Content Area* (4th edition). Boston, MA: Allyn & Bacon.

Olson, Carol Booth. (2003) *The Reading/Writing Connection: Strategies for Teaching and Learning in the Secondary Classroom*. New York, NY: Allyn & Bacon/Longman.

Villanueva, Victor. (1997). *Cross Talk in Comp Theory: A Reader*. Urbana, IL: National Council of Teachers of English.

Language, Linguistics, and Literacy

Berko Gleason, Jean (Ed.). (2000). *The Development of Language* (5th edition). Boston, MA: Allyn & Bacon.

Cooper, J. David. (2000). *Literacy: Helping Children to Construct Meaning* (4th edition). Boston, MA: Houghton Mifflin.

English-Language Arts Content Standards for California Public Schools, Kindergarten Through Grade Twelve. (1998). Sacramento, CA: California Department of Education.

Hoff, Erika. (1996). *Language Development.* Belmont, CA: Wadsworth Publishing Co.

Lightbown, Patsy M., and Speda, Nina. (1993). *How Languages Are Learned.* New York, NY: Oxford University Press.

Moore, David; Moore, Sharon; Cunningham, Patricia; and Cunningham, James. (2003). *Developing Readers and Writers in the Content Area* (4th edition). Boston, MA: Allyn & Bacon.

Olson, Carol Booth. (2003) *The Reading/Writing Connection: Strategies for Teaching and Learning in the Secondary Classroom.* New York, NY: Allyn & Bacon/Longman.

Yoopp, Ruth Helen, and Yopp, Hallie Kay. (2001). *Literature-Based Reading Activities* (3rd edition). Boston, MA: Allyn & Bacon.

Other Resources of Interest

Copi, Irving M., and Cohen, Carl. (1990). *Introduction to Logic* (8th edition). New York, NY: Macmillan.

Curriculum Frameworks and Instructional Resources. (2001). Sacramento, CA: California Department of Education.

Donoahue, Z.; Tassell, M.; and Patterson, L. (Eds.). (1996). *Research in the Classroom: Talk, Texts, and Inquiry.* Newark, DE: International Reading Association.